Dynamite Entertainment Presents

EDUARDO RISSO • CARLOS TRILLO

BORDERLINE™

VOLUME I

Dynamite Entertainment Presents

EDUARDO RISSO • CARLOS TRILLO

BORDERLINE™

VOLUME I

ART AND STORY BY
EDUARDO RISSO AND
CARLOS TRILLO

TRANSLATION
IVAN BRANDON

INTRODUCTION
BRIAN AZZARELLO

LETTERING
JASON ULLMEYER

SPECIAL THANKS TO
MARIA BARRUCCI

DYNAMITE ENTERTAINMENT
NICK BARRUCCI — PRESIDENT
JUAN COLLADO — CHIEF OPERATING OFFICER
JOSEPH RYBANDT — DIRECTOR OF MARKETING
JOSH JOHNSON — CREATIVE DIRECTOR
JASON ULLMEYER — GRAPHIC DESIGNER

DYNAMITE
ENTERTAINMENT™

First Printing
ISBN-10: 1-933305-05-3
ISBN-13: 9-781933-305059
10 9 8 7 6 5 4 3 2 1

To find a comic shop in your area, call the comic shop locator service toll-free 1-888-266-4226

INTRODUCTION

BY BRIAN AZZARELLO

"The dog can talk."

"Excuse me?" was all I could growl, hearing this.

The tall man in the tight suit, its pinstripes not draping nicely at all, winked at me. "It's true," he grinned, pulling the leash. "This dog can talk. Ask him a question."

Me and the dog looked at each other. He cocked his head first. "Is it embarrassing to have a man following you around with a plastic bag in his hand full of your business?" I wondered. Out loud.

The dog said nothing. He whined a bit, tugged on his line, his nails scratching hard on the concrete. Down the block, another tree, another shrub, another corner of a building. All waiting. For him.

Through a cloud of gun-metal cigar smoke, I corrected the man in the ill-fitting suit. "Your dog can't talk." The man slowly shook his head, as the dog pulled him towards territory fresh with possibilities. "No friend. You're not listening."

Ah. So this was about language–communication, culturally speaking. But then, what interesting isn't? The rub–and it's a hell of a one–is it depends where you live. If you happen to call a nation that speaks American your home, well we are in the all day business of exporting culture. Importing? Mmmm... not so much.

And the trouble with that is we have less to talk about than the rest of the world does. Every book I've written has been translated into dozens of languages, meaning–if the care to–people all over the world can talk about them. That makes me feel real warm, as a comic writer. But it's a feeling that's denied to comic writers who don't write in American, as far as America is concerned. (And don't think I'm ignorant of the 800 lb. gorilla named Manga that's got me in a corner, either. He doesn't fit into my argument, much less the room, so let's ignore him like we still have the chance.)

Case in point, the writer of BORDERLINE, Carlos Trillo. Sure, we've been able to read a handful of his work, but just a handful of this Argentine author's remarkable career–one that's spanned over thirty years–is not nearly enough. His stories manage not to be just viscerally gripping, but political commentaries that are socially aware. In other words–and in any language–he has something to say. Are you listening?

As for his partner in this book, Eduardo Risso... well, words... he doesn't need words. I'll humbly use these to describe him though: The greatest visual story-teller alive. Put that in any language; the proof is on the page. It's in the inky shadows that pull you along, the subtle expressions that suck you into the cast's inner lives. You can be as deaf to words as the main character Crash (or is she Lisa? Trillo deftly leaves that distinction up to you.) Read with just your eyes. You'll see what I'm saying.

So what we have here in BORDERLINE is a dystopian future, brought to life by two immensely talented Argentine creators, translated into American for the first time. And it's about time. While you read it, pay attention. Consider the words, get lost in the pictures; you may just hear something. As bleak as the story may seem to be, it has a heart. Beating.

Woof.

Azz

Brian Azzarello is a writer living in Chicago. He and Eduardo Risso have won multiple Eisner & Harvey awards for their acclaimed series 100 BULLETS, *published by* DC/Vertigo. *Other work includes* HELLBLAZER, BATMAN, SUPERMAN, *and* LOVELESS. *He has two cats, who incessantly tell him how much they hate him every morning until he feeds them.*

0

AFA

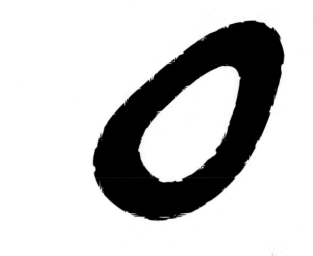

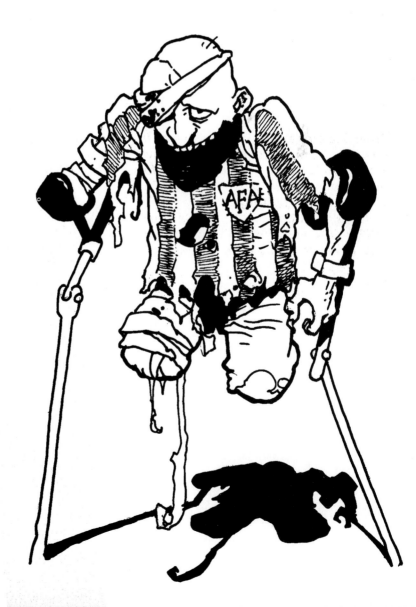

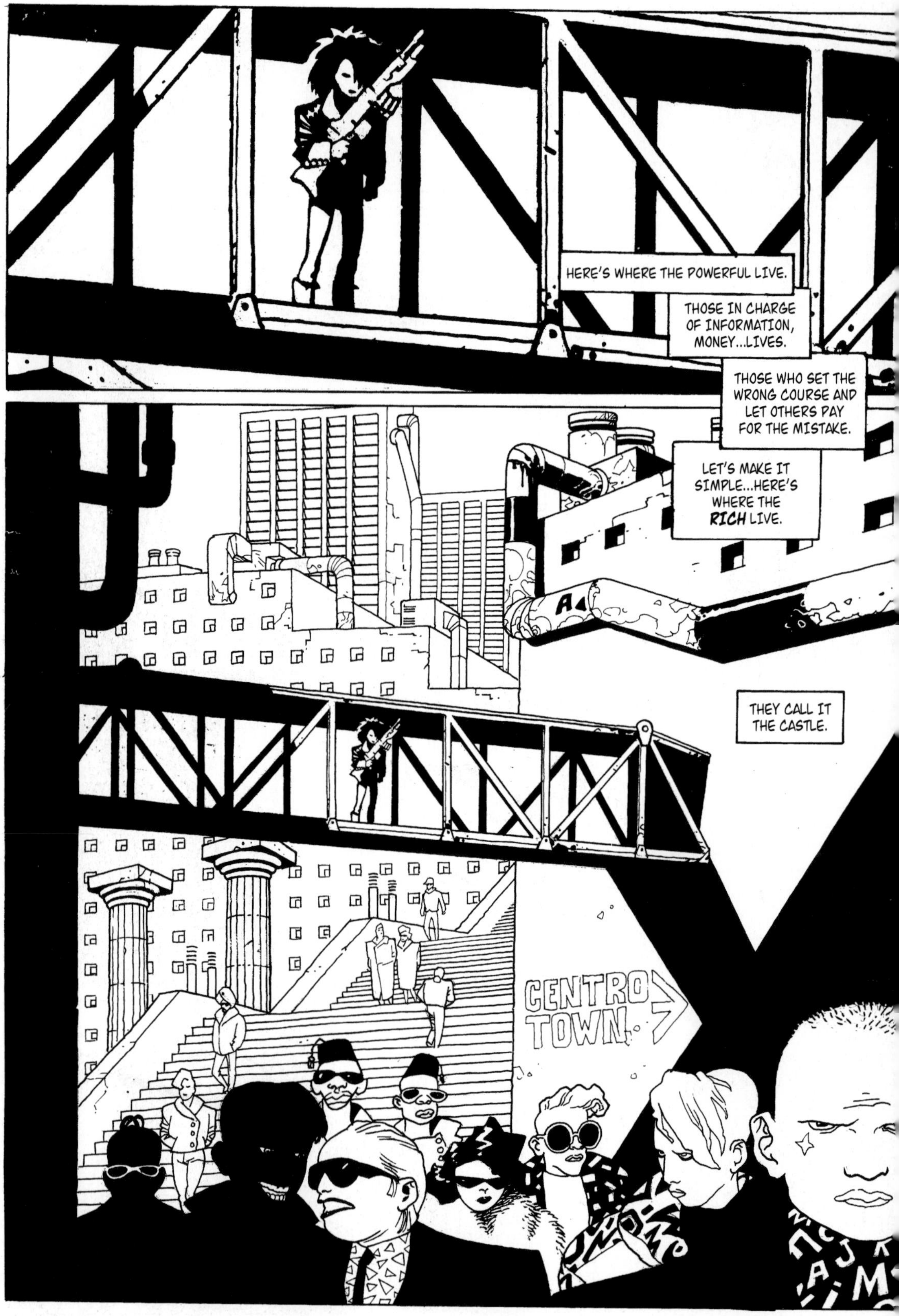
HERE'S WHERE THE POWERFUL LIVE.
THOSE IN CHARGE OF INFORMATION, MONEY...LIVES.
THOSE WHO SET THE WRONG COURSE AND LET OTHERS PAY FOR THE MISTAKE.
LET'S MAKE IT SIMPLE...HERE'S WHERE THE **RICH** LIVE.
THEY CALL IT THE CASTLE.
CENTRO TOWN

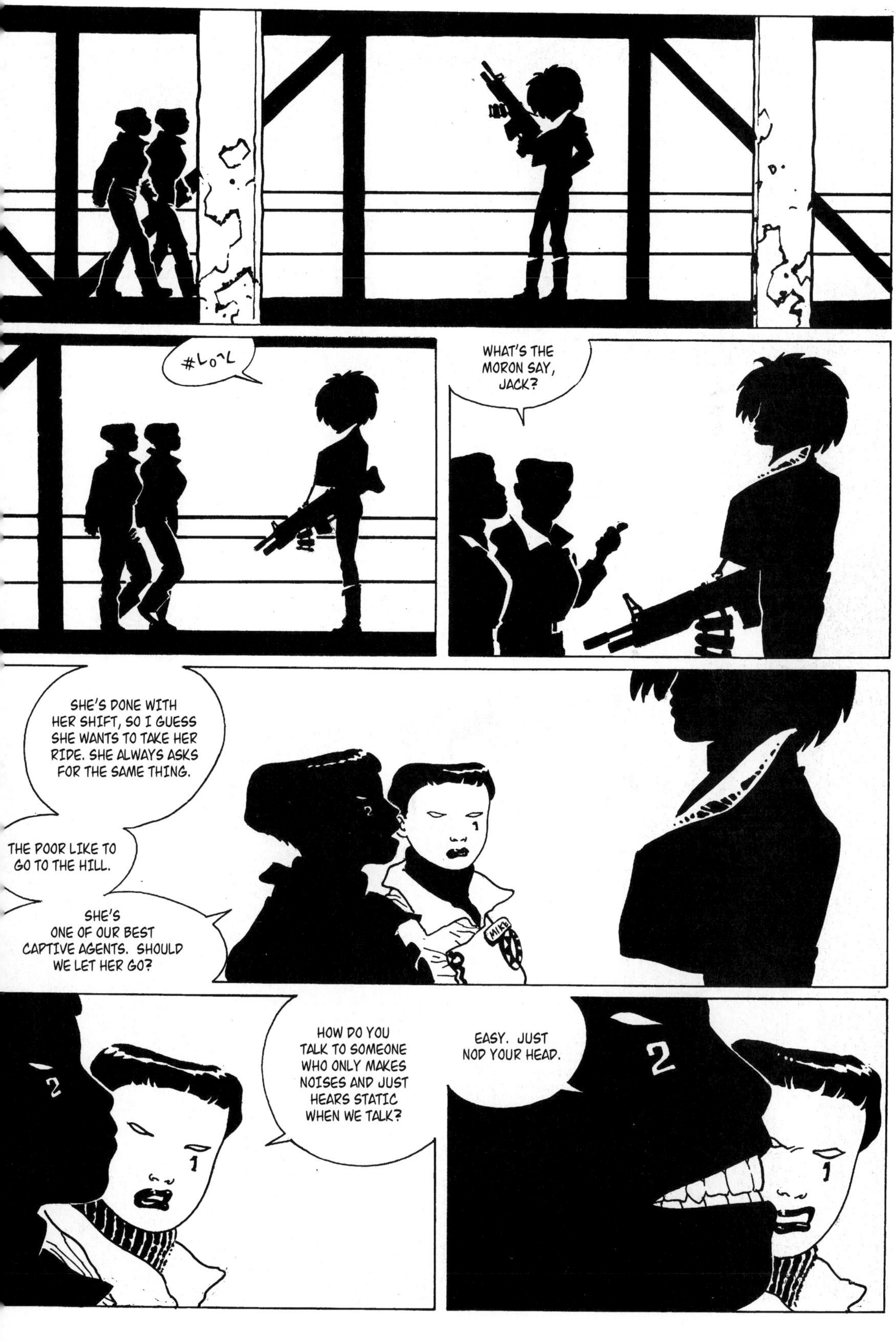
#Lo~L
WHAT'S THE MORON SAY, JACK?
SHE'S DONE WITH HER SHIFT, SO I GUESS SHE WANTS TO TAKE HER RIDE. SHE ALWAYS ASKS FOR THE SAME THING.
THE POOR LIKE TO GO TO THE HILL.
SHE'S ONE OF OUR BEST CAPTIVE AGENTS. SHOULD WE LET HER GO?
MIKE
HOW DO YOU TALK TO SOMEONE WHO ONLY MAKES NOISES AND JUST HEARS STATIC WHEN WE TALK?
EASY. JUST NOD YOUR HEAD.

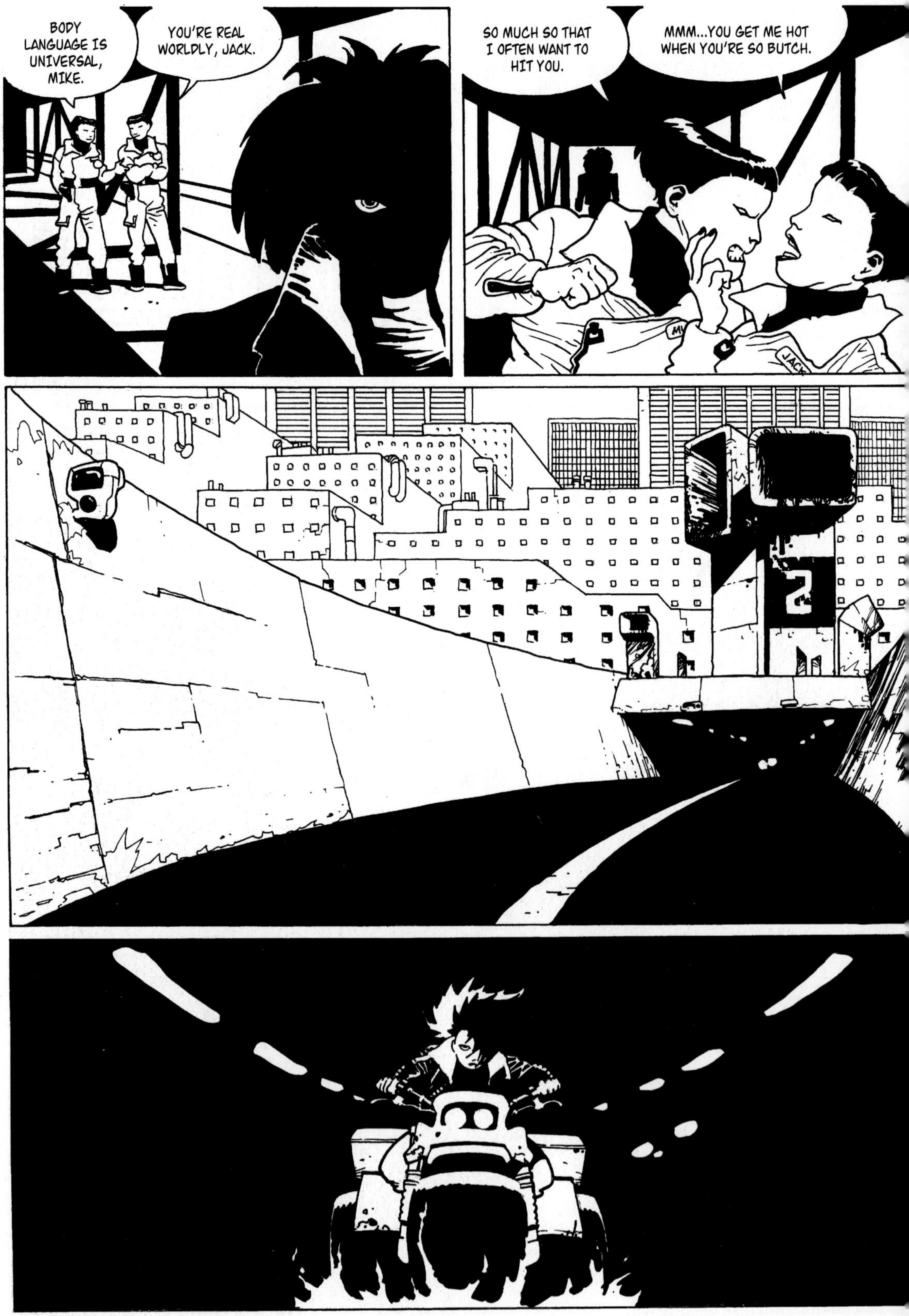
BODY LANGUAGE IS UNIVERSAL, MIKE.
YOU'RE REAL WORLDLY, JACK.
SO MUCH SO THAT I OFTEN WANT TO HIT YOU.
MMM...YOU GET ME HOT WHEN YOU'RE SO BUTCH.
JACK
2

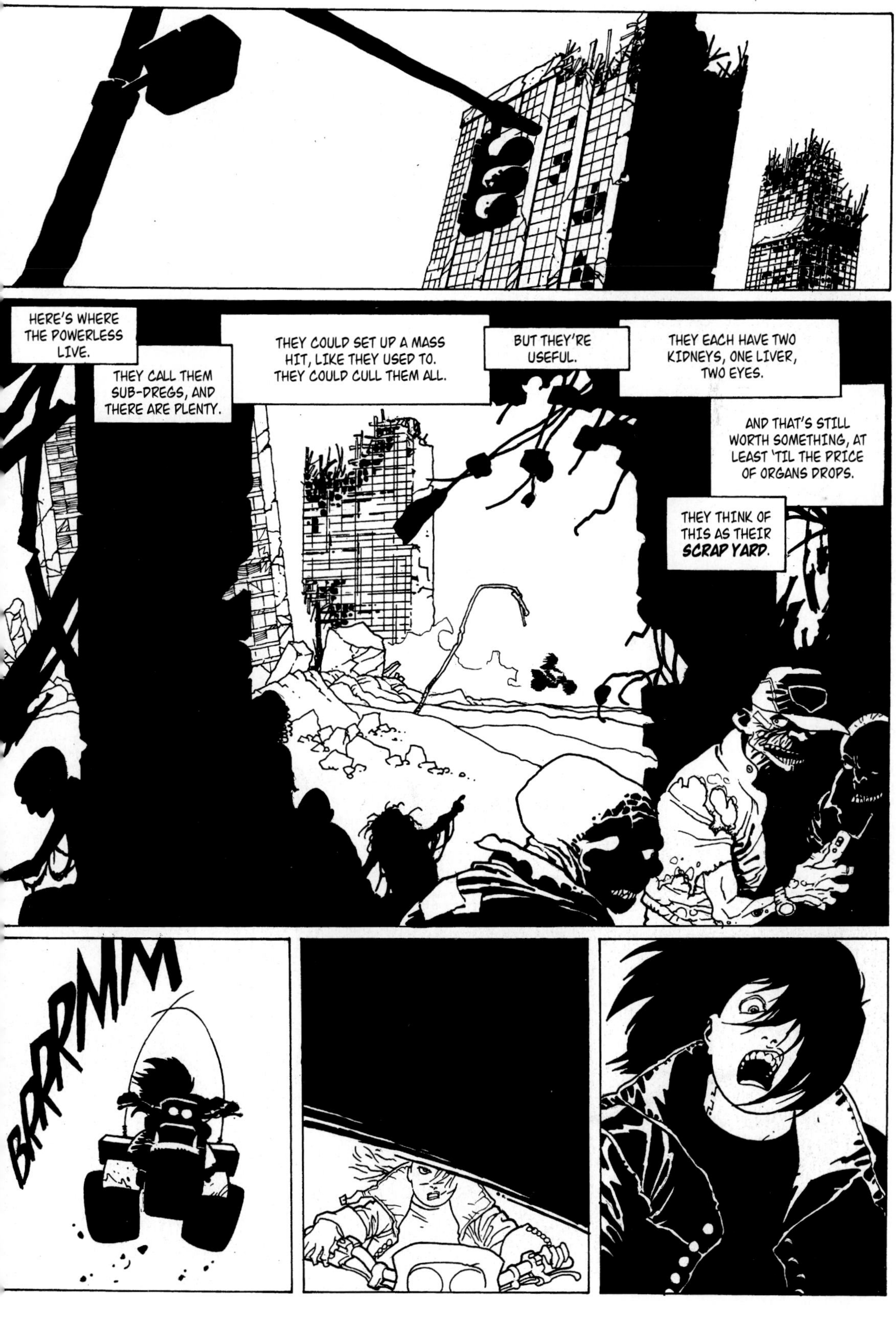
HERE'S WHERE THE POWERLESS LIVE.
THEY CALL THEM SUB-DREGS, AND THERE ARE PLENTY.
THEY COULD SET UP A MASS HIT, LIKE THEY USED TO. THEY COULD CULL THEM ALL.
BUT THEY'RE USEFUL.
THEY EACH HAVE TWO KIDNEYS, ONE LIVER, TWO EYES.
AND THAT'S STILL WORTH SOMETHING, AT LEAST 'TIL THE PRICE OF ORGANS DROPS.
THEY THINK OF THIS AS THEIR **SCRAP YARD**.
BRRRMM

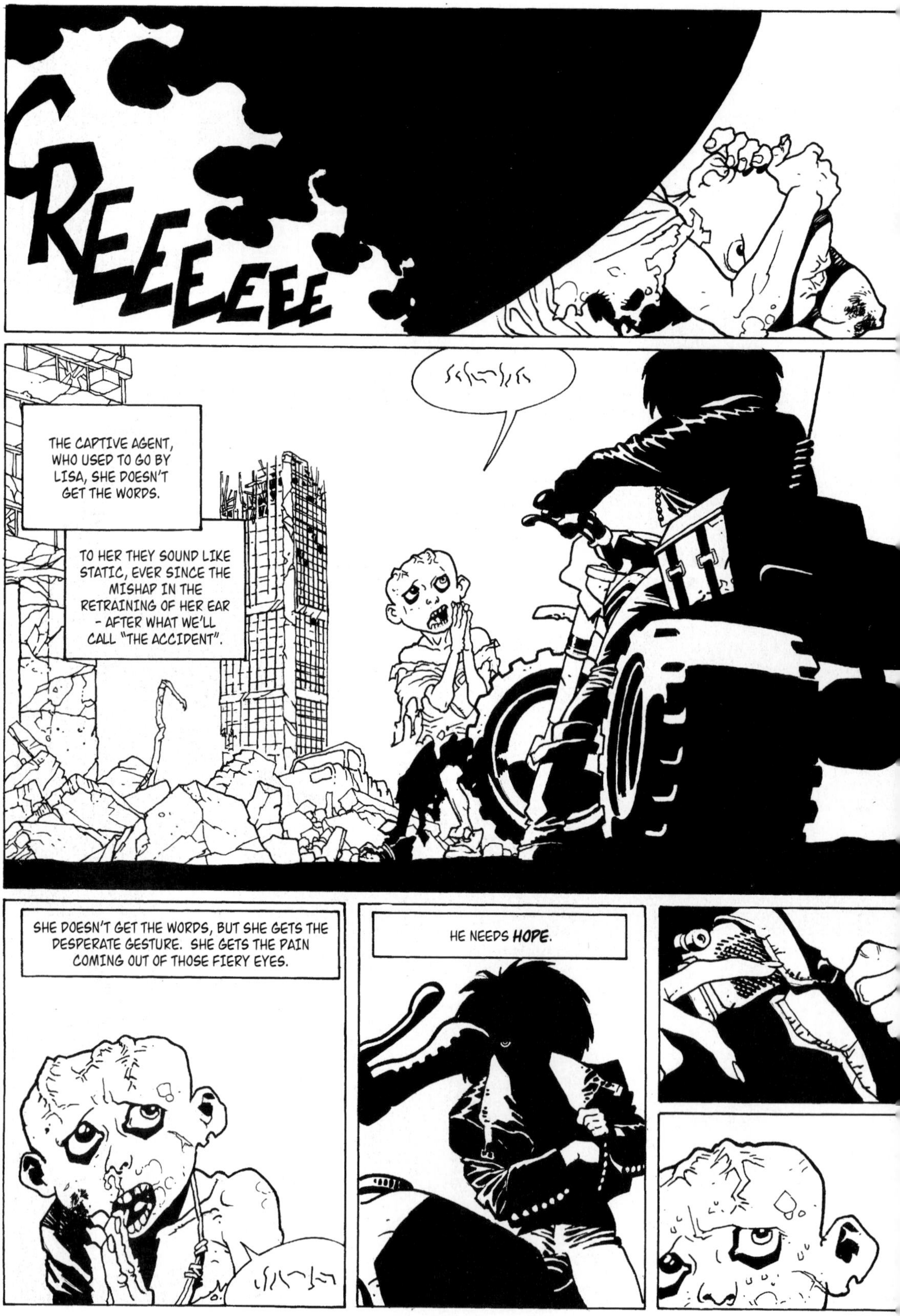
REEEEEE
THE CAPTIVE AGENT, WHO USED TO GO BY LISA, SHE DOESN'T GET THE WORDS.
TO HER THEY SOUND LIKE STATIC, EVER SINCE THE MISHAP IN THE RETRAINING OF HER EAR - AFTER WHAT WE'LL CALL "THE ACCIDENT".
SHE DOESN'T GET THE WORDS, BUT SHE GETS THE DESPERATE GESTURE. SHE GETS THE PAIN COMING OUT OF THOSE FIERY EYES.
HE NEEDS **HOPE**.

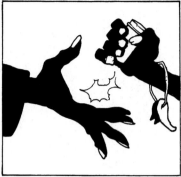

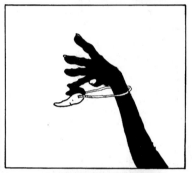

THE CAPTIVE AGENTS OF THE ELITE SQUAD ARE AUTHORIZED TO PRESCRIBE SMALL DOSES OF HOPE TO THE SUB-DREGS.

HOPE.

THE DRUG THAT LETS THEM THINK IT'S ALL GETTING BETTER. THAT HAPPINESS IS ABOUT TO UNLOAD ON THE WORLD.

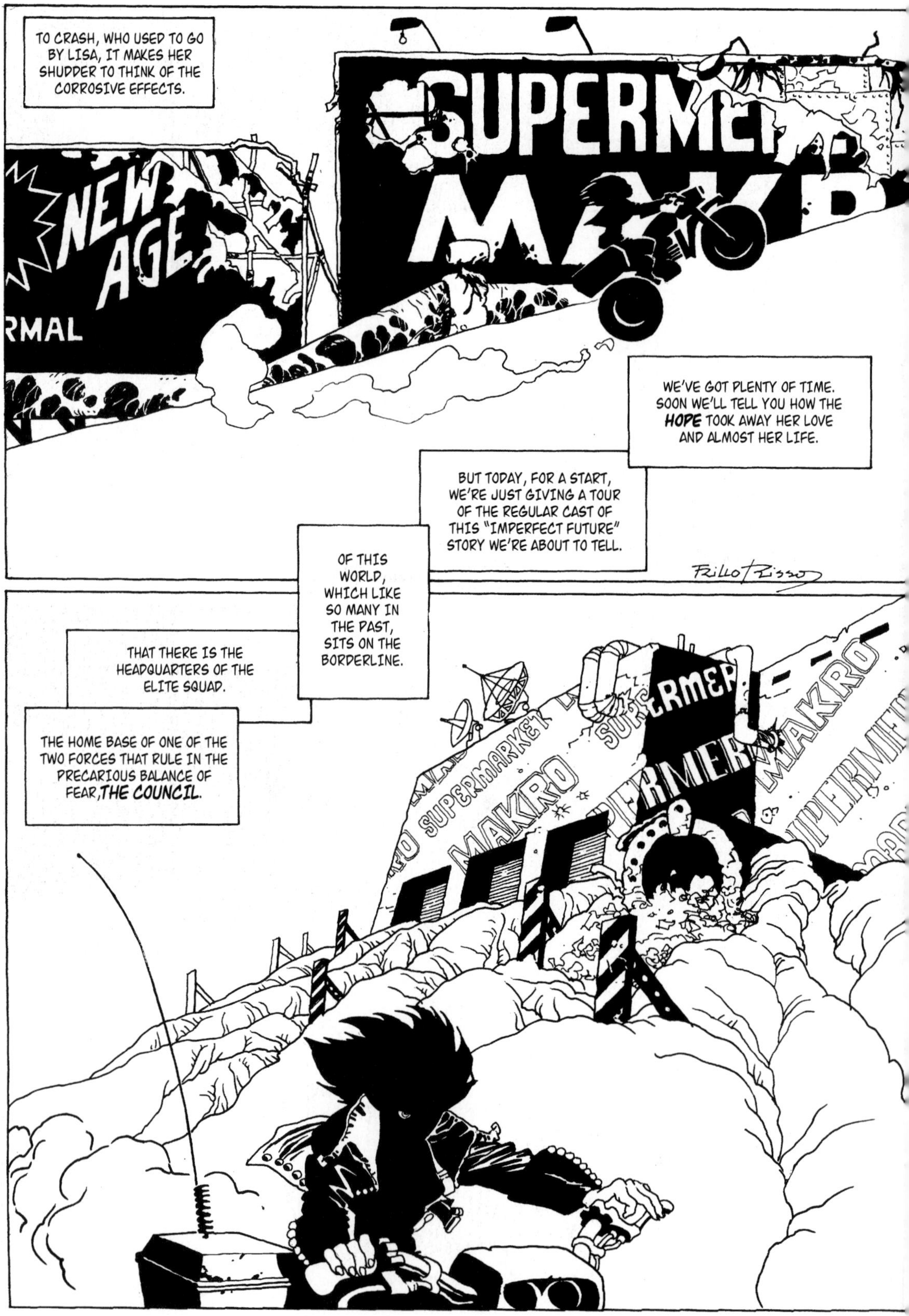
TO CRASH, WHO USED TO GO BY LISA, IT MAKES HER SHUDDER TO THINK OF THE CORROSIVE EFFECTS.
SUPERME
NEW AGE
RMAL
WE'VE GOT PLENTY OF TIME. SOON WE'LL TELL YOU HOW THE **HOPE** TOOK AWAY HER LOVE AND ALMOST HER LIFE.
BUT TODAY, FOR A START, WE'RE JUST GIVING A TOUR OF THE REGULAR CAST OF THIS "IMPERFECT FUTURE" STORY WE'RE ABOUT TO TELL.
OF THIS WORLD, WHICH LIKE SO MANY IN THE PAST, SITS ON THE BORDERLINE.
Frillo/Risso
THAT THERE IS THE HEADQUARTERS OF THE ELITE SQUAD.
THE HOME BASE OF ONE OF THE TWO FORCES THAT RULE IN THE PRECARIOUS BALANCE OF FEAR, **THE COUNCIL**.
SUPERMARKET
MAKRO
SUPERMER

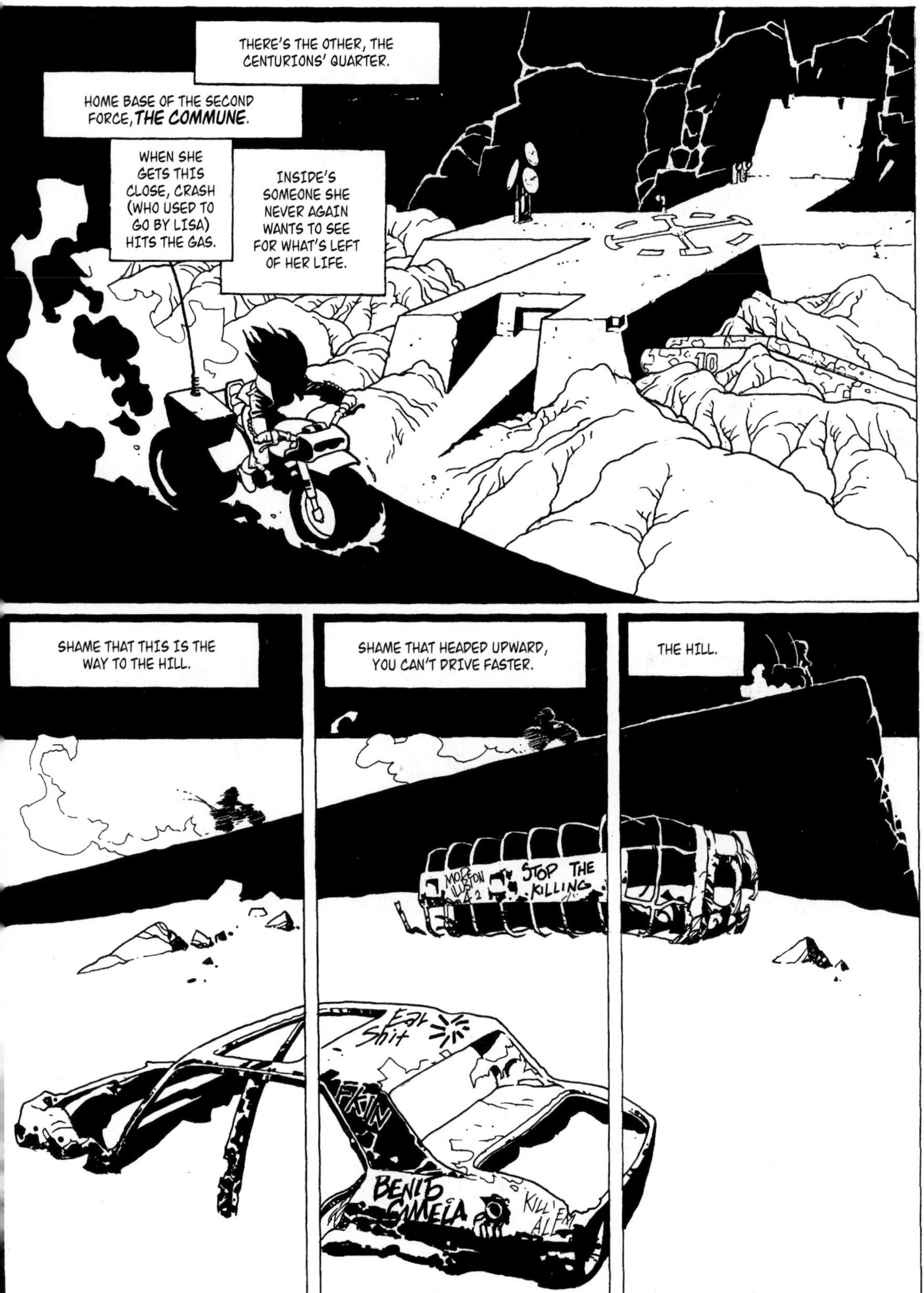
THERE'S THE OTHER, THE CENTURIONS' QUARTER.
HOME BASE OF THE SECOND FORCE, **THE COMMUNE**.
WHEN SHE GETS THIS CLOSE, CRASH (WHO USED TO GO BY LISA) HITS THE GAS.
INSIDE'S SOMEONE SHE NEVER AGAIN WANTS TO SEE FOR WHAT'S LEFT OF HER LIFE.
SHAME THAT THIS IS THE WAY TO THE HILL.
SHAME THAT HEADED UPWARD, YOU CAN'T DRIVE FASTER.
THE HILL.
STOP THE KILLING
Eat Shit
FKIN
BENITO CAMELA
KILL 'EM ALL

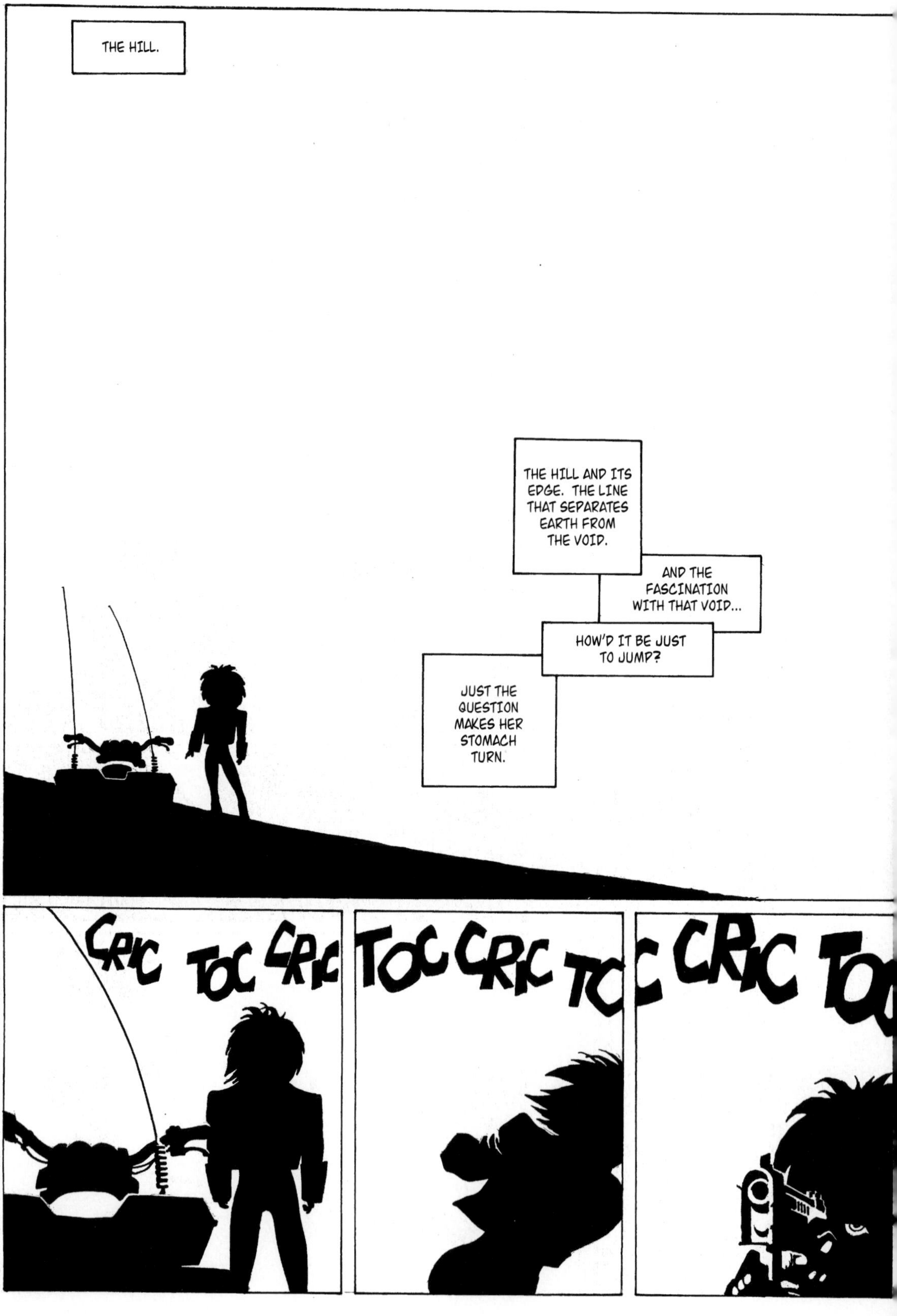
THE HILL.
THE HILL AND ITS EDGE. THE LINE THAT SEPARATES EARTH FROM THE VOID.
AND THE FASCINATION WITH THAT VOID...
HOW'D IT BE JUST TO JUMP?
JUST THE QUESTION MAKES HER STOMACH TURN.
CRIC TOC CRIC TOC CRIC TOC CRIC TOC

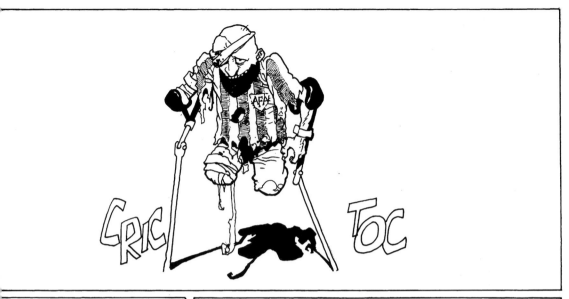

CRIC   TOC

TAC

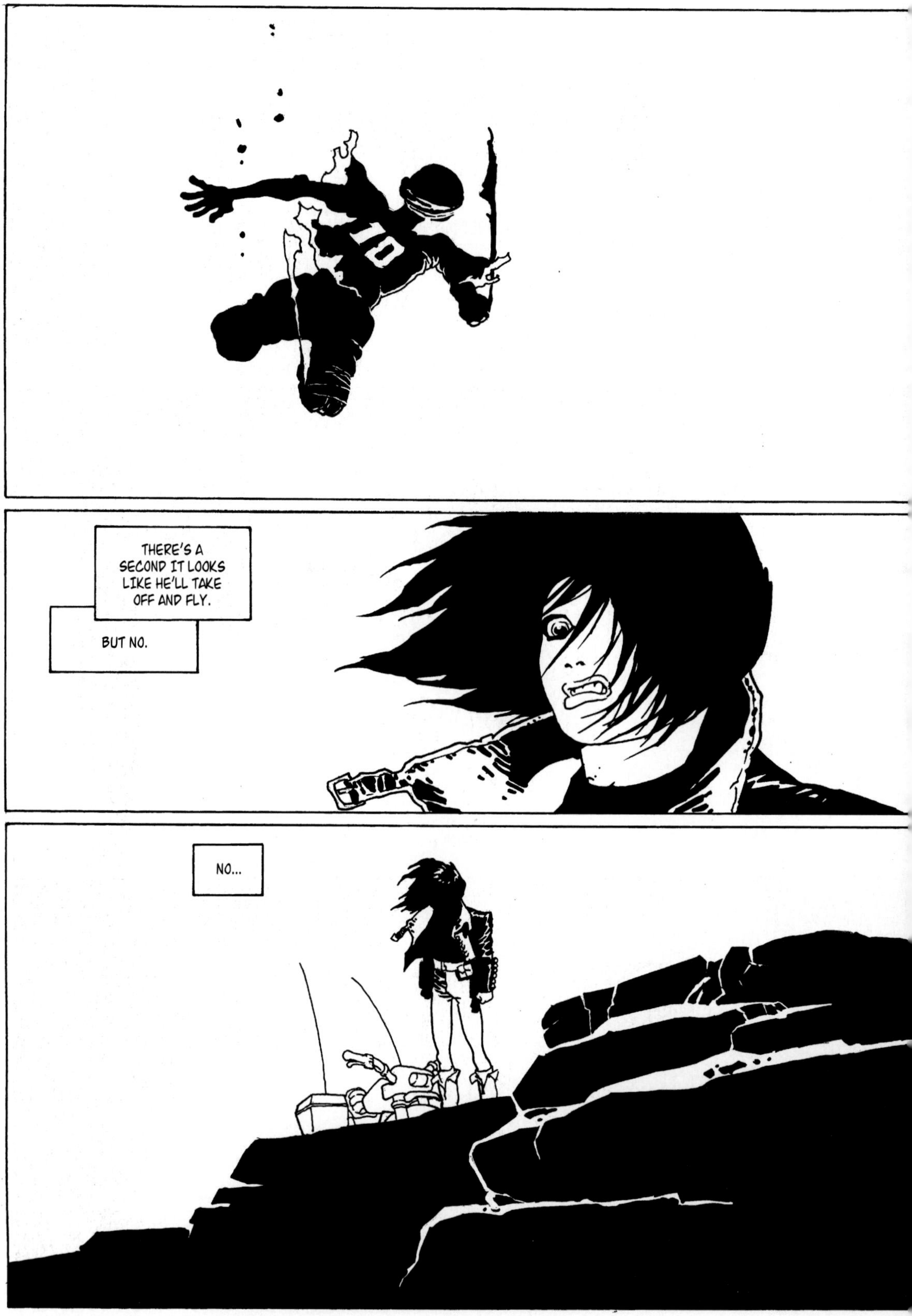
THERE'S A SECOND IT LOOKS LIKE HE'LL TAKE OFF AND FLY.
BUT NO.
NO...

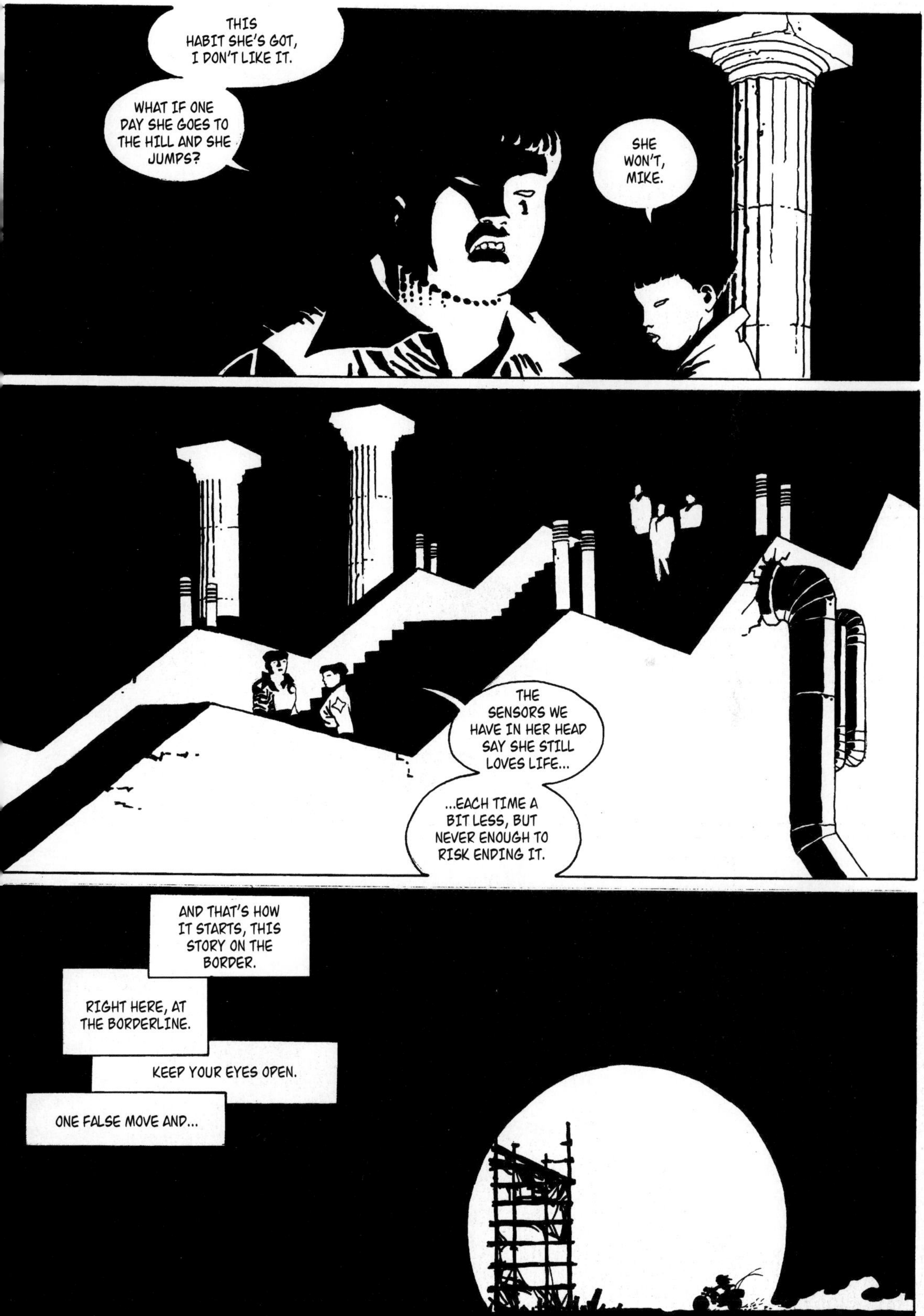
THIS HABIT SHE'S GOT, I DON'T LIKE IT.
WHAT IF ONE DAY SHE GOES TO THE HILL AND SHE JUMPS?
SHE WON'T, MIKE.
THE SENSORS WE HAVE IN HER HEAD SAY SHE STILL LOVES LIFE...
...EACH TIME A BIT LESS, BUT NEVER ENOUGH TO RISK ENDING IT.
AND THAT'S HOW IT STARTS, THIS STORY ON THE BORDER.
RIGHT HERE, AT THE BORDERLINE.
KEEP YOUR EYES OPEN.
ONE FALSE MOVE AND...

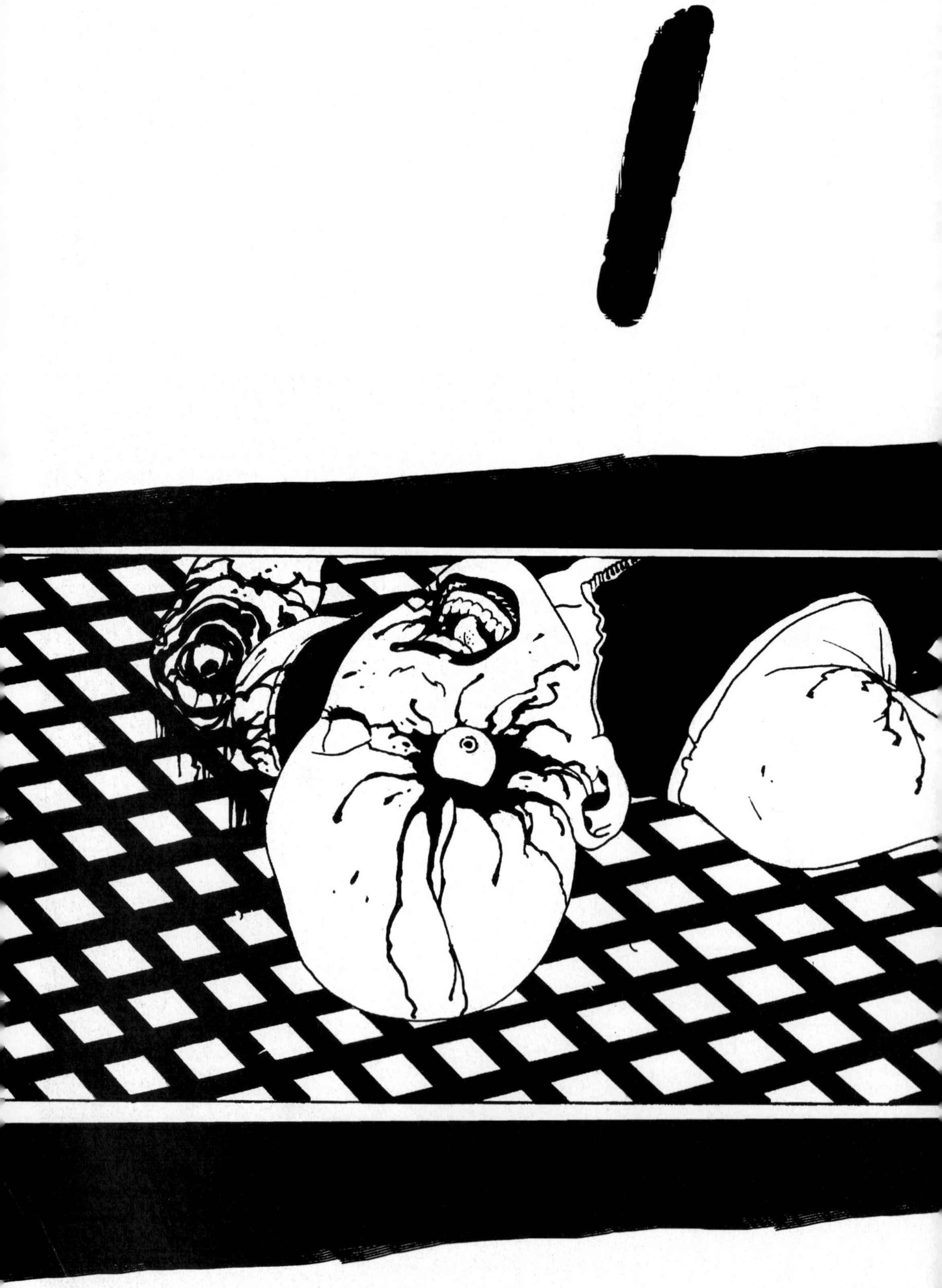

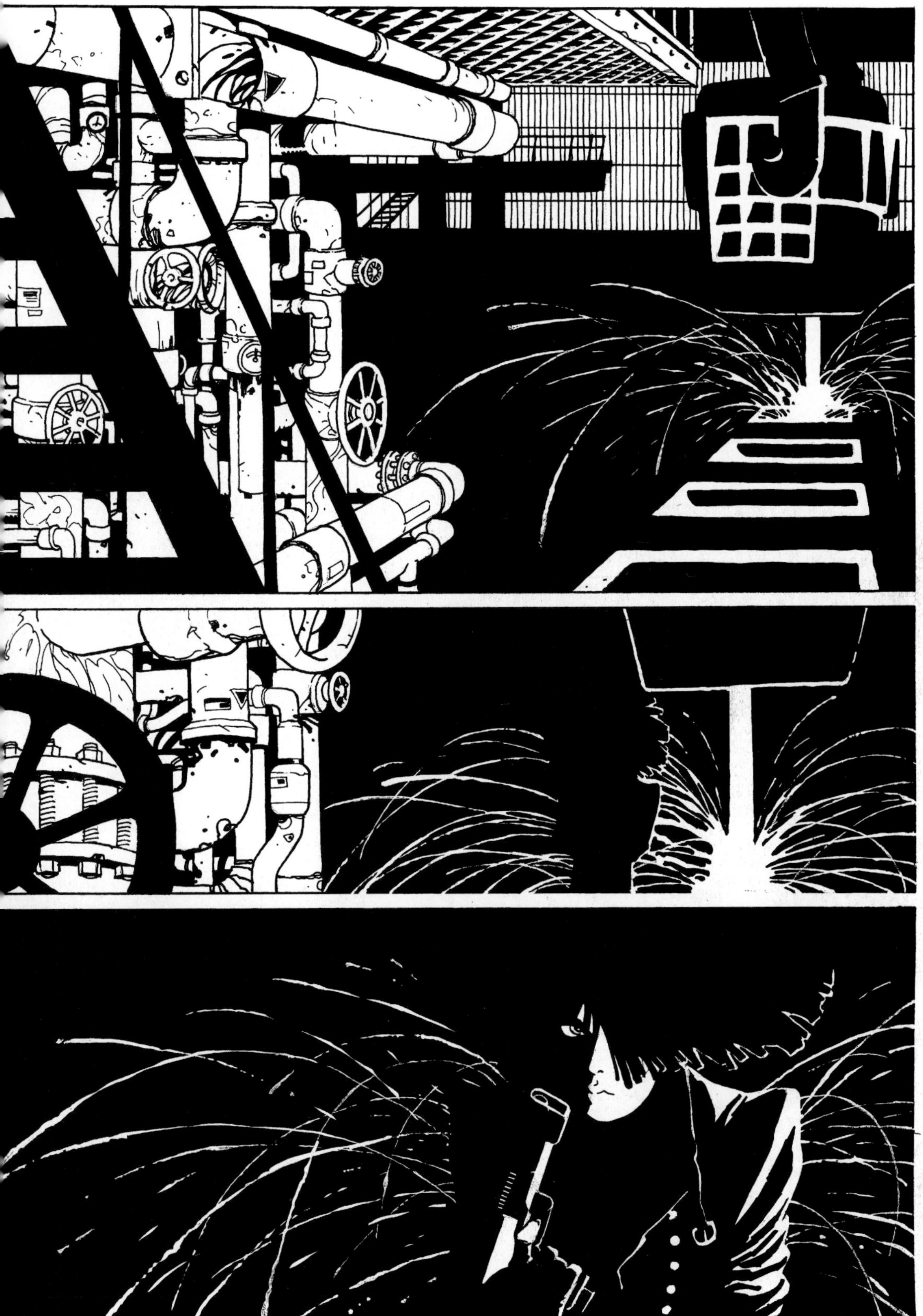

PLIC!

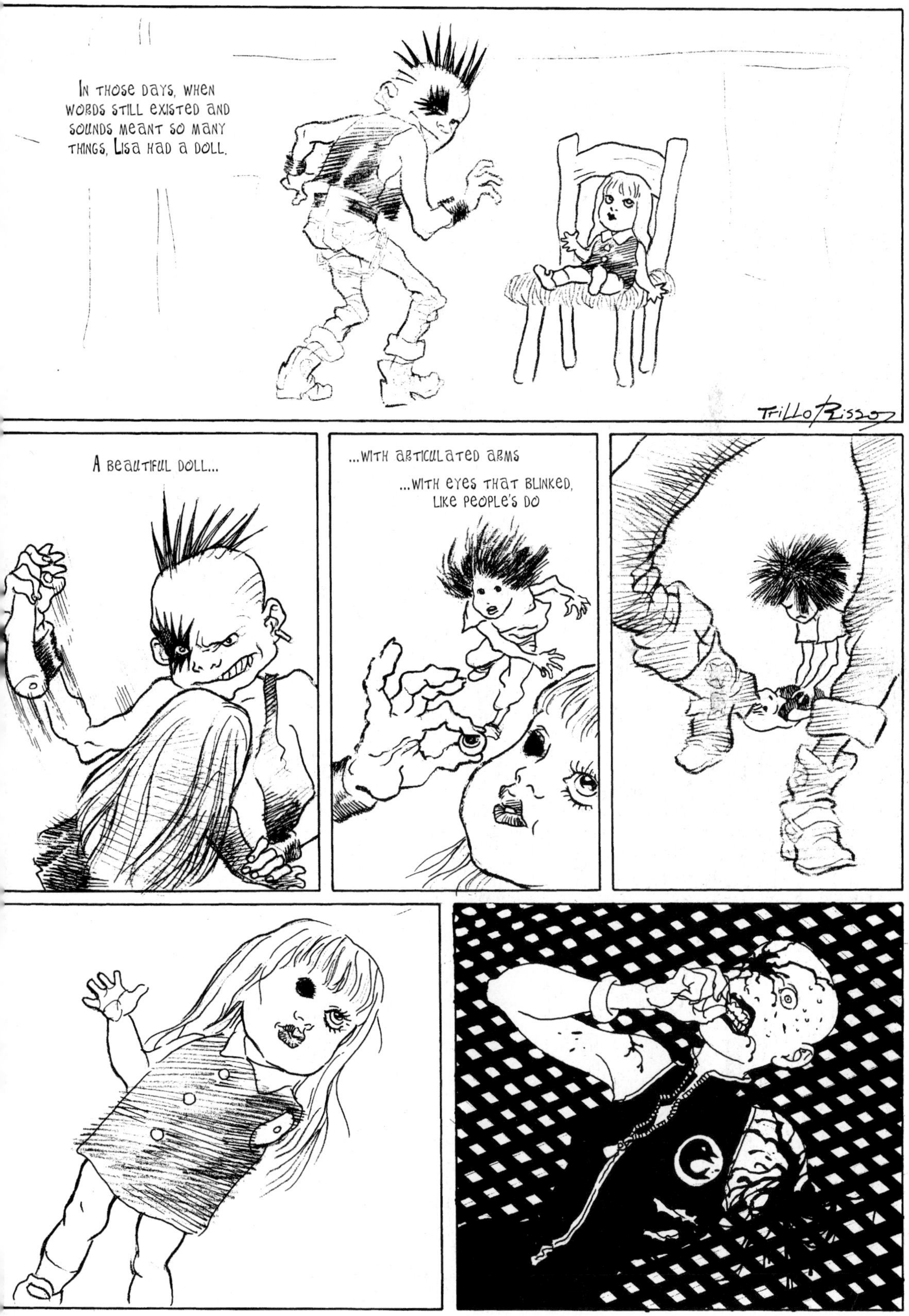
In those days, when words still existed and sounds meant so many things, Lisa had a doll.
TrilloRisso
A beautiful doll...
...with articulated arms
...with eyes that blinked, like people's do

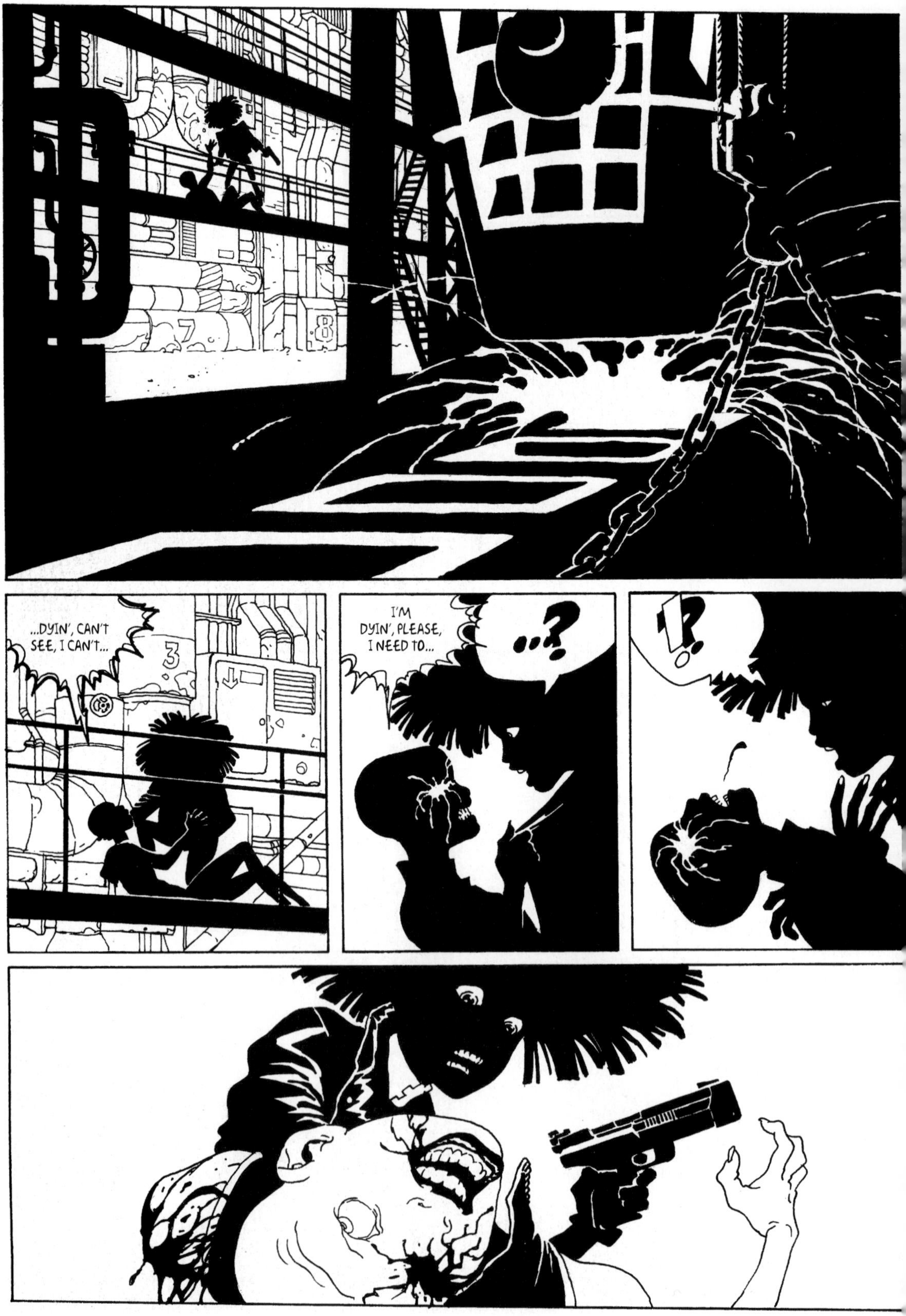
...DYIN', CAN'T SEE, I CAN'T...
I'M DYIN', PLEASE, I NEED TO...
..?
!?

In those days of words, it all hurt the same as in these days of silence.

And tears burned the skin until later the sky raining acid made crying redundant.

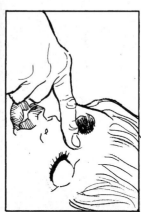

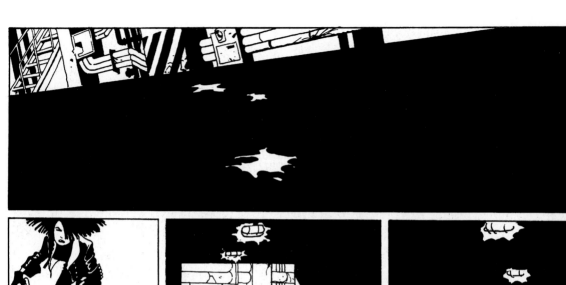

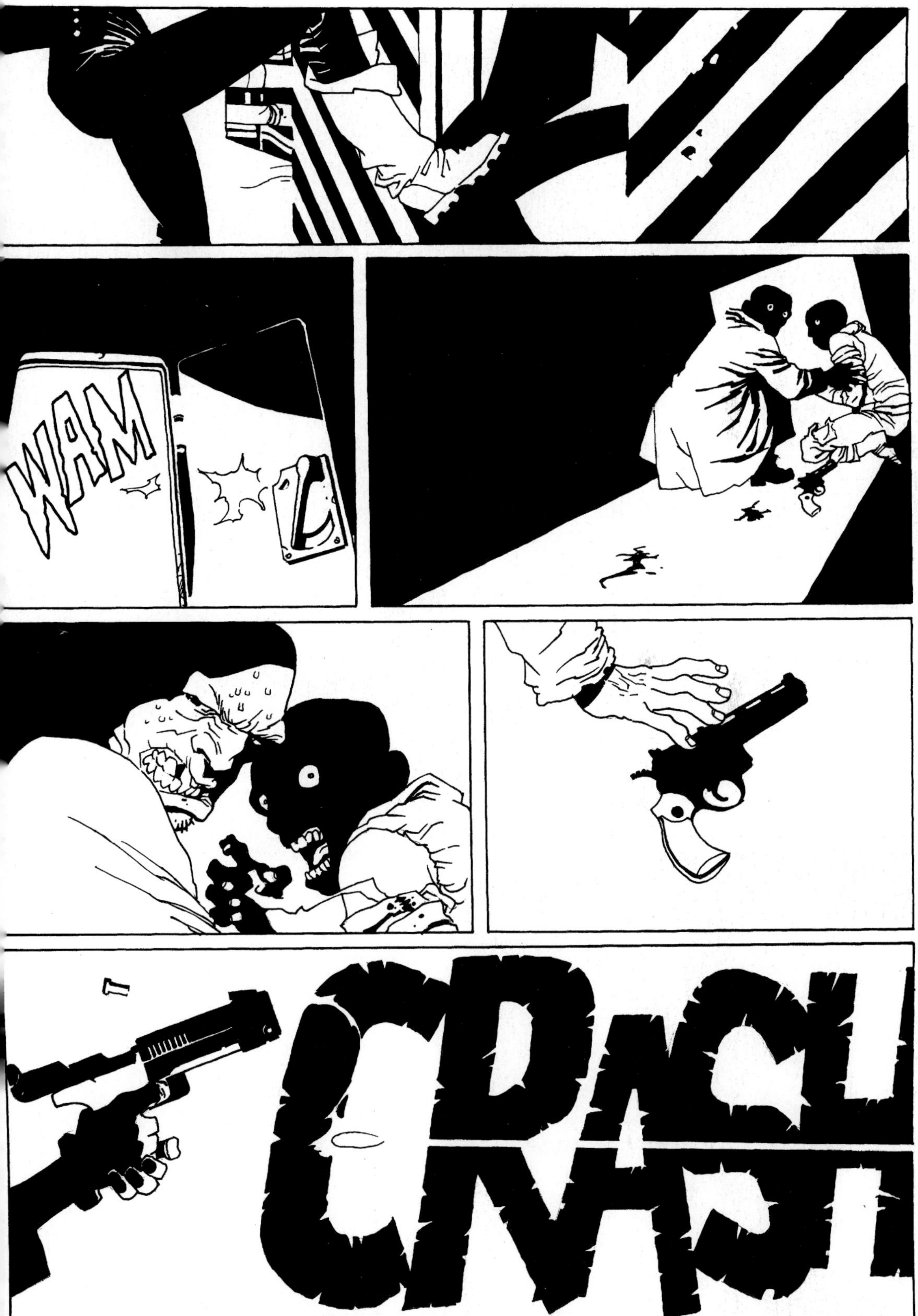
WAM

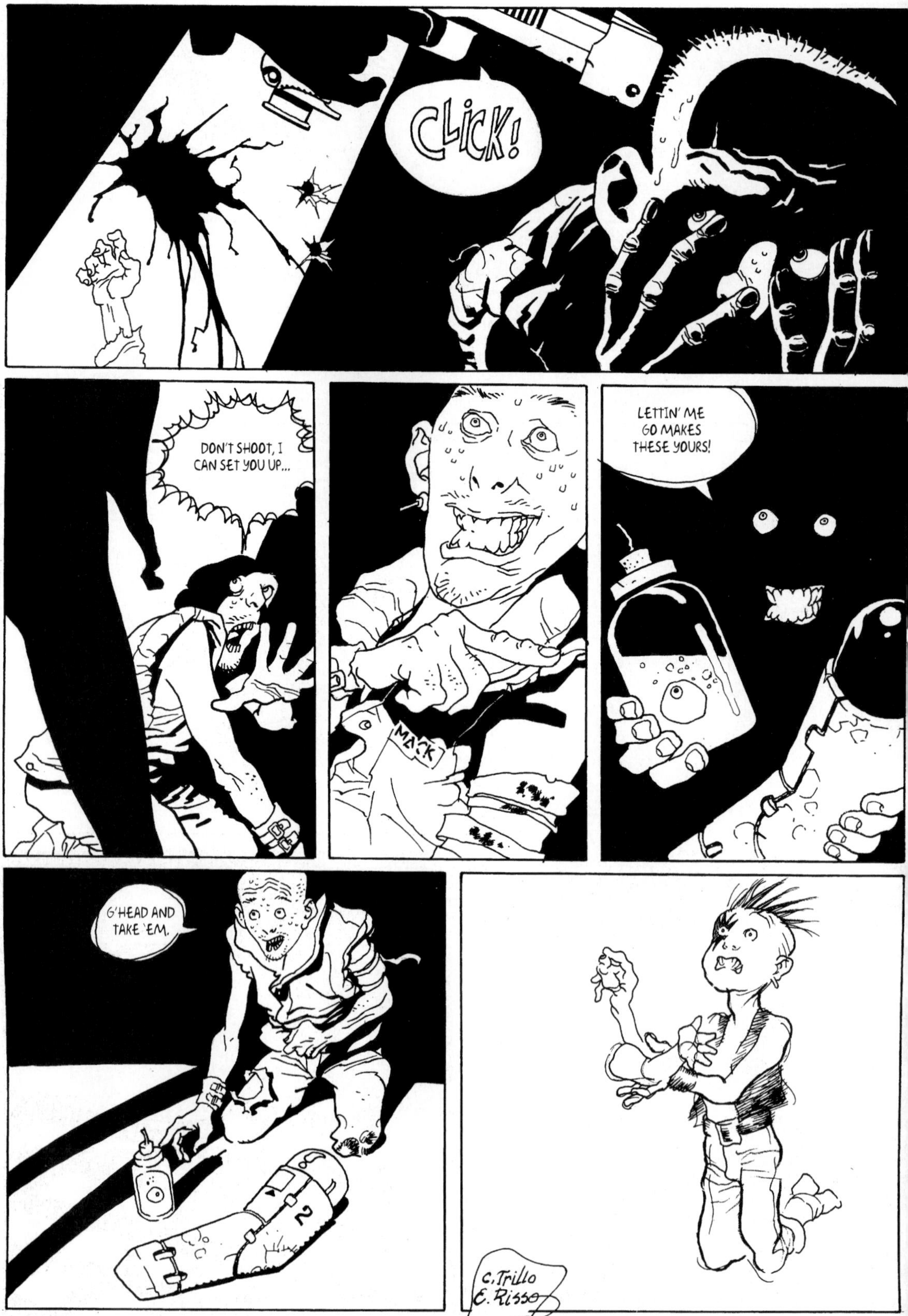
CLICK!
DON'T SHOOT, I CAN SET YOU UP...
MACK
LETTIN' ME GO MAKES THESE YOURS!
G'HEAD AND TAKE 'EM.
C. Trillo
E. Risso

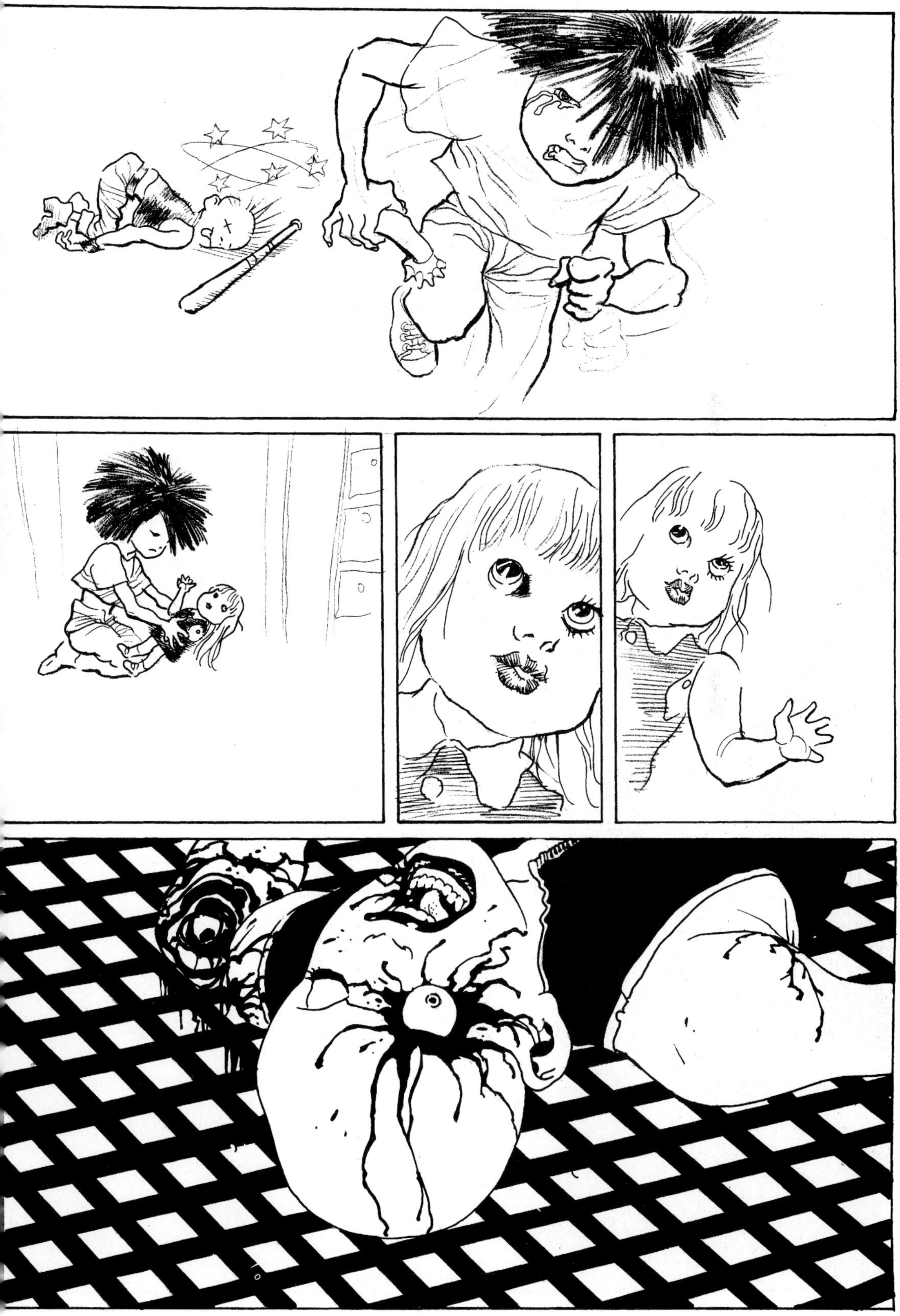

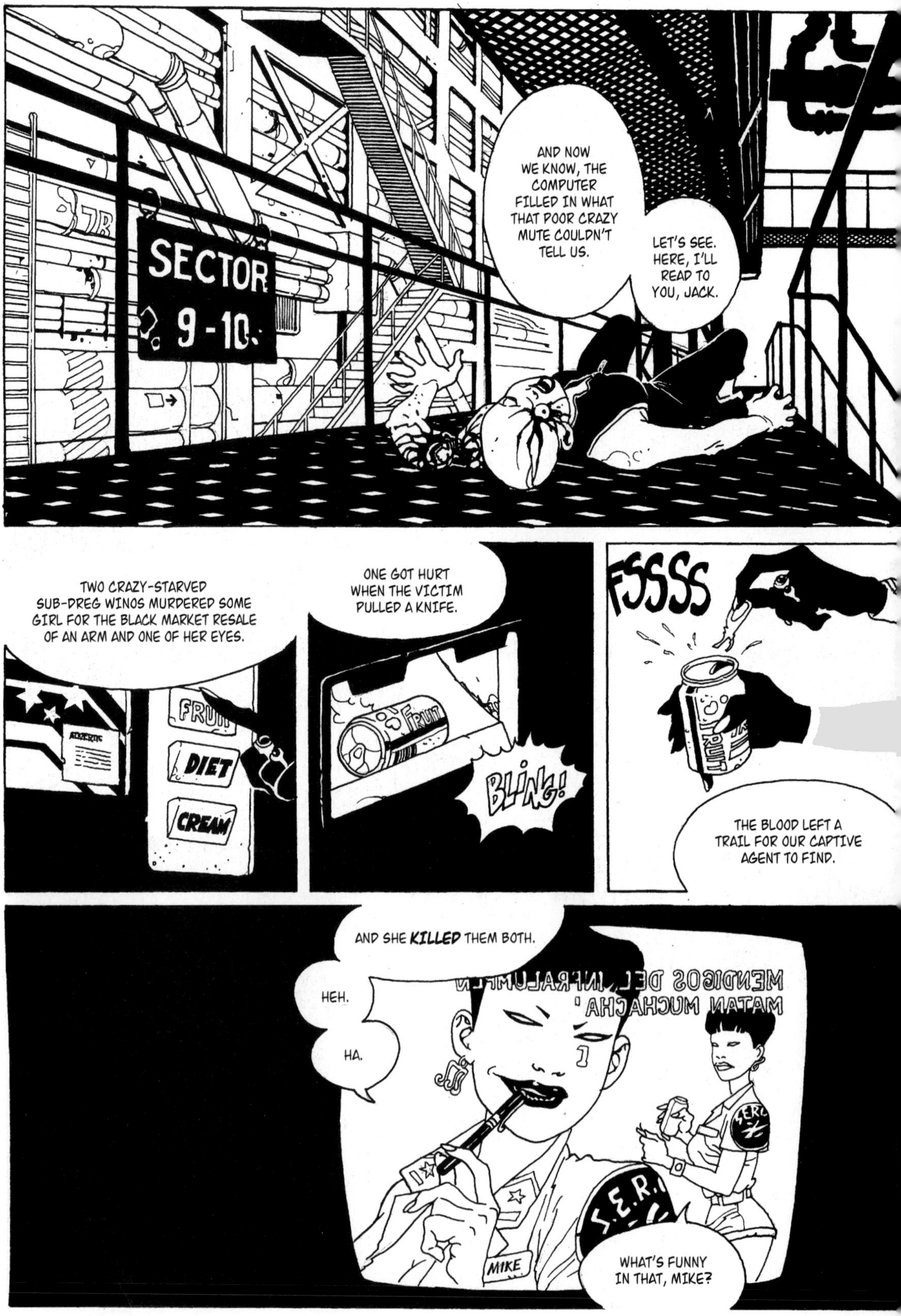
SECTOR
9-10
AND NOW WE KNOW, THE COMPUTER FILLED IN WHAT THAT POOR CRAZY MUTE COULDN'T TELL US.
LET'S SEE. HERE, I'LL READ TO YOU, JACK.
TWO CRAZY-STARVED SUB-DREG WINOS MURDERED SOME GIRL FOR THE BLACK MARKET RESALE OF AN ARM AND ONE OF HER EYES.
FRUIT
DIET
CREAM
ONE GOT HURT WHEN THE VICTIM PULLED A KNIFE.
FRUIT
BLING!
FSSSS
THE BLOOD LEFT A TRAIL FOR OUR CAPTIVE AGENT TO FIND.
AND SHE **KILLED** THEM BOTH.
HEH.
HA.
MIKE
S.E.R.
WHAT'S FUNNY IN THAT, MIKE?

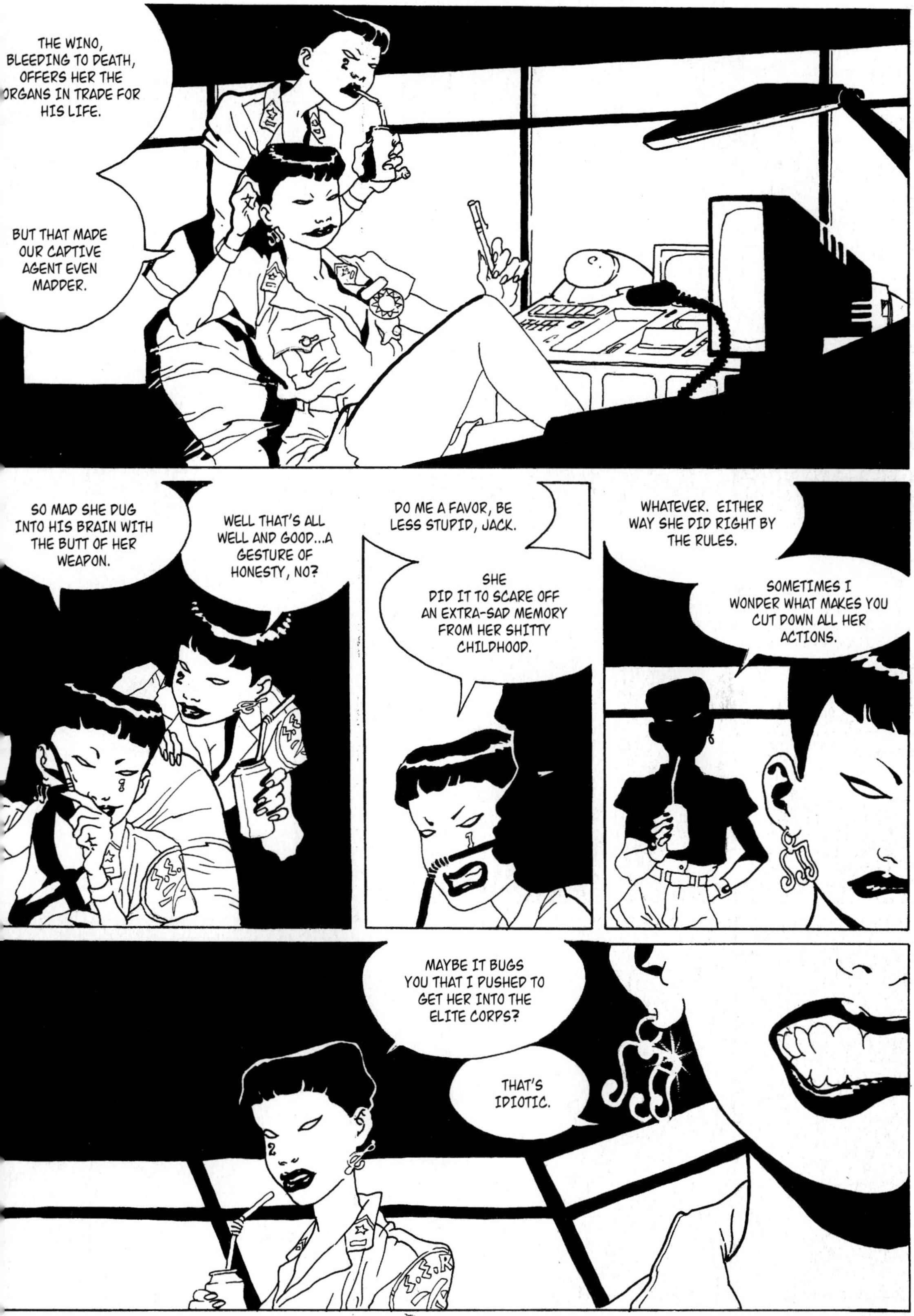
THE WINO, BLEEDING TO DEATH, OFFERS HER THE ORGANS IN TRADE FOR HIS LIFE.
BUT THAT MADE OUR CAPTIVE AGENT EVEN MADDER.
SO MAD SHE DUG INTO HIS BRAIN WITH THE BUTT OF HER WEAPON.
WELL THAT'S ALL WELL AND GOOD...A GESTURE OF HONESTY, NO?
DO ME A FAVOR, BE LESS STUPID, JACK.
SHE DID IT TO SCARE OFF AN EXTRA-SAD MEMORY FROM HER SHITTY CHILDHOOD.
WHATEVER. EITHER WAY SHE DID RIGHT BY THE RULES.
SOMETIMES I WONDER WHAT MAKES YOU CUT DOWN ALL HER ACTIONS.
MAYBE IT BUGS YOU THAT I PUSHED TO GET HER INTO THE ELITE CORPS?
THAT'S IDIOTIC.

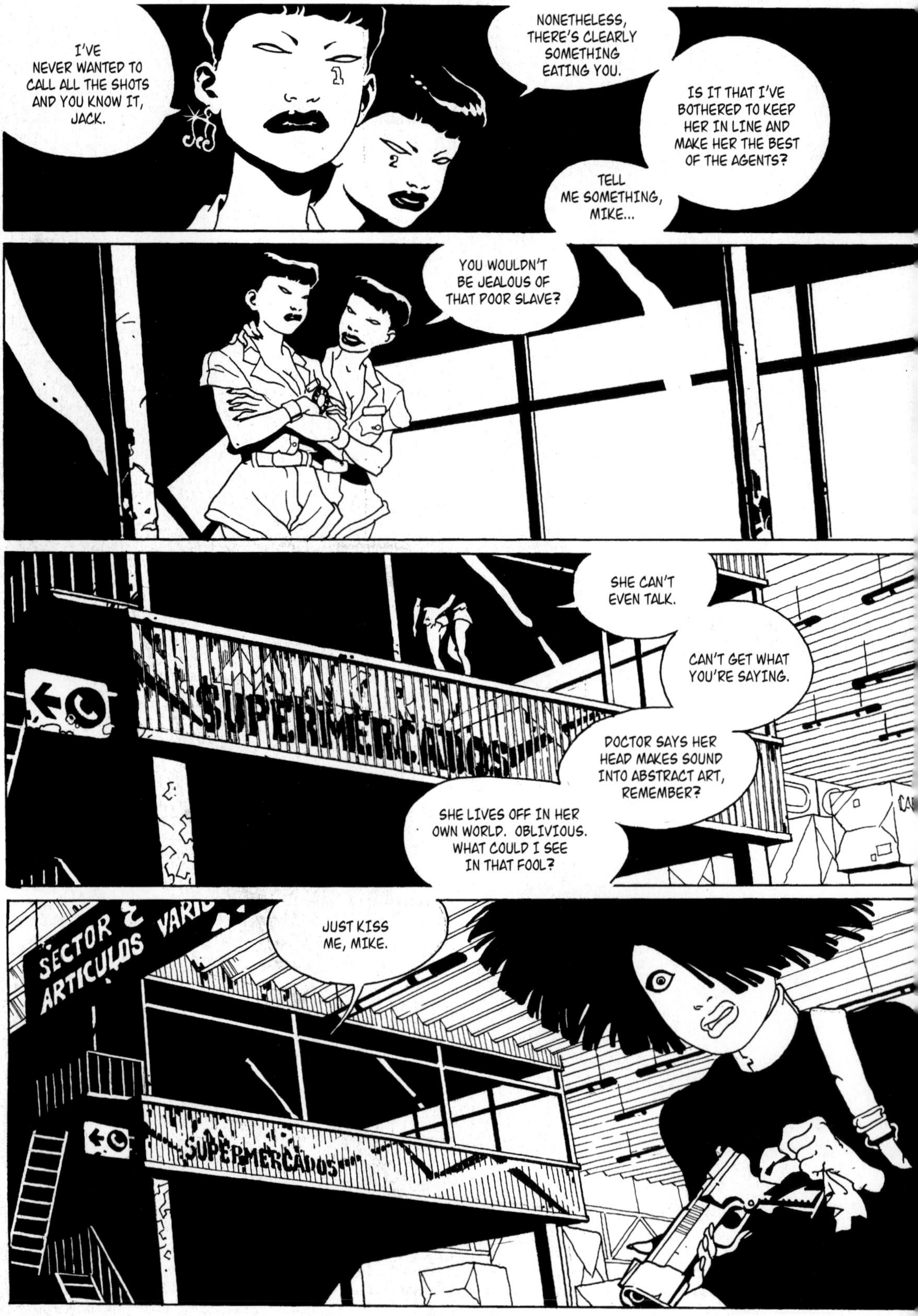

I'VE NEVER WANTED TO CALL ALL THE SHOTS AND YOU KNOW IT, JACK.
NONETHELESS, THERE'S CLEARLY SOMETHING EATING YOU.
IS IT THAT I'VE BOTHERED TO KEEP HER IN LINE AND MAKE HER THE BEST OF THE AGENTS?
TELL ME SOMETHING, MIKE...
YOU WOULDN'T BE JEALOUS OF THAT POOR SLAVE?
SUPERMERCADOS
SHE CAN'T EVEN TALK.
CAN'T GET WHAT YOU'RE SAYING.
DOCTOR SAYS HER HEAD MAKES SOUND INTO ABSTRACT ART, REMEMBER?
SHE LIVES OFF IN HER OWN WORLD. OBLIVIOUS. WHAT COULD I SEE IN THAT FOOL?
SECTOR &
ARTICULOS
JUST KISS ME, MIKE.
SUPERMERCADOS

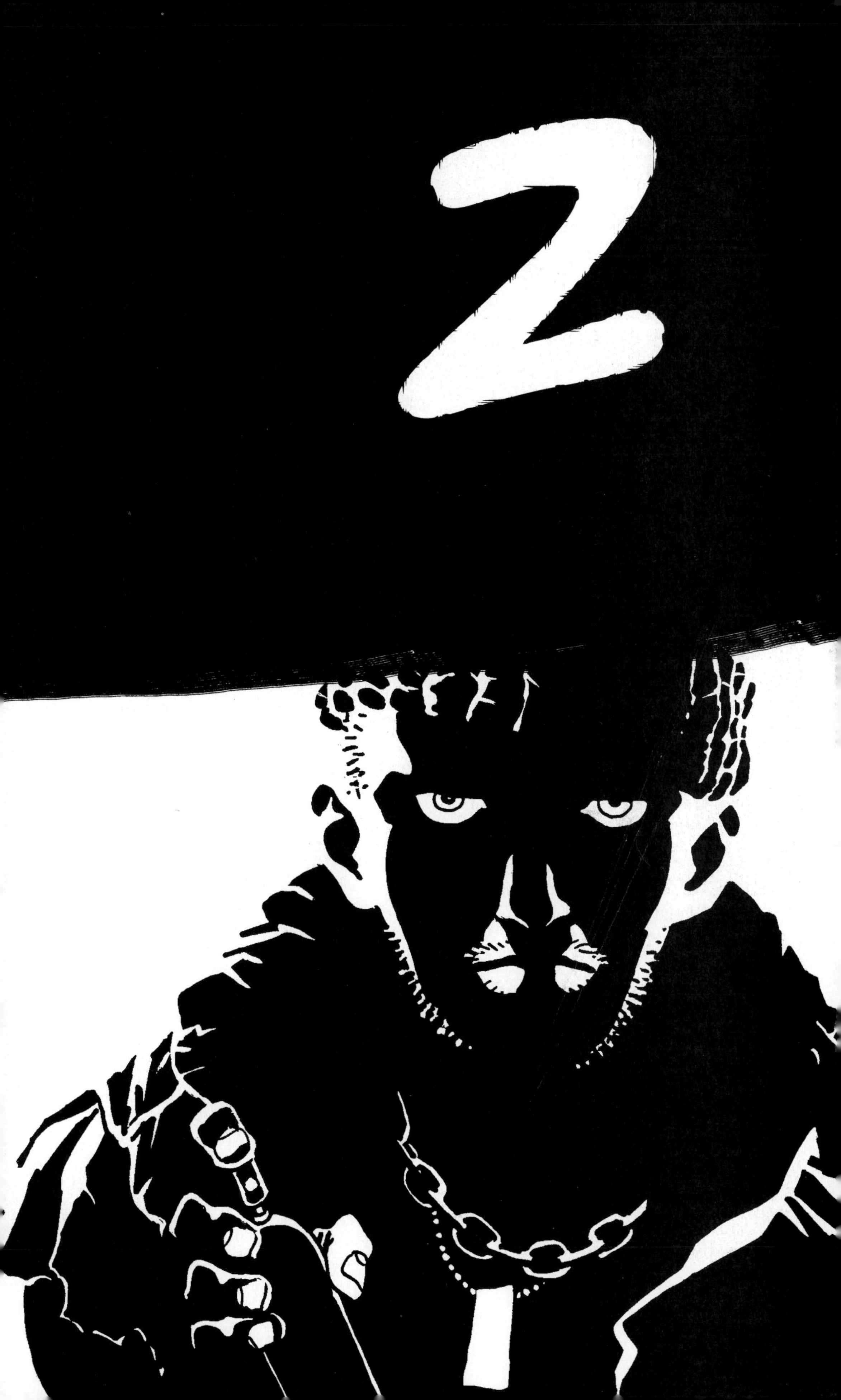
Z

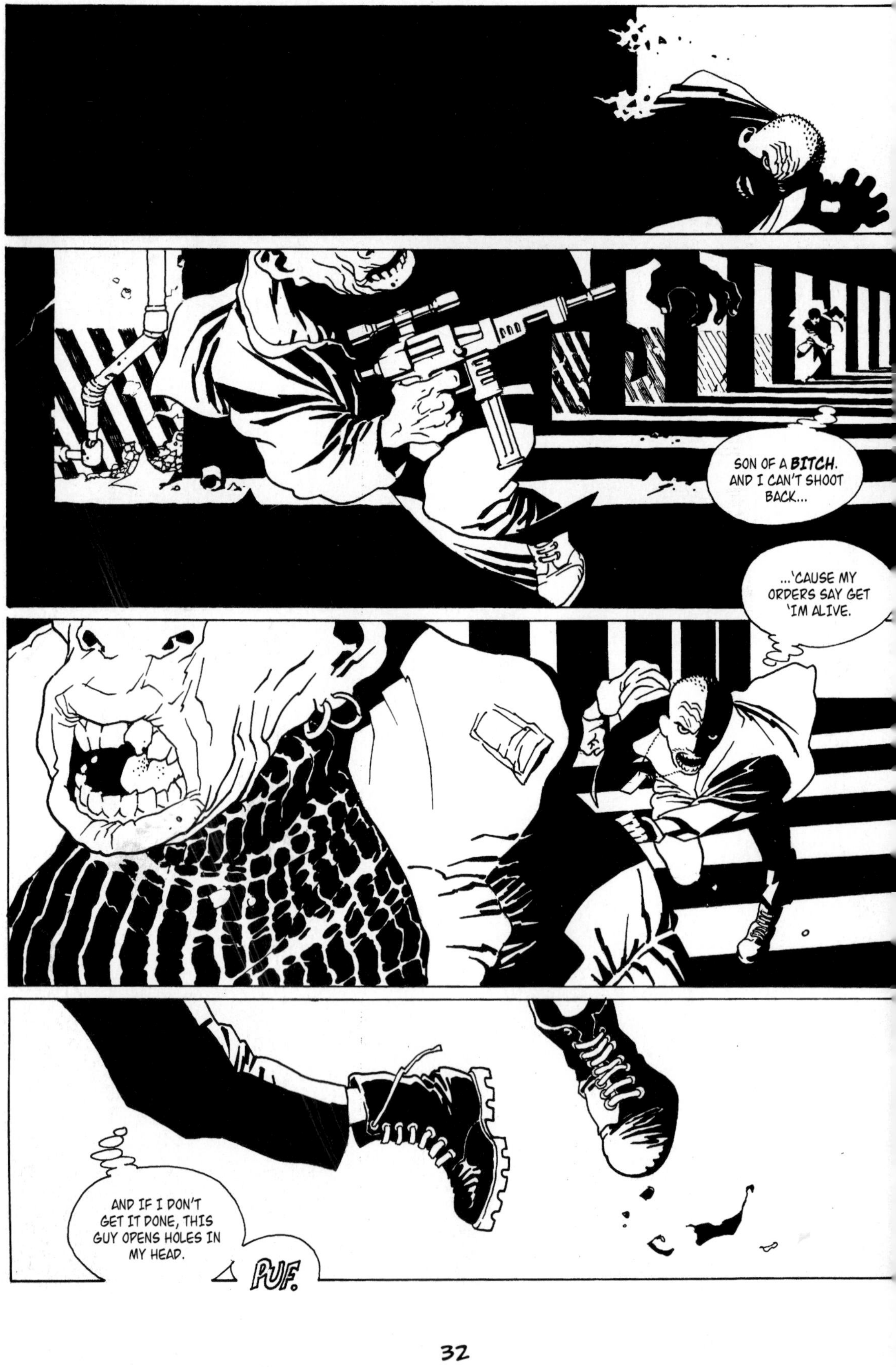
SON OF A BITCH. AND I CAN'T SHOOT BACK...
...'CAUSE MY ORDERS SAY GET 'IM ALIVE.
AND IF I DON'T GET IT DONE, THIS GUY OPENS HOLES IN MY HEAD.
PUF.

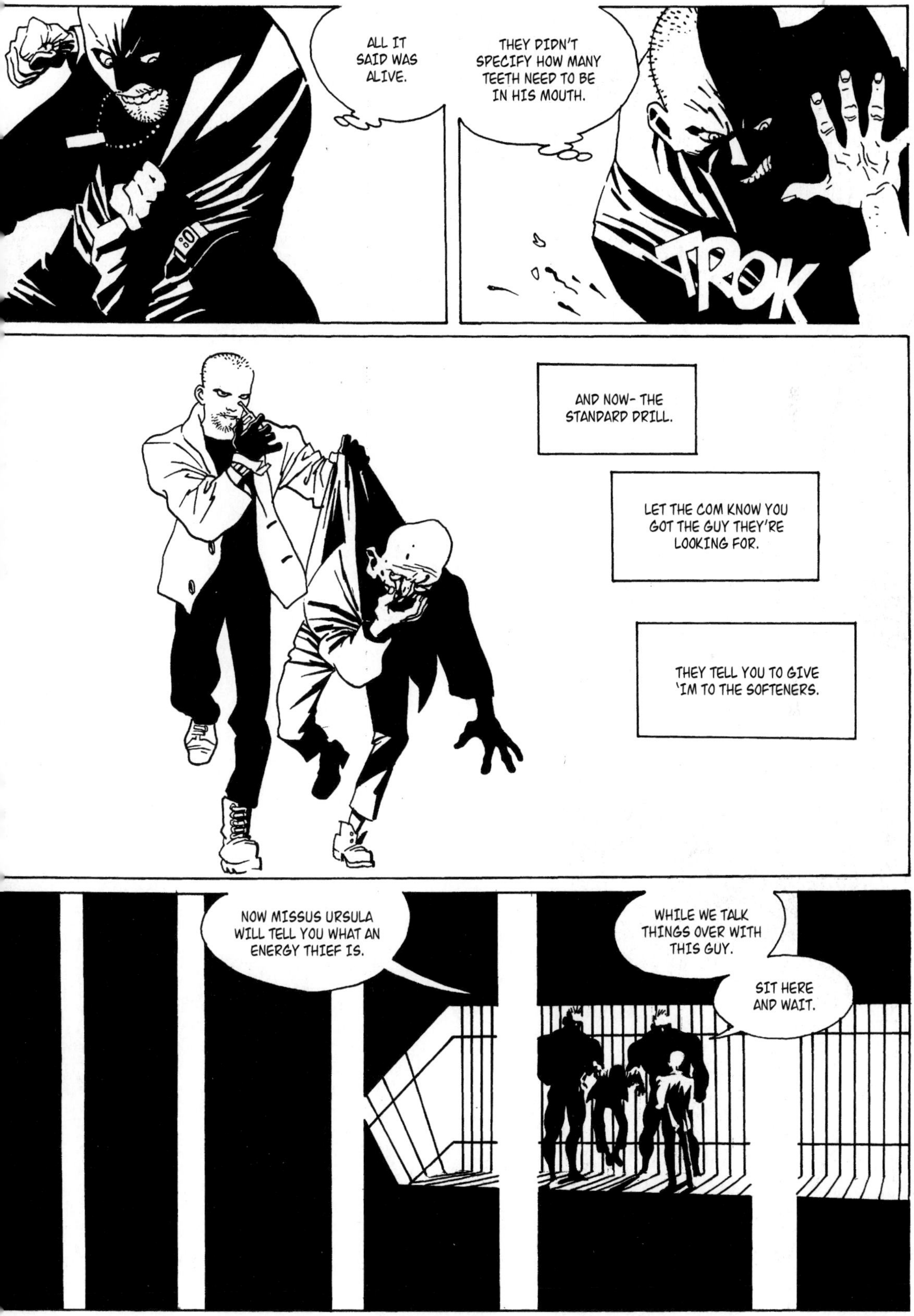

ALL IT SAID WAS ALIVE.
THEY DIDN'T SPECIFY HOW MANY TEETH NEED TO BE IN HIS MOUTH.
TROK
AND NOW- THE STANDARD DRILL.
LET THE COM KNOW YOU GOT THE GUY THEY'RE LOOKING FOR.
THEY TELL YOU TO GIVE 'IM TO THE SOFTENERS.
NOW MISSUS URSULA WILL TELL YOU WHAT AN ENERGY THIEF IS.
WHILE WE TALK THINGS OVER WITH THIS GUY.
SIT HERE AND WAIT.

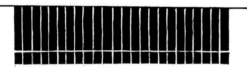

AHEM.

I'M URSULA. COMMAND INFO.

YOU'RE THE NEW TEN YEAR?

LIKE YOU OUGHT TO KNOW BUT SURELY DON'T, ALL ENERGY IS THE EXCLUSIVE PROPERTY OF THE STATE.

NOBODY USES WITHOUT FIRST GETTING SPECIAL PERMISSION FROM THE LAW.

OUTSIDE THE LAW, SOME BUY IT OFF THIEVES.

OUR TASK IS TO FIGHT THOSE THAT SIPHON THE NETWORK. THOSE THAT STEAL THE PROPERTY OF THE STATE.

THAT ONE YOU GOT, TODAY...

AAAAAAHHAAAKGH

HEAR THAT? WITH SUCH GOOD LUNGS HE'LL RAT OUT HIS GROUP IN NO TIME.

YOU SEE, NO ONE LASTS MORE THAN A HALF HOUR WITH THE SOFTENERS.

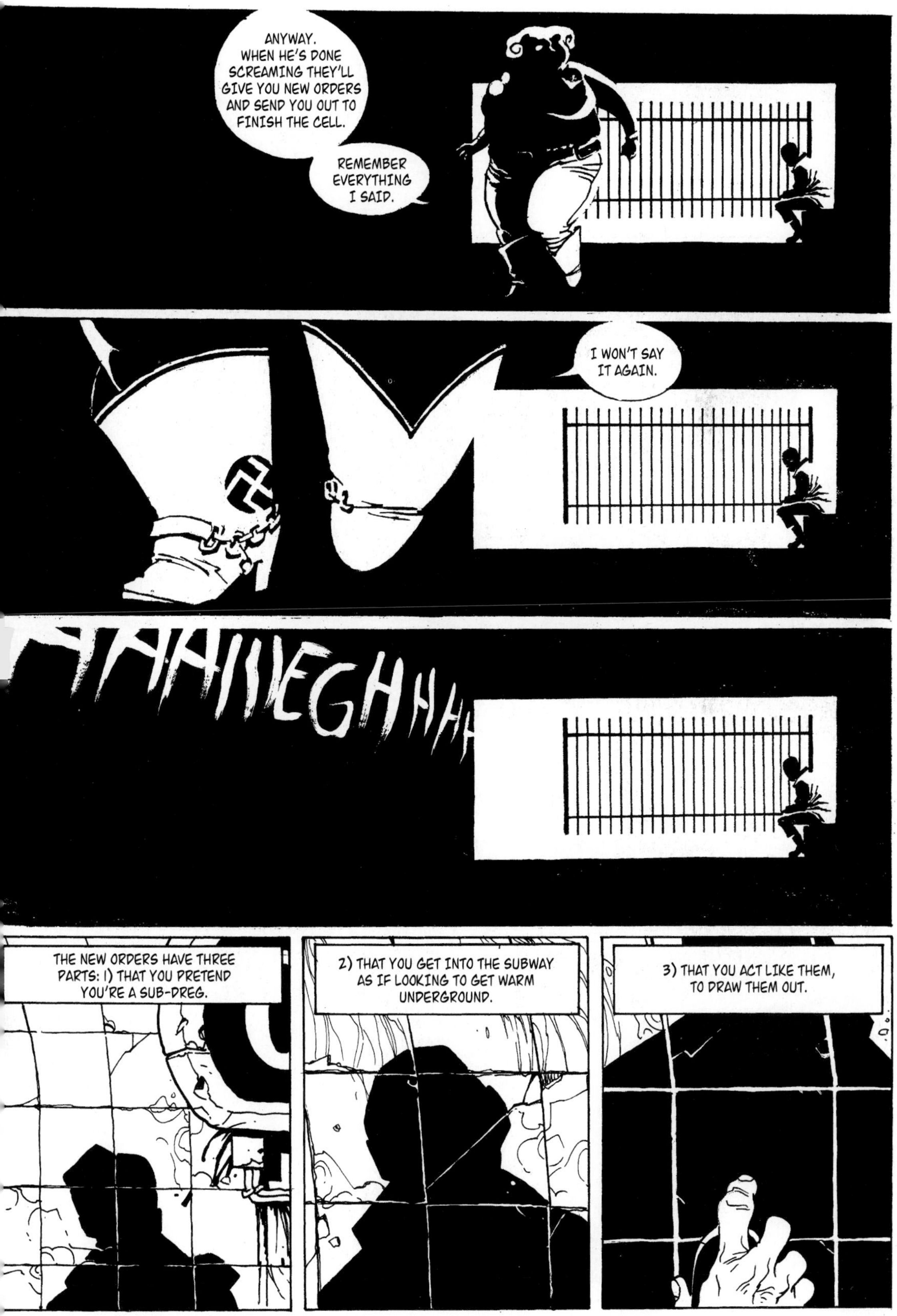

ANYWAY. WHEN HE'S DONE SCREAMING THEY'LL GIVE YOU NEW ORDERS AND SEND YOU OUT TO FINISH THE CELL.
REMEMBER EVERYTHING I SAID.
I WON'T SAY IT AGAIN.
AAAAIIEGHHHH
THE NEW ORDERS HAVE THREE PARTS: 1) THAT YOU PRETEND YOU'RE A SUB-DREG.
2) THAT YOU GET INTO THE SUBWAY AS IF LOOKING TO GET WARM UNDERGROUND.
3) THAT YOU ACT LIKE THEM, TO DRAW THEM OUT.

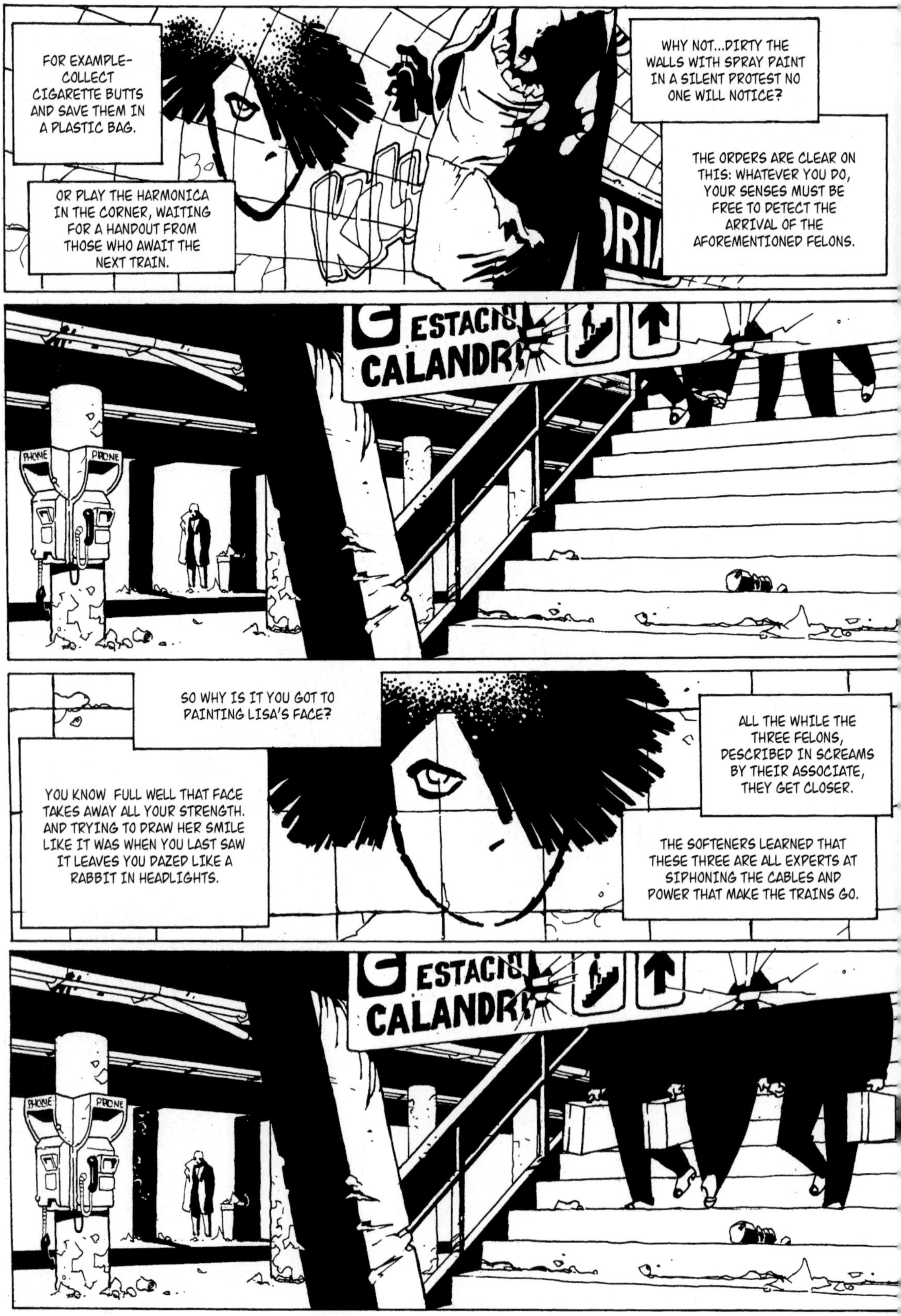

FOR EXAMPLE- COLLECT CIGARETTE BUTTS AND SAVE THEM IN A PLASTIC BAG.
OR PLAY THE HARMONICA IN THE CORNER, WAITING FOR A HANDOUT FROM THOSE WHO AWAIT THE NEXT TRAIN.
WHY NOT...DIRTY THE WALLS WITH SPRAY PAINT IN A SILENT PROTEST NO ONE WILL NOTICE?
THE ORDERS ARE CLEAR ON THIS: WHATEVER YOU DO, YOUR SENSES MUST BE FREE TO DETECT THE ARRIVAL OF THE AFOREMENTIONED FELONS.
ESTACIO
CALANDR
PHONE
PHONE
SO WHY IS IT YOU GOT TO PAINTING LISA'S FACE?
YOU KNOW FULL WELL THAT FACE TAKES AWAY ALL YOUR STRENGTH. AND TRYING TO DRAW HER SMILE LIKE IT WAS WHEN YOU LAST SAW IT LEAVES YOU DAZED LIKE A RABBIT IN HEADLIGHTS.
ALL THE WHILE THE THREE FELONS, DESCRIBED IN SCREAMS BY THEIR ASSOCIATE, THEY GET CLOSER.
THE SOFTENERS LEARNED THAT THESE THREE ARE ALL EXPERTS AT SIPHONING THE CABLES AND POWER THAT MAKE THE TRAINS GO.
ESTACIO
CALANDR
PHONE
PHONE

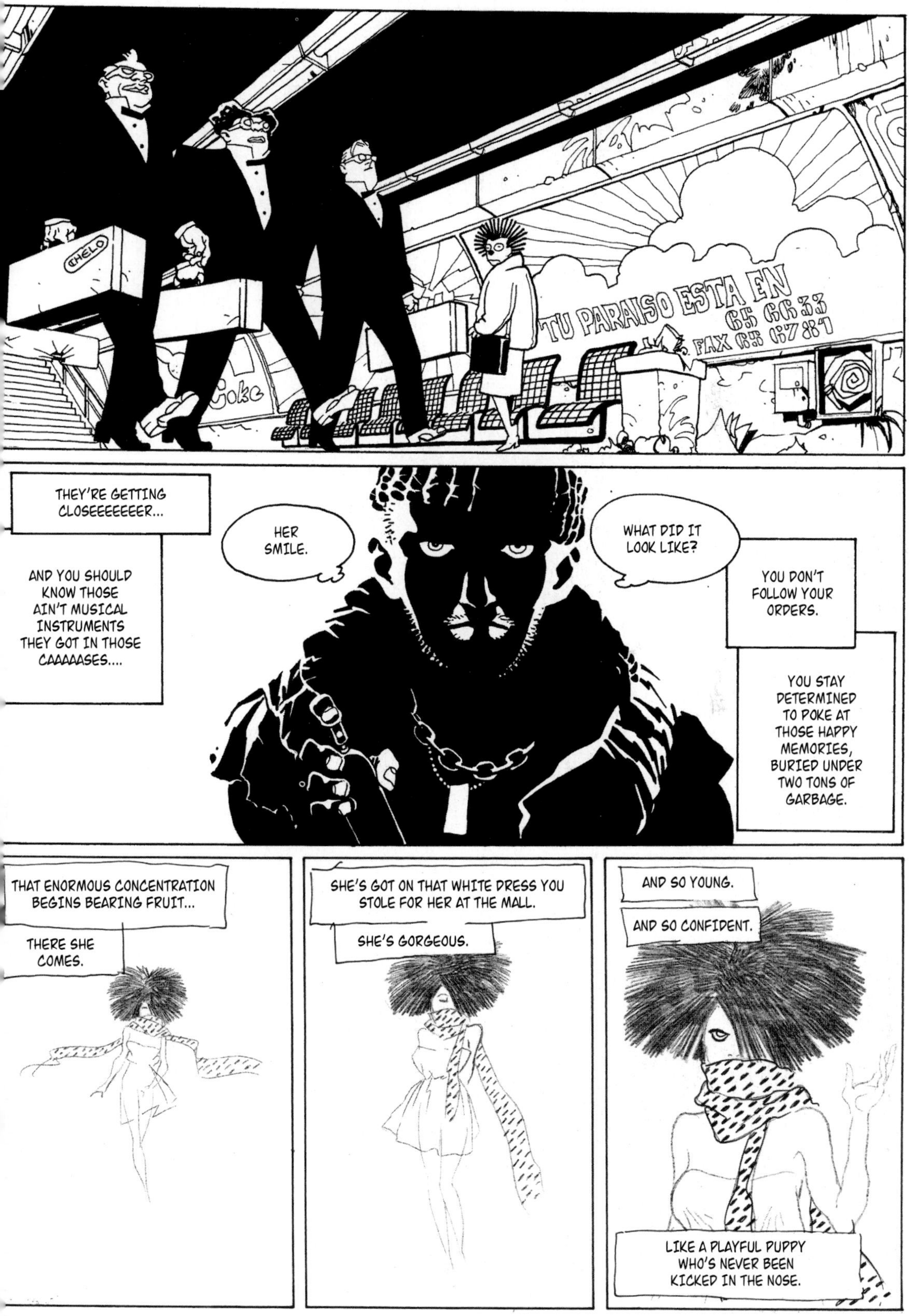
CHELO
TU PARAISO ESTA EN
65 66 33
FAX 65 67 87
Coke
THEY'RE GETTING CLOSEEEEEEER...
AND YOU SHOULD KNOW THOSE AIN'T MUSICAL INSTRUMENTS THEY GOT IN THOSE CAAAAASES....
HER SMILE.
WHAT DID IT LOOK LIKE?
YOU DON'T FOLLOW YOUR ORDERS.
YOU STAY DETERMINED TO POKE AT THOSE HAPPY MEMORIES, BURIED UNDER TWO TONS OF GARBAGE.
THAT ENORMOUS CONCENTRATION BEGINS BEARING FRUIT...
THERE SHE COMES.
SHE'S GOT ON THAT WHITE DRESS YOU STOLE FOR HER AT THE MALL.
SHE'S GORGEOUS.
AND SO YOUNG.
AND SO CONFIDENT.
LIKE A PLAYFUL PUPPY WHO'S NEVER BEEN KICKED IN THE NOSE.

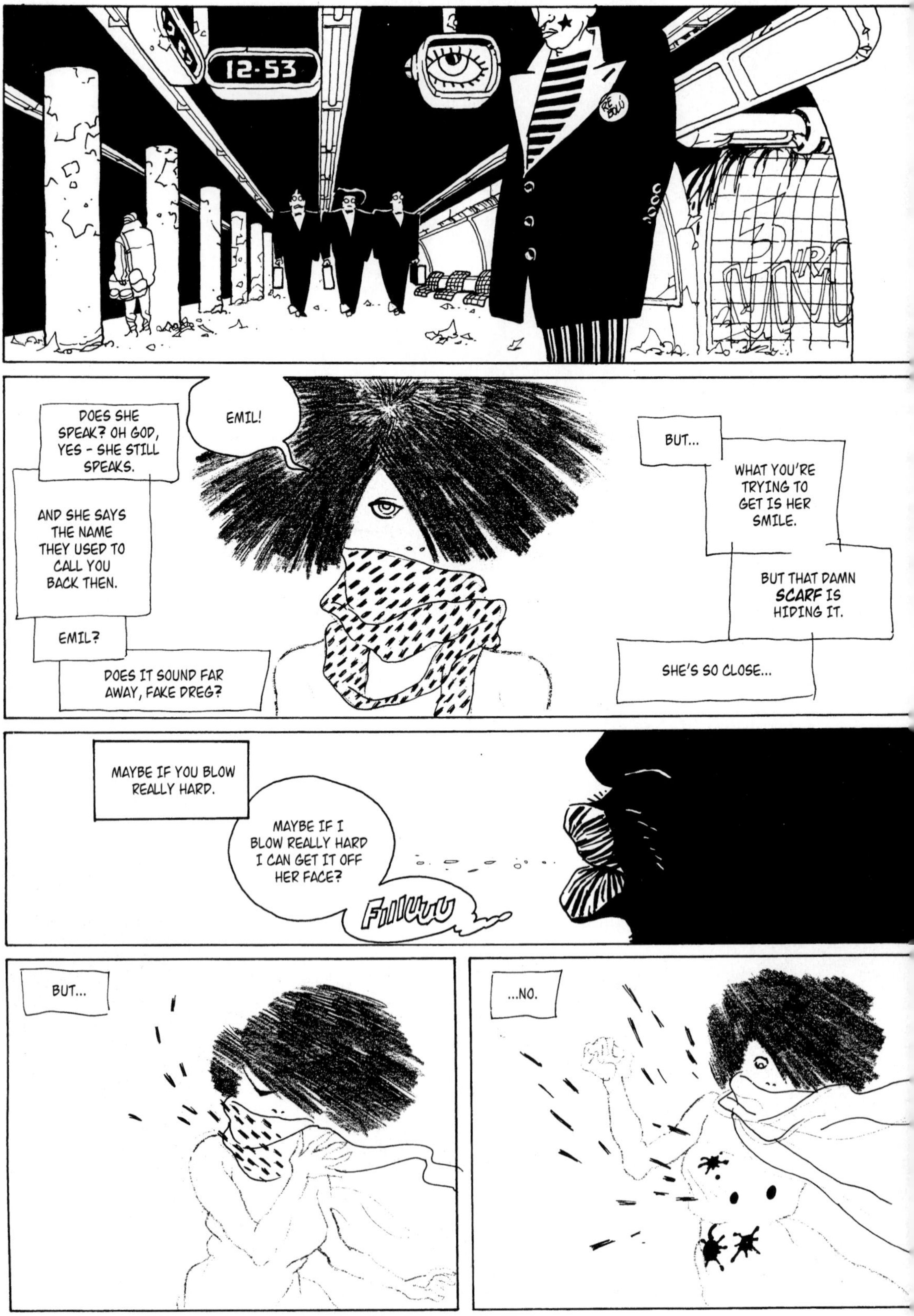
12-53
DOES SHE SPEAK? OH GOD, YES - SHE STILL SPEAKS.
EMIL!
AND SHE SAYS THE NAME THEY USED TO CALL YOU BACK THEN.
EMIL?
DOES IT SOUND FAR AWAY, FAKE DREG?
BUT...
WHAT YOU'RE TRYING TO GET IS HER SMILE.
BUT THAT DAMN SCARF IS HIDING IT.
SHE'S SO CLOSE...
MAYBE IF YOU BLOW REALLY HARD.
MAYBE IF I BLOW REALLY HARD I CAN GET IT OFF HER FACE?
FIIIUUU
BUT...
...NO.

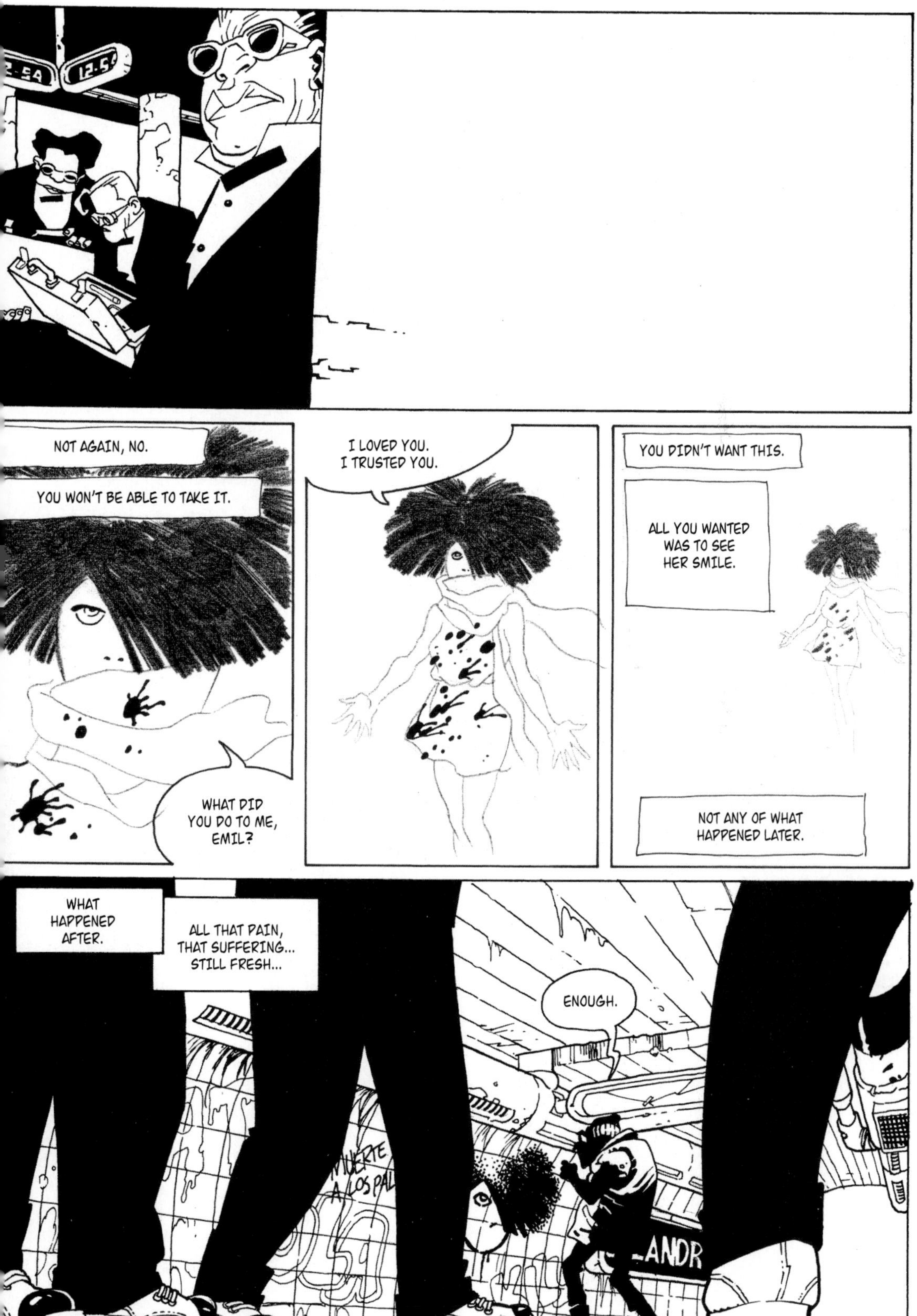

12.54
12.5
NOT AGAIN, NO.
YOU WON'T BE ABLE TO TAKE IT.
WHAT DID YOU DO TO ME, EMIL?
I LOVED YOU. I TRUSTED YOU.
YOU DIDN'T WANT THIS.
ALL YOU WANTED WAS TO SEE HER SMILE.
NOT ANY OF WHAT HAPPENED LATER.
WHAT HAPPENED AFTER.
ALL THAT PAIN, THAT SUFFERING... STILL FRESH...
ENOUGH.
MUERTE A LOS PA
LANDR

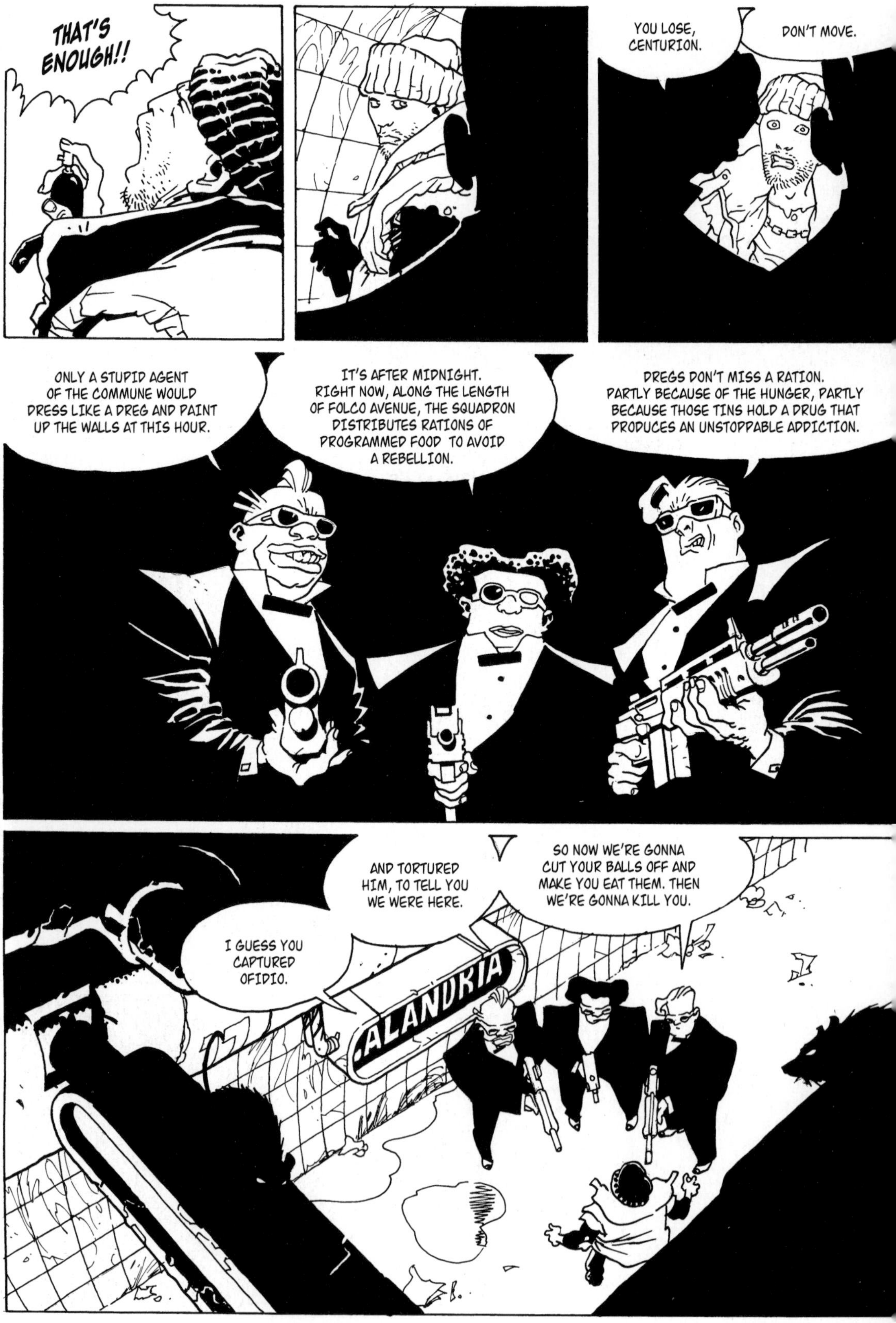
THAT'S ENOUGH!!
YOU LOSE, CENTURION.
DON'T MOVE.
ONLY A STUPID AGENT OF THE COMMUNE WOULD DRESS LIKE A DREG AND PAINT UP THE WALLS AT THIS HOUR.
IT'S AFTER MIDNIGHT. RIGHT NOW, ALONG THE LENGTH OF FOLCO AVENUE, THE SQUADRON DISTRIBUTES RATIONS OF PROGRAMMED FOOD TO AVOID A REBELLION.
DREGS DON'T MISS A RATION. PARTLY BECAUSE OF THE HUNGER, PARTLY BECAUSE THOSE TINS HOLD A DRUG THAT PRODUCES AN UNSTOPPABLE ADDICTION.
I GUESS YOU CAPTURED OFIDIO.
AND TORTURED HIM, TO TELL YOU WE WERE HERE.
SO NOW WE'RE GONNA CUT YOUR BALLS OFF AND MAKE YOU EAT THEM. THEN WE'RE GONNA KILL YOU.
ALANDRIA

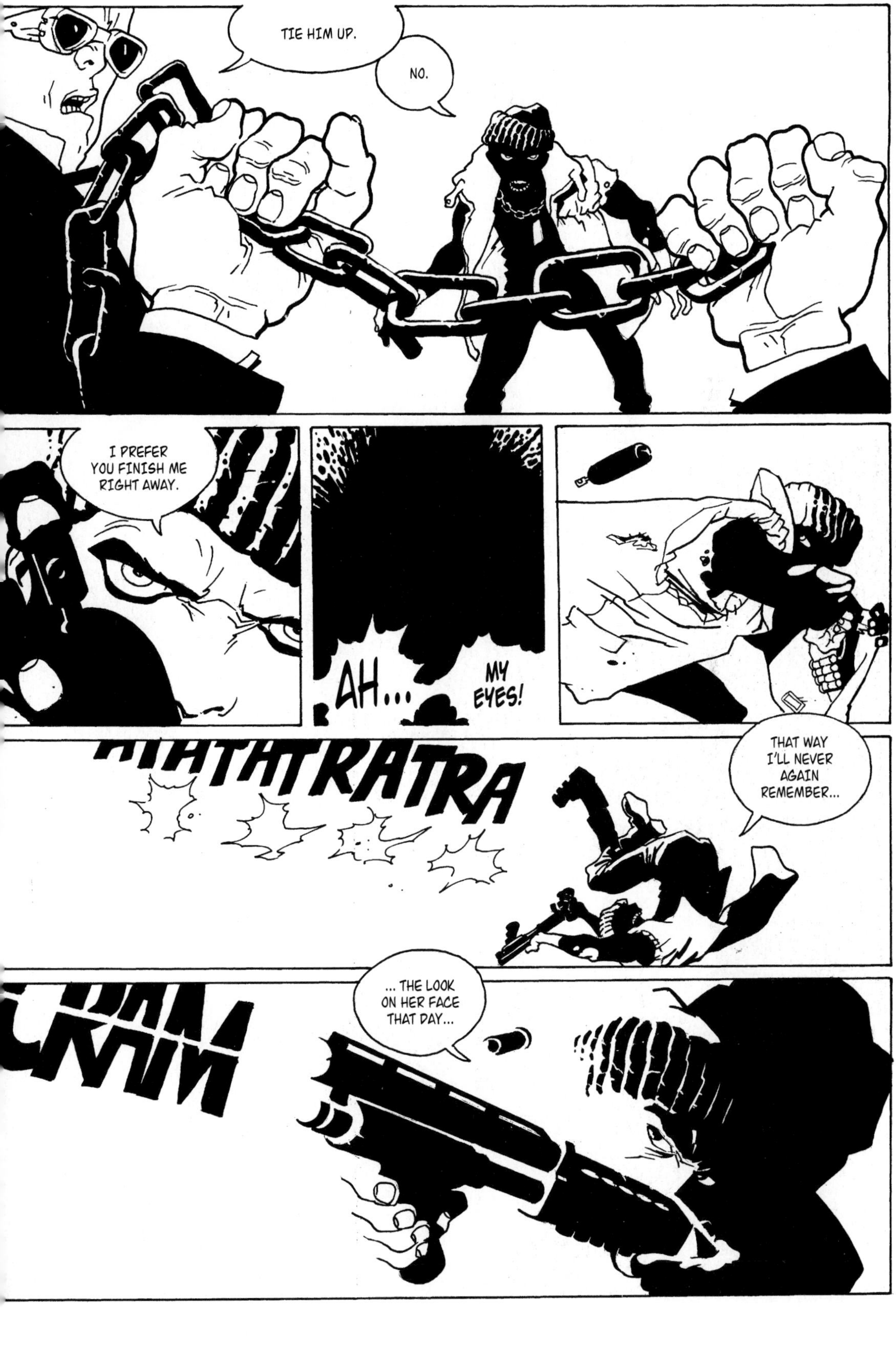
TIE HIM UP.
NO.
I PREFER YOU FINISH ME RIGHT AWAY.
AH...
MY EYES!
TATATRATRA
THAT WAY I'LL NEVER AGAIN REMEMBER...
BRAM
... THE LOOK ON HER FACE THAT DAY...

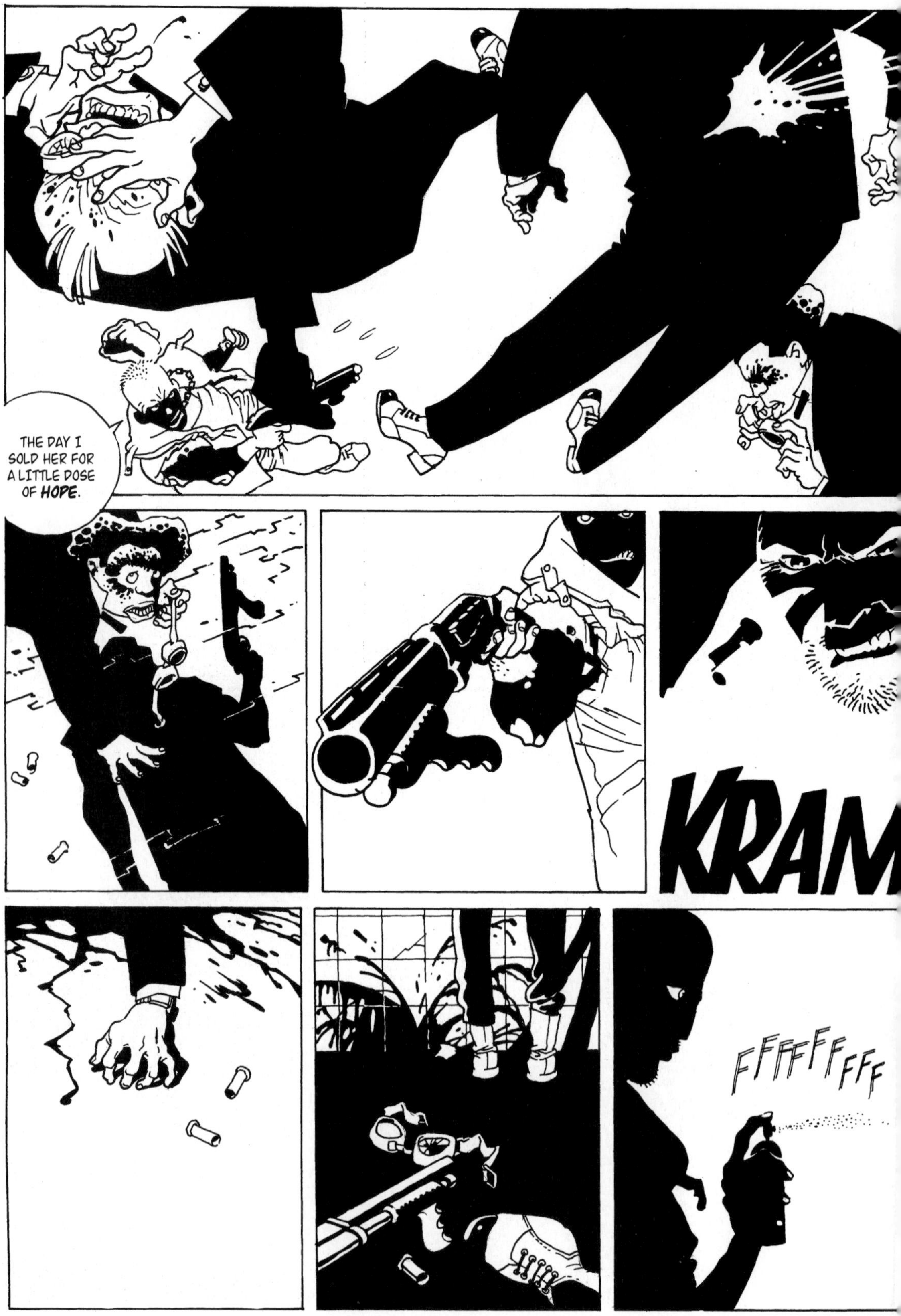
THE DAY I SOLD HER FOR A LITTLE DOSE OF HOPE.
KRAM
FFFFFFFFFF

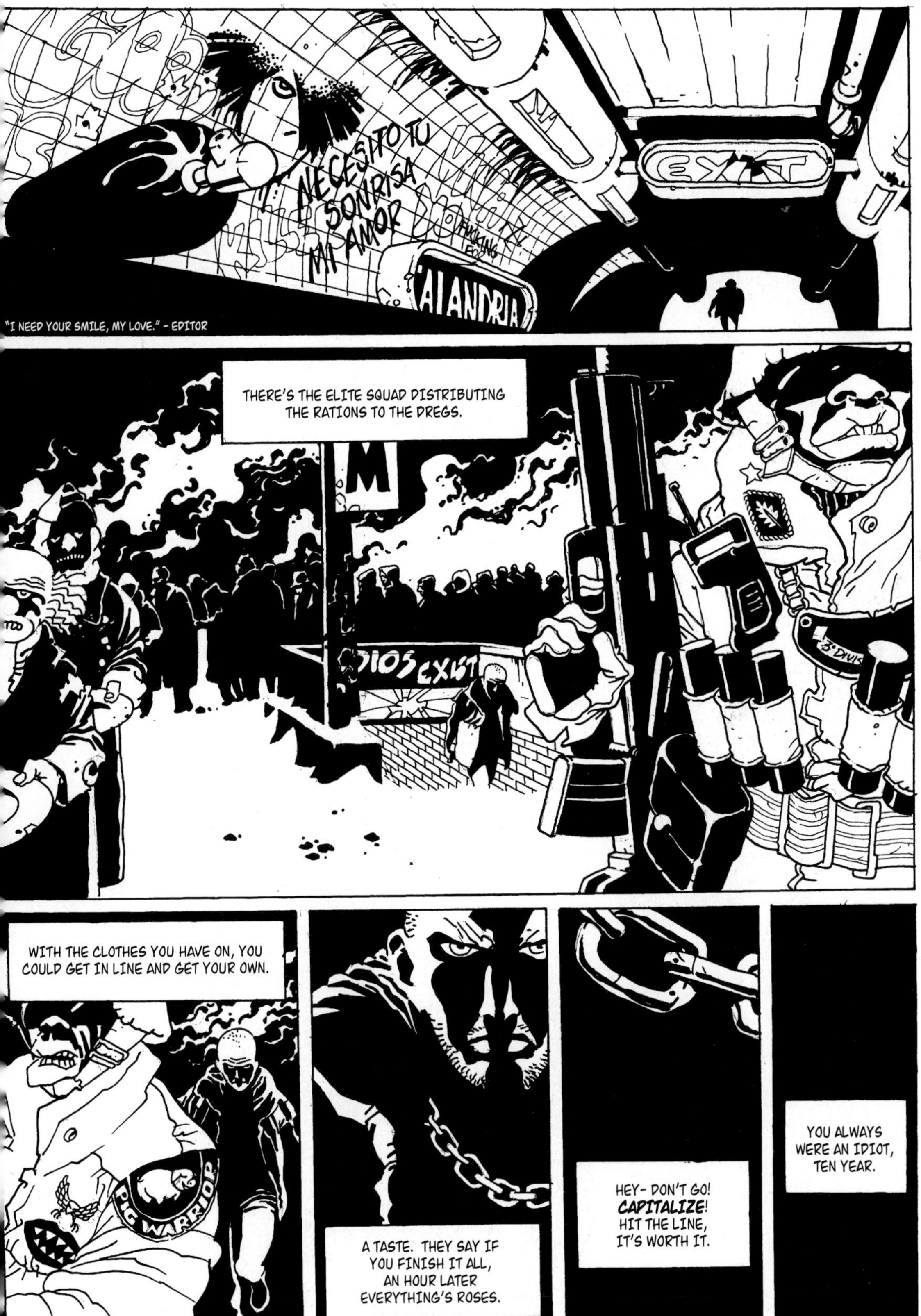
NECESITO TU SONRISA MI AMOR
EXIT
ALANDRIA
"I NEED YOUR SMILE, MY LOVE." - EDITOR
THERE'S THE ELITE SQUAD DISTRIBUTING THE RATIONS TO THE DREGS.
M
DIOS EXIST
WITH THE CLOTHES YOU HAVE ON, YOU COULD GET IN LINE AND GET YOUR OWN.
PIG WARRIOR
A TASTE. THEY SAY IF YOU FINISH IT ALL, AN HOUR LATER EVERYTHING'S ROSES.
HEY- DON'T GO! **CAPITALIZE**! HIT THE LINE, IT'S WORTH IT.
YOU ALWAYS WERE AN IDIOT, TEN YEAR.

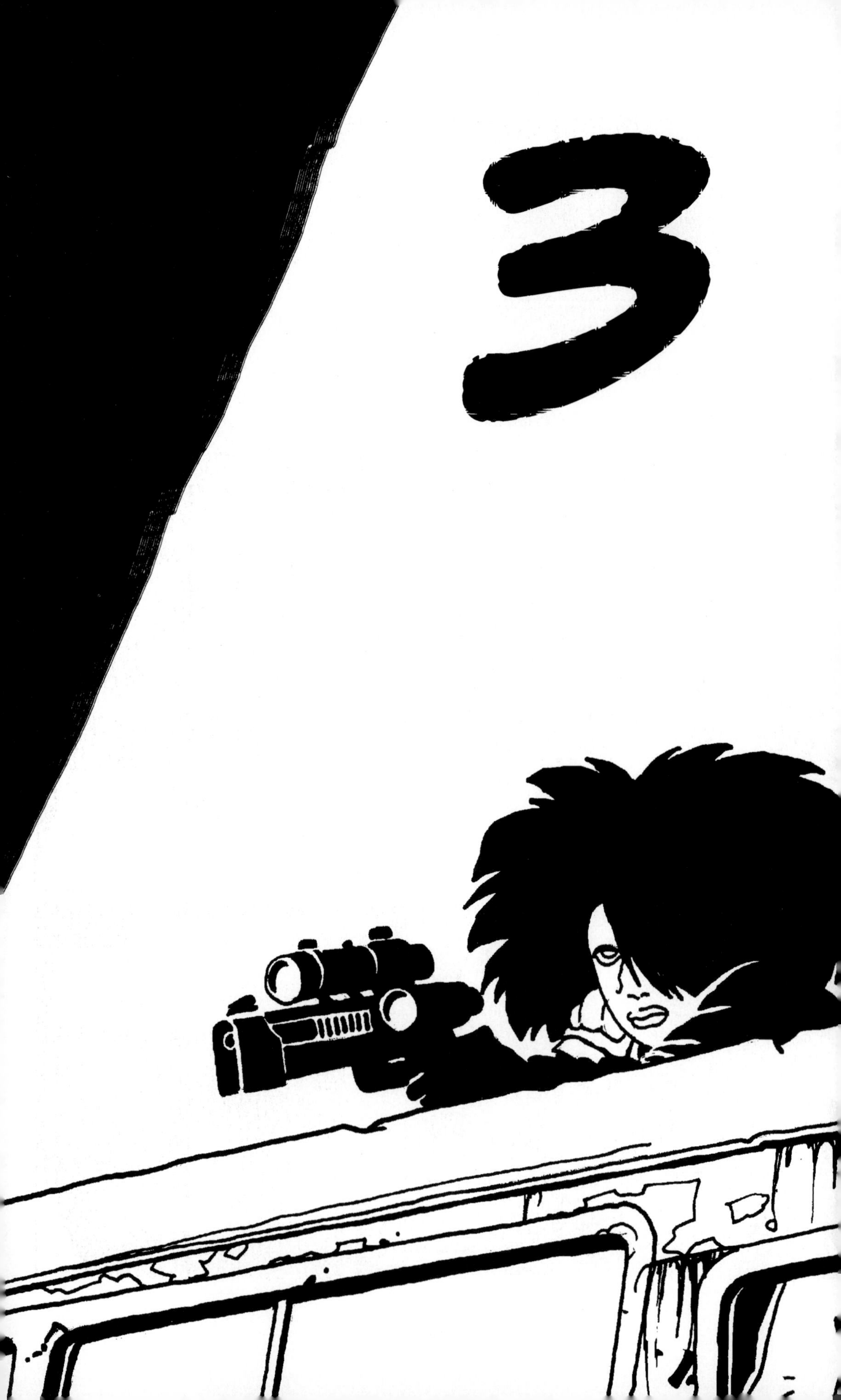
3

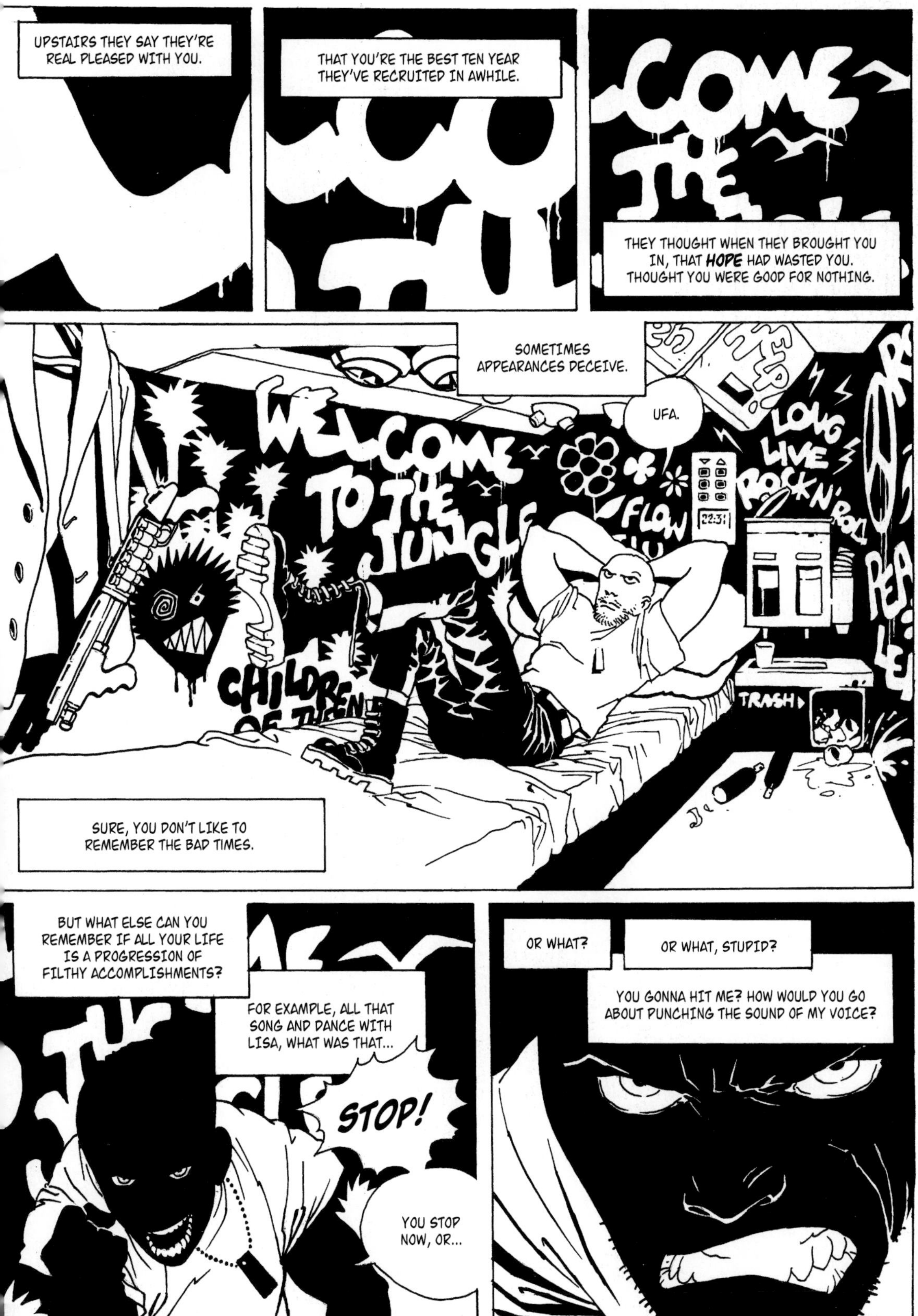
UPSTAIRS THEY SAY THEY'RE REAL PLEASED WITH YOU.
THAT YOU'RE THE BEST TEN YEAR THEY'VE RECRUITED IN AWHILE.
THEY THOUGHT WHEN THEY BROUGHT YOU IN, THAT **HOPE** HAD WASTED YOU. THOUGHT YOU WERE GOOD FOR NOTHING.
SOMETIMES APPEARANCES DECEIVE.
UFA.
WELCOME TO THE JUNGLE
LONG LIVE ROCK N' ROLL
TRASH
SURE, YOU DON'T LIKE TO REMEMBER THE BAD TIMES.
BUT WHAT ELSE CAN YOU REMEMBER IF ALL YOUR LIFE IS A PROGRESSION OF FILTHY ACCOMPLISHMENTS?
FOR EXAMPLE, ALL THAT SONG AND DANCE WITH LISA, WHAT WAS THAT...
STOP!
YOU STOP NOW, OR...
OR WHAT?
OR WHAT, STUPID?
YOU GONNA HIT ME? HOW WOULD YOU GO ABOUT PUNCHING THE SOUND OF MY VOICE?

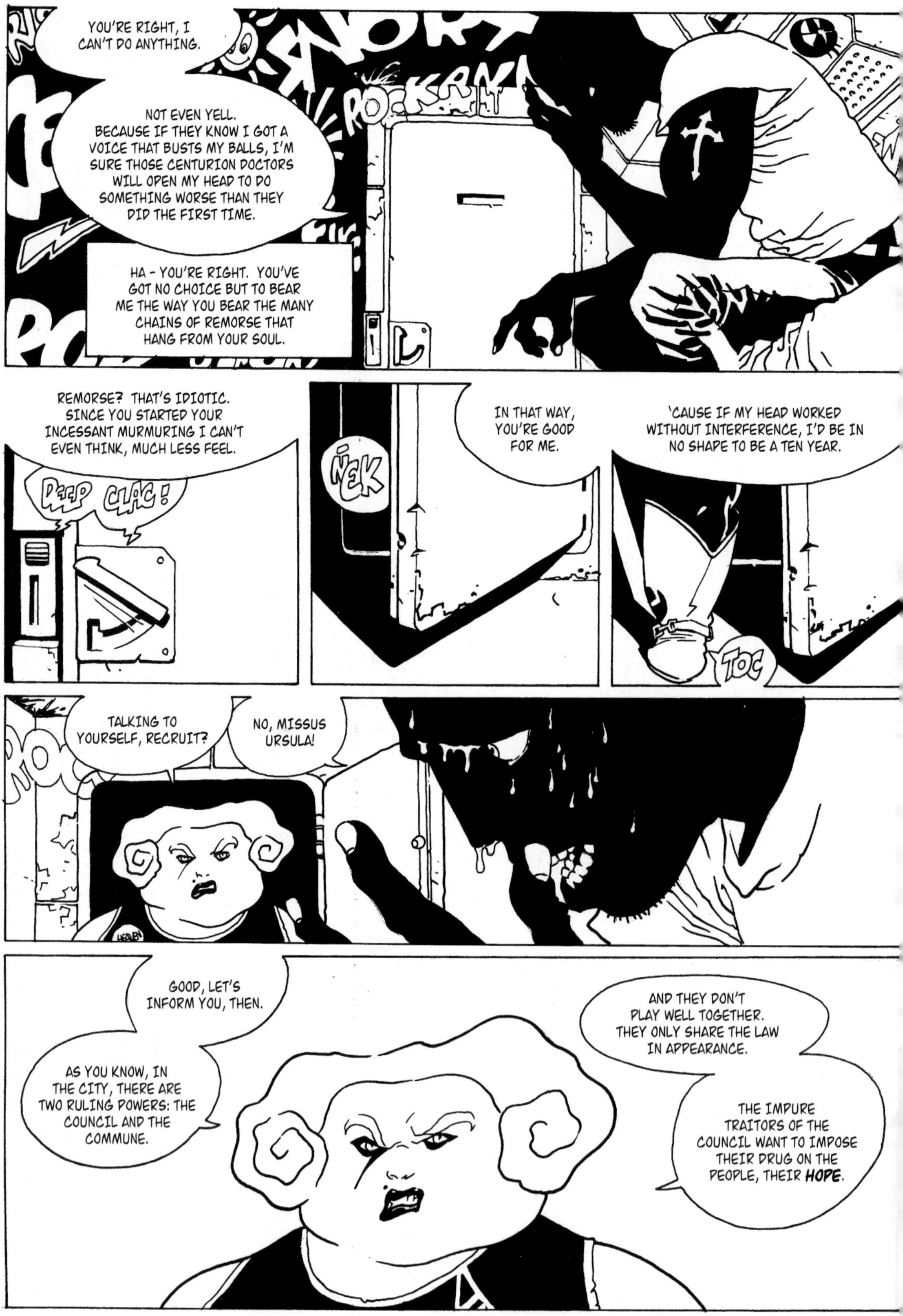

YOU'RE RIGHT, I CAN'T DO ANYTHING.
NOT EVEN YELL. BECAUSE IF THEY KNOW I GOT A VOICE THAT BUSTS MY BALLS, I'M SURE THOSE CENTURION DOCTORS WILL OPEN MY HEAD TO DO SOMETHING WORSE THAN THEY DID THE FIRST TIME.
HA - YOU'RE RIGHT. YOU'VE GOT NO CHOICE BUT TO BEAR ME THE WAY YOU BEAR THE MANY CHAINS OF REMORSE THAT HANG FROM YOUR SOUL.
REMORSE? THAT'S IDIOTIC. SINCE YOU STARTED YOUR INCESSANT MURMURING I CAN'T EVEN THINK, MUCH LESS FEEL.
CLAC!
ÑEK
IN THAT WAY, YOU'RE GOOD FOR ME.
'CAUSE IF MY HEAD WORKED WITHOUT INTERFERENCE, I'D BE IN NO SHAPE TO BE A TEN YEAR.
TOC
TALKING TO YOURSELF, RECRUIT?
NO, MISSUS URSULA!
GOOD, LET'S INFORM YOU, THEN.
AS YOU KNOW, IN THE CITY, THERE ARE TWO RULING POWERS: THE COUNCIL AND THE COMMUNE.
AND THEY DON'T PLAY WELL TOGETHER. THEY ONLY SHARE THE LAW IN APPEARANCE.
THE IMPURE TRAITORS OF THE COUNCIL WANT TO IMPOSE THEIR DRUG ON THE PEOPLE, THEIR **HOPE**.

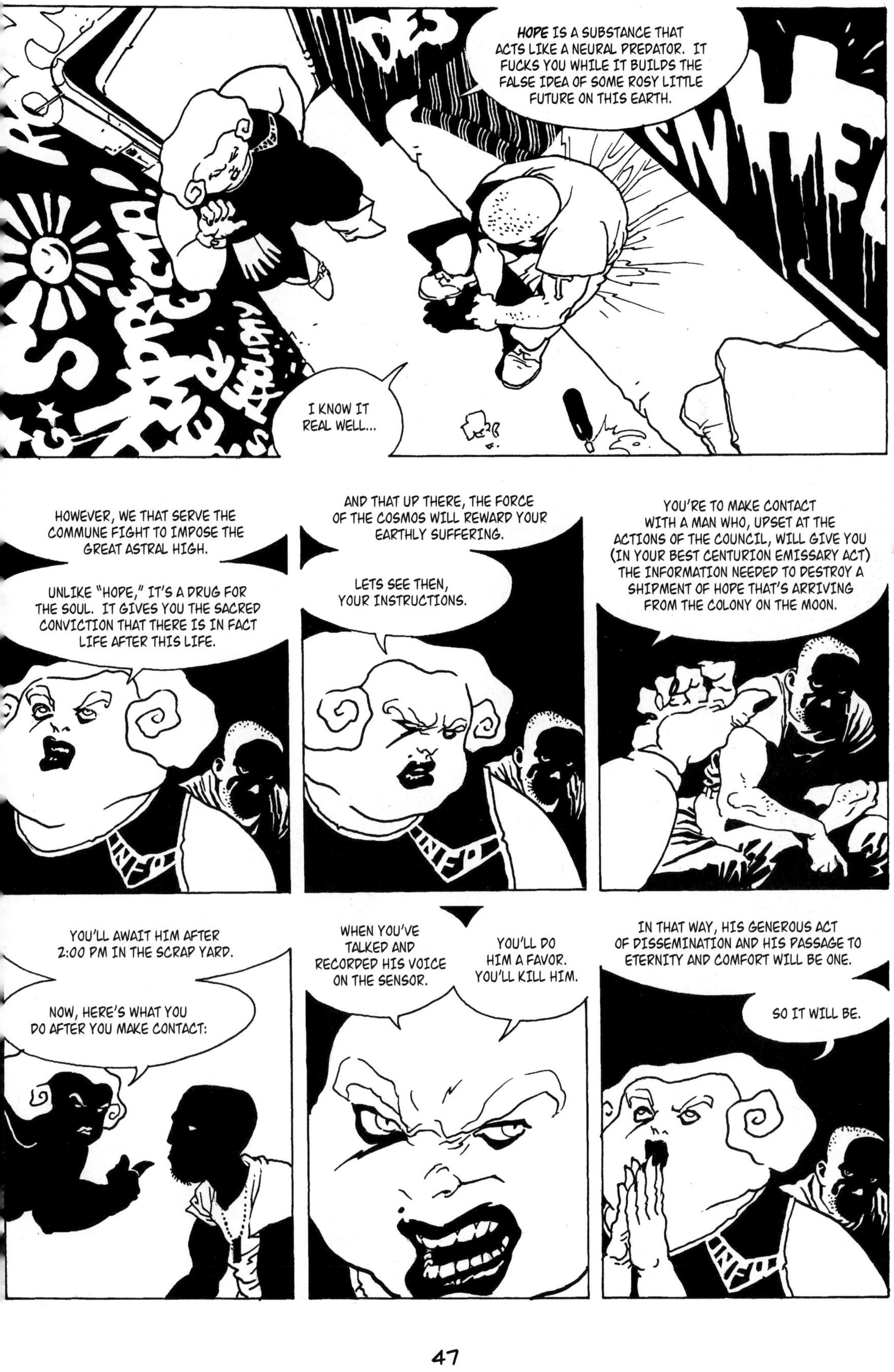
HOPE IS A SUBSTANCE THAT ACTS LIKE A NEURAL PREDATOR. IT FUCKS YOU WHILE IT BUILDS THE FALSE IDEA OF SOME ROSY LITTLE FUTURE ON THIS EARTH.
I KNOW IT REAL WELL...
HOWEVER, WE THAT SERVE THE COMMUNE FIGHT TO IMPOSE THE GREAT ASTRAL HIGH.
UNLIKE "HOPE," IT'S A DRUG FOR THE SOUL. IT GIVES YOU THE SACRED CONVICTION THAT THERE IS IN FACT LIFE AFTER THIS LIFE.
AND THAT UP THERE, THE FORCE OF THE COSMOS WILL REWARD YOUR EARTHLY SUFFERING.
LETS SEE THEN, YOUR INSTRUCTIONS.
YOU'RE TO MAKE CONTACT WITH A MAN WHO, UPSET AT THE ACTIONS OF THE COUNCIL, WILL GIVE YOU (IN YOUR BEST CENTURION EMISSARY ACT) THE INFORMATION NEEDED TO DESTROY A SHIPMENT OF HOPE THAT'S ARRIVING FROM THE COLONY ON THE MOON.
YOU'LL AWAIT HIM AFTER 2:00 PM IN THE SCRAP YARD.
NOW, HERE'S WHAT YOU DO AFTER YOU MAKE CONTACT:
WHEN YOU'VE TALKED AND RECORDED HIS VOICE ON THE SENSOR.
YOU'LL DO HIM A FAVOR. YOU'LL KILL HIM.
IN THAT WAY, HIS GENEROUS ACT OF DISSEMINATION AND HIS PASSAGE TO ETERNITY AND COMFORT WILL BE ONE.
SO IT WILL BE.

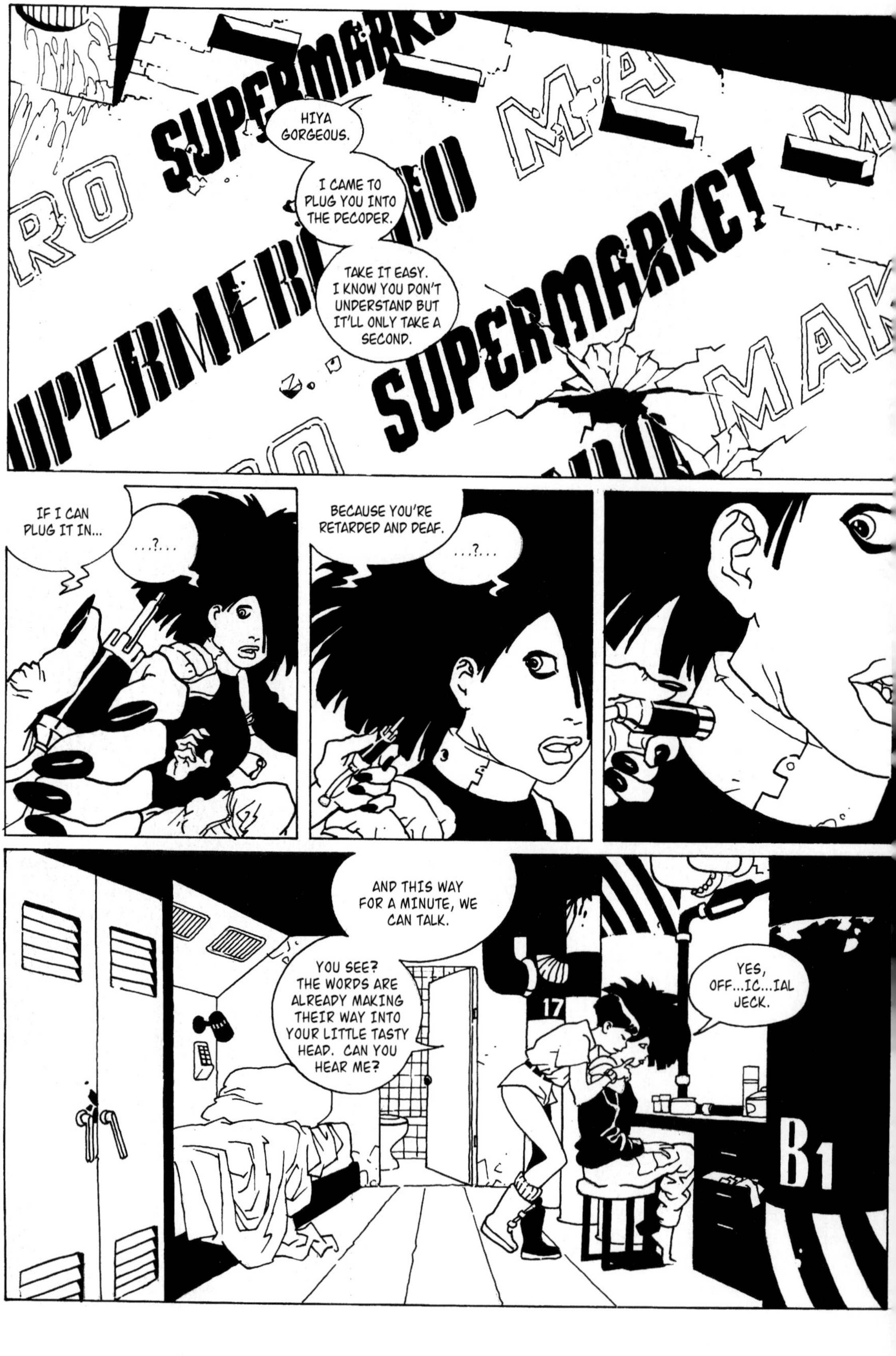
SUPERMARKET
HIYA GORGEOUS.
I CAME TO PLUG YOU INTO THE DECODER.
TAKE IT EASY. I KNOW YOU DON'T UNDERSTAND BUT IT'LL ONLY TAKE A SECOND.
SUPERMARKET
IF I CAN PLUG IT IN...
...?...
BECAUSE YOU'RE RETARDED AND DEAF.
...?...
AND THIS WAY FOR A MINUTE, WE CAN TALK.
YOU SEE? THE WORDS ARE ALREADY MAKING THEIR WAY INTO YOUR LITTLE TASTY HEAD. CAN YOU HEAR ME?
YES, OFF...IC...IAL JECK.
17
B1

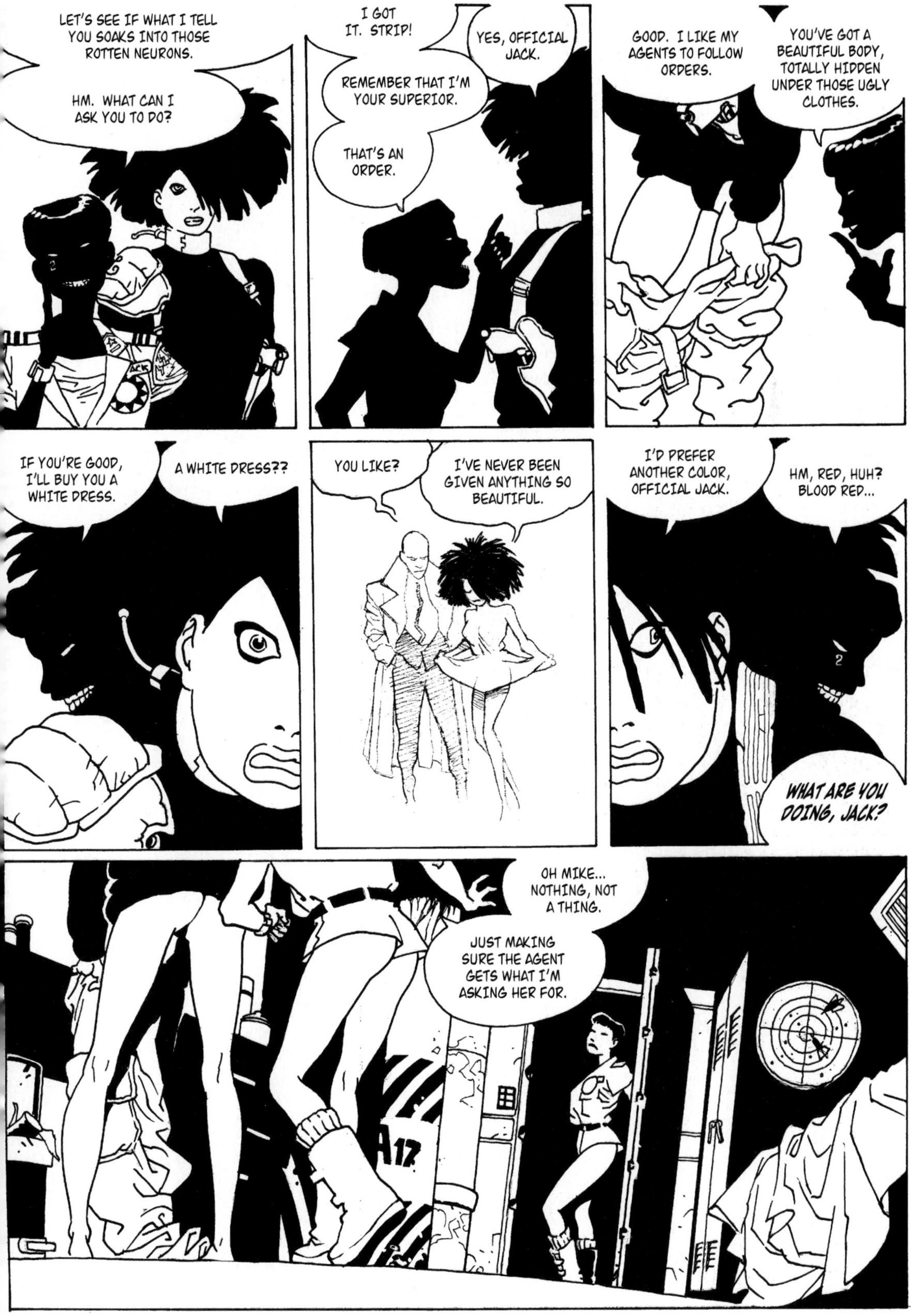
LET'S SEE IF WHAT I TELL YOU SOAKS INTO THOSE ROTTEN NEURONS.
HM. WHAT CAN I ASK YOU TO DO?
I GOT IT. STRIP!
REMEMBER THAT I'M YOUR SUPERIOR.
THAT'S AN ORDER.
YES, OFFICIAL JACK.
GOOD. I LIKE MY AGENTS TO FOLLOW ORDERS.
YOU'VE GOT A BEAUTIFUL BODY, TOTALLY HIDDEN UNDER THOSE UGLY CLOTHES.
IF YOU'RE GOOD, I'LL BUY YOU A WHITE DRESS.
A WHITE DRESS??
YOU LIKE?
I'VE NEVER BEEN GIVEN ANYTHING SO BEAUTIFUL.
I'D PREFER ANOTHER COLOR, OFFICIAL JACK.
HM, RED, HUH? BLOOD RED...
WHAT ARE YOU DOING, JACK?
OH MIKE... NOTHING, NOT A THING.
JUST MAKING SURE THE AGENT GETS WHAT I'M ASKING HER FOR.
A17

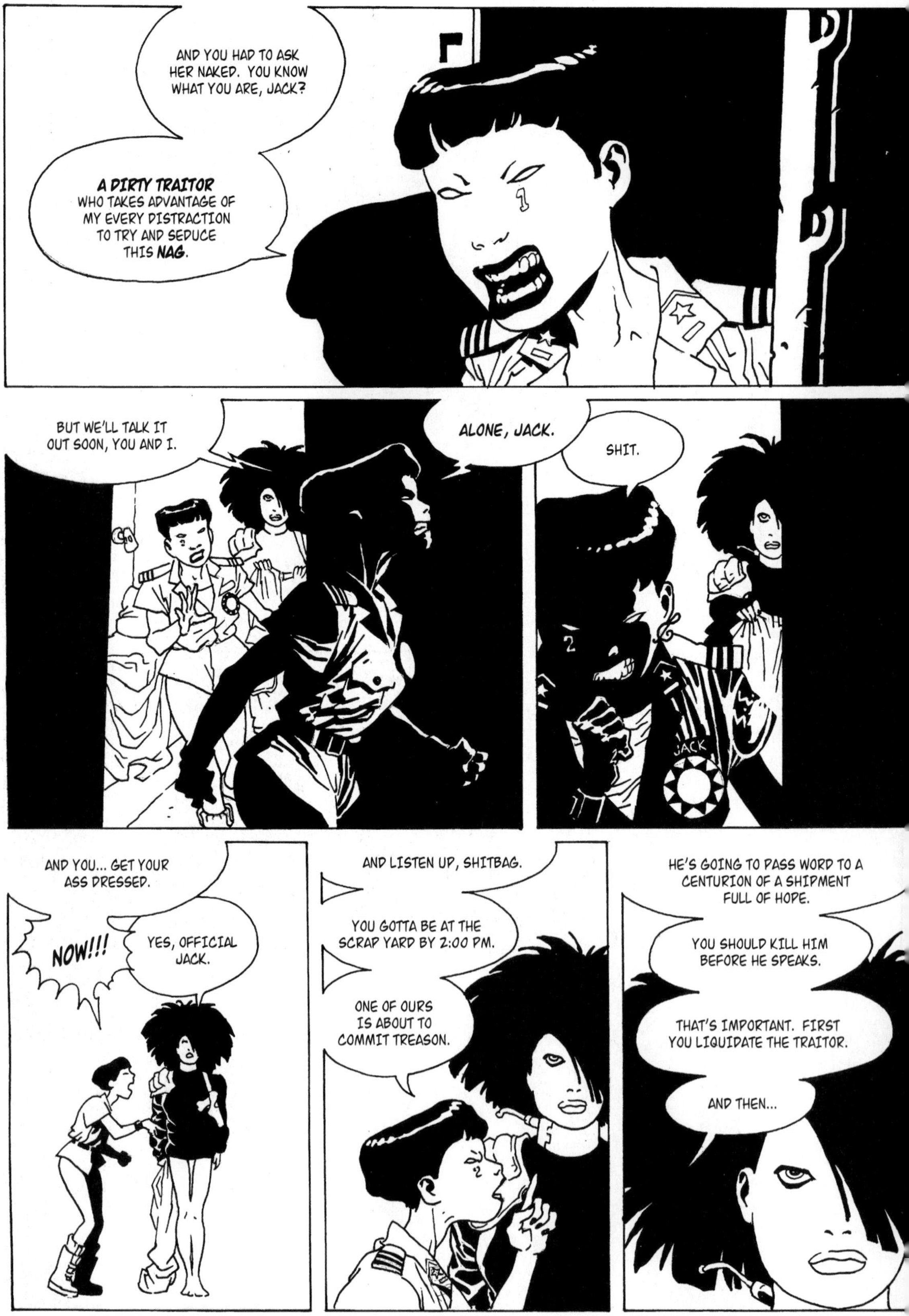

AND YOU HAD TO ASK HER NAKED. YOU KNOW WHAT YOU ARE, JACK?
A DIRTY TRAITOR WHO TAKES ADVANTAGE OF MY EVERY DISTRACTION TO TRY AND SEDUCE THIS NAG.
BUT WE'LL TALK IT OUT SOON, YOU AND I.
ALONE, JACK.
SHIT.
JACK
AND YOU... GET YOUR ASS DRESSED.
NOW!!!
YES, OFFICIAL JACK.
AND LISTEN UP, SHITBAG.
YOU GOTTA BE AT THE SCRAP YARD BY 2:00 PM.
ONE OF OURS IS ABOUT TO COMMIT TREASON.
HE'S GOING TO PASS WORD TO A CENTURION OF A SHIPMENT FULL OF HOPE.
YOU SHOULD KILL HIM BEFORE HE SPEAKS.
THAT'S IMPORTANT. FIRST YOU LIQUIDATE THE TRAITOR.
AND THEN...

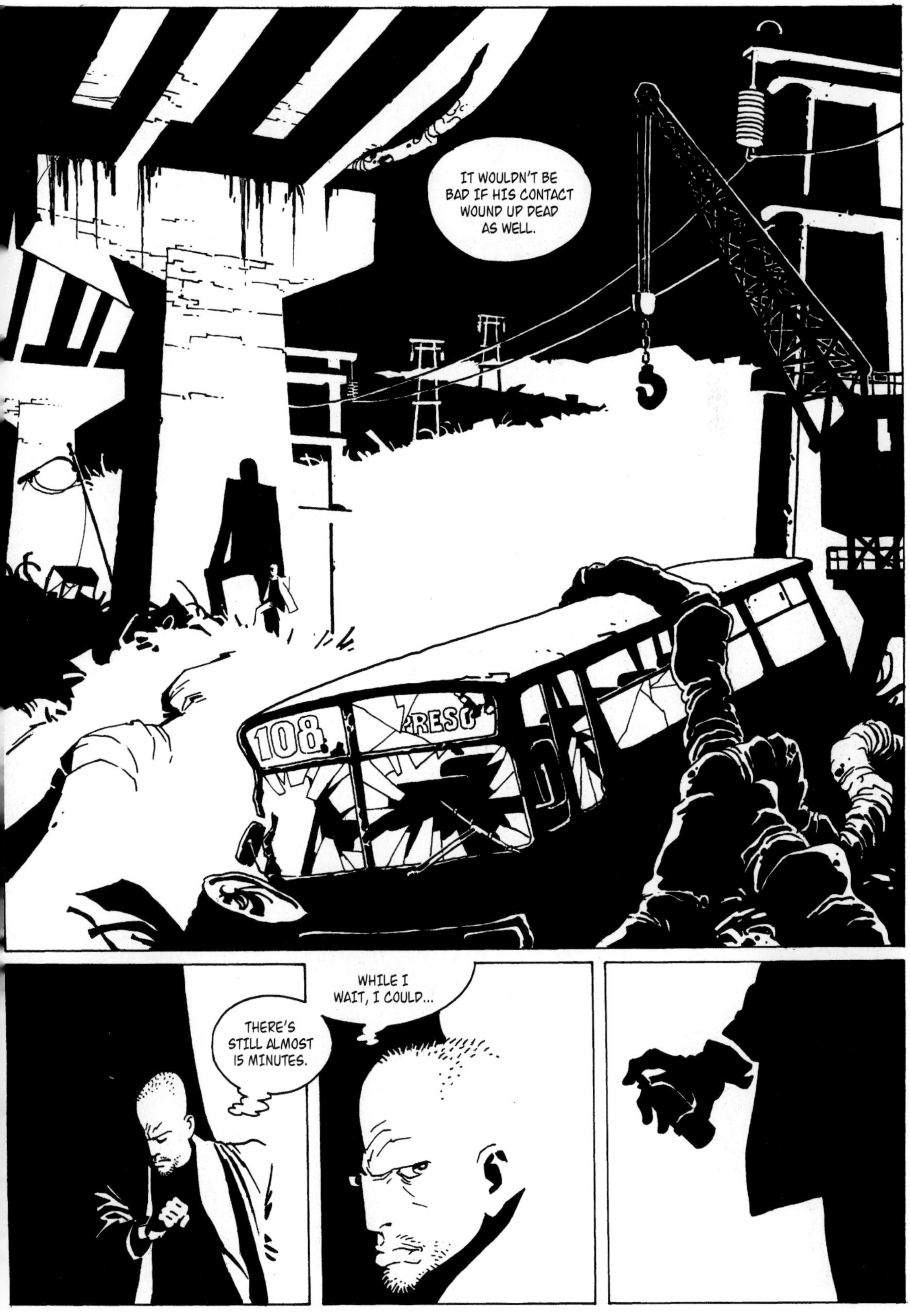
IT WOULDN'T BE BAD IF HIS CONTACT WOUND UP DEAD AS WELL.
108
RESO
THERE'S STILL ALMOST 15 MINUTES.
WHILE I WAIT, I COULD...

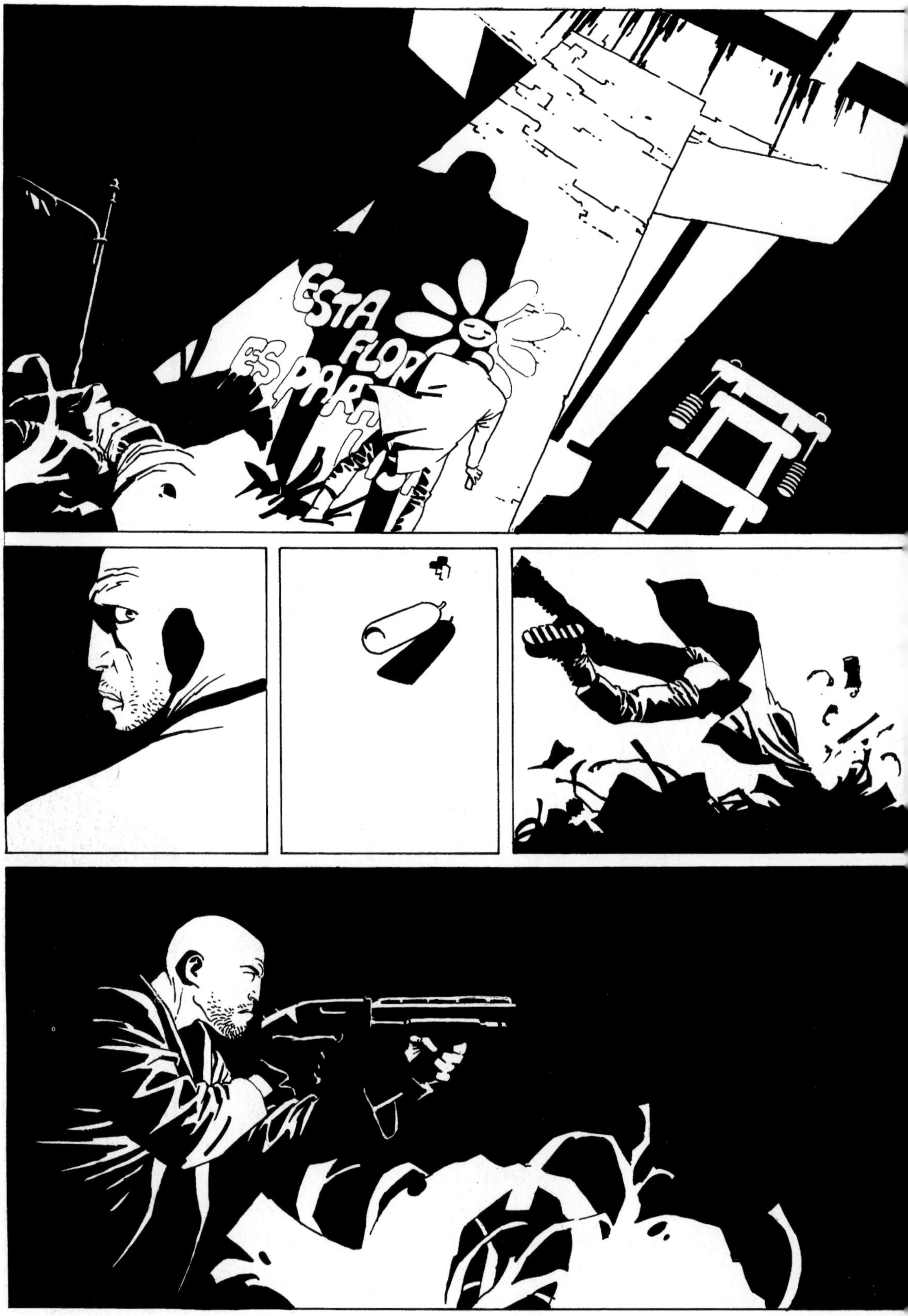
ESTA FLOR
ES PAR

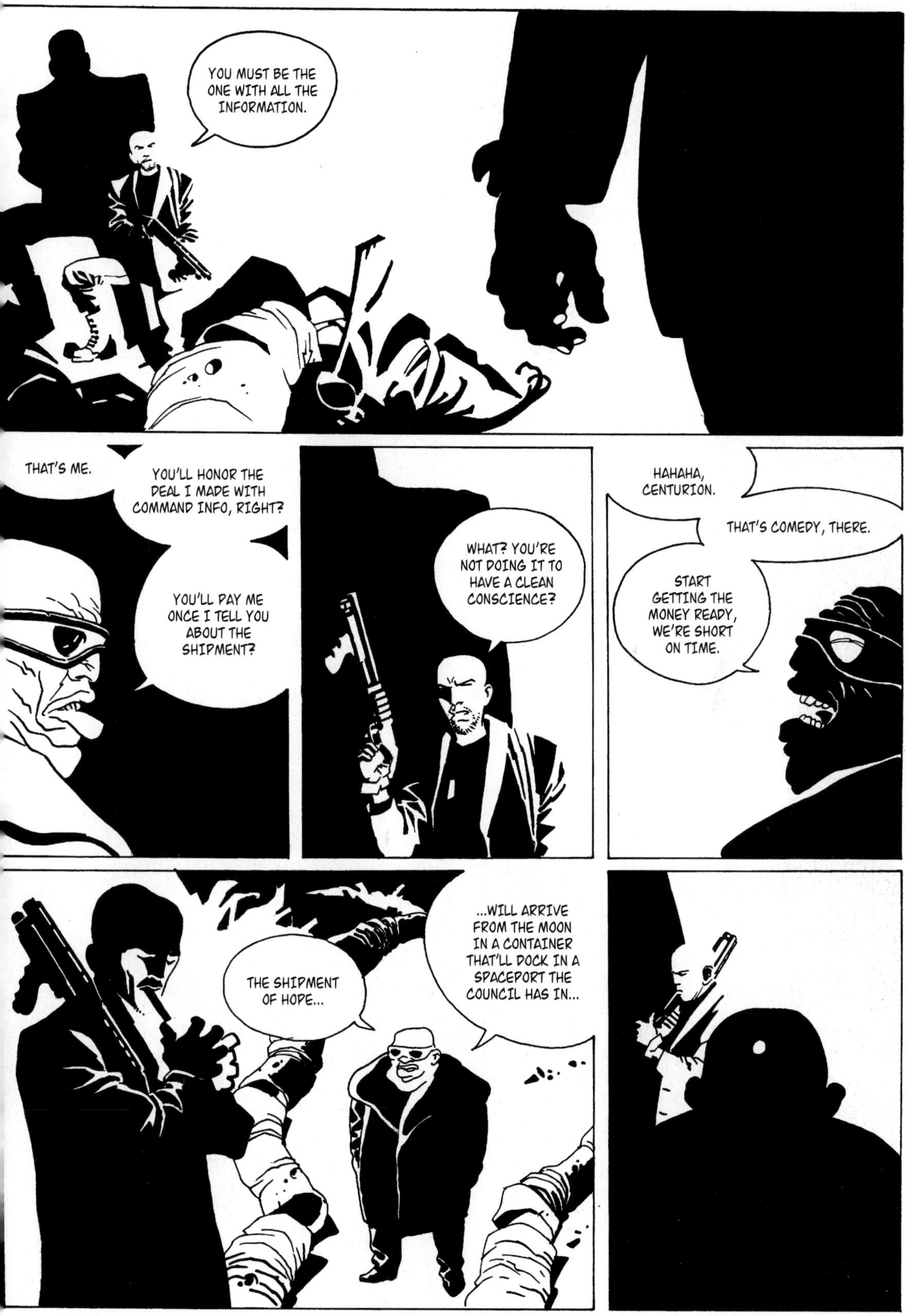
YOU MUST BE THE ONE WITH ALL THE INFORMATION.
THAT'S ME.
YOU'LL HONOR THE DEAL I MADE WITH COMMAND INFO, RIGHT?
YOU'LL PAY ME ONCE I TELL YOU ABOUT THE SHIPMENT?
WHAT? YOU'RE NOT DOING IT TO HAVE A CLEAN CONSCIENCE?
HAHAHA, CENTURION.
THAT'S COMEDY, THERE.
START GETTING THE MONEY READY, WE'RE SHORT ON TIME.
THE SHIPMENT OF HOPE...
...WILL ARRIVE FROM THE MOON IN A CONTAINER THAT'LL DOCK IN A SPACEPORT THE COUNCIL HAS IN...

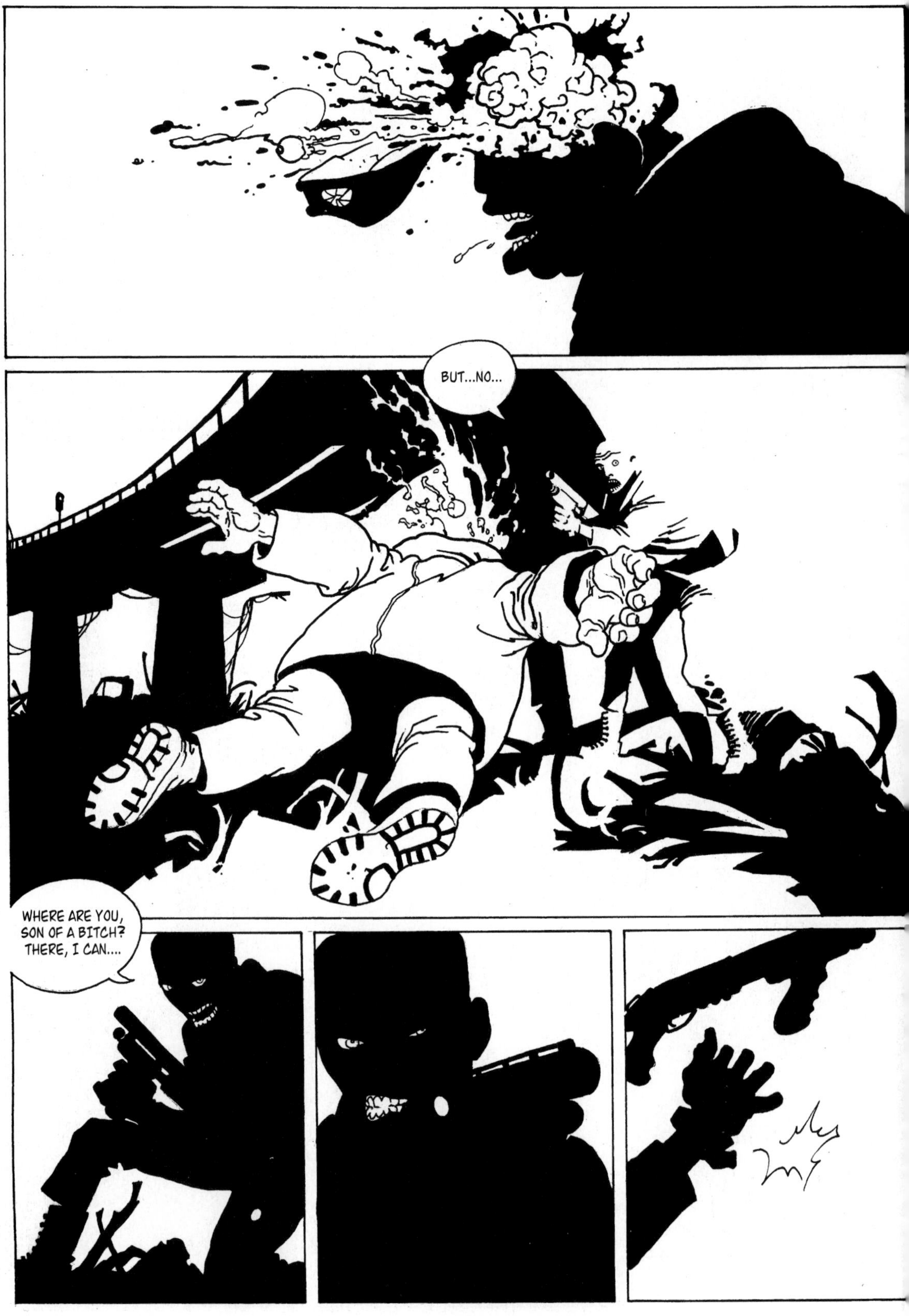
BUT...NO...
WHERE ARE YOU, SON OF A BITCH? THERE, I CAN....

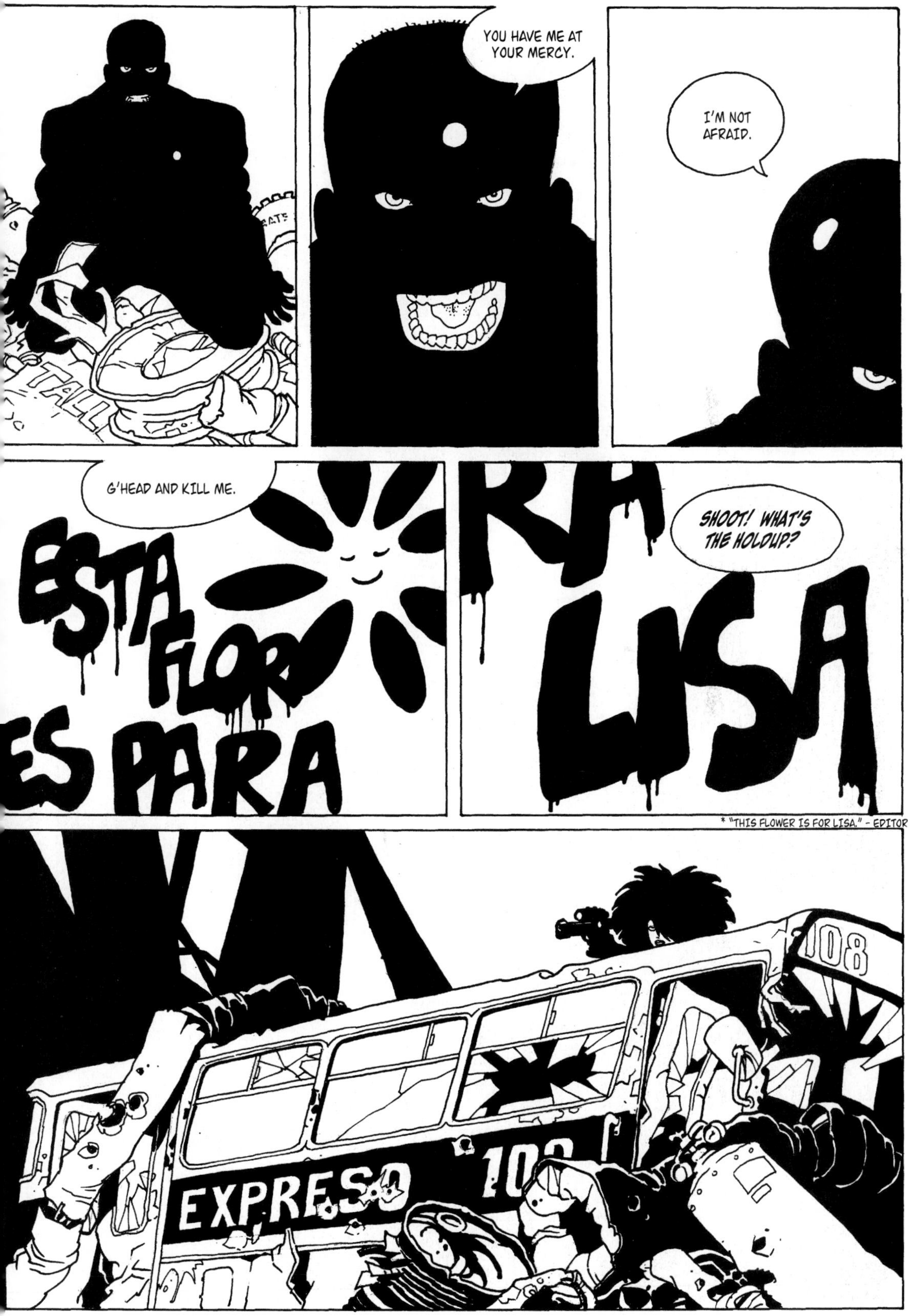
YOU HAVE ME AT YOUR MERCY.
I'M NOT AFRAID.
G'HEAD AND KILL ME.
ESTA FLOR ES PARA
LISA
SHOOT! WHAT'S THE HOLDUP?
* "THIS FLOWER IS FOR LISA." - EDITOR
108
EXPRESO

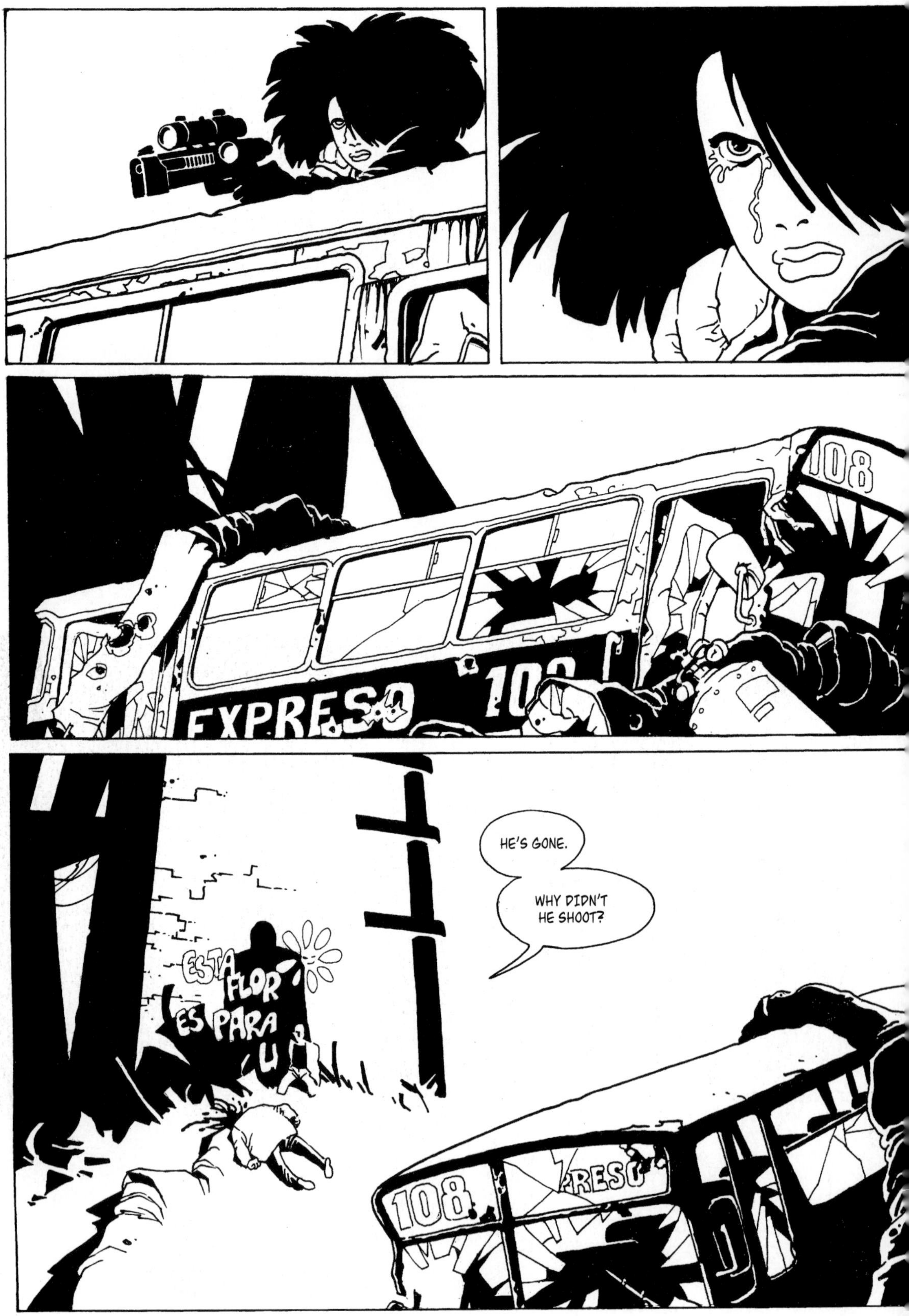
EXPRESO 108
108
HE'S GONE.
WHY DIDN'T HE SHOOT?
ESTA FLOR ES PARA U
108
RESO

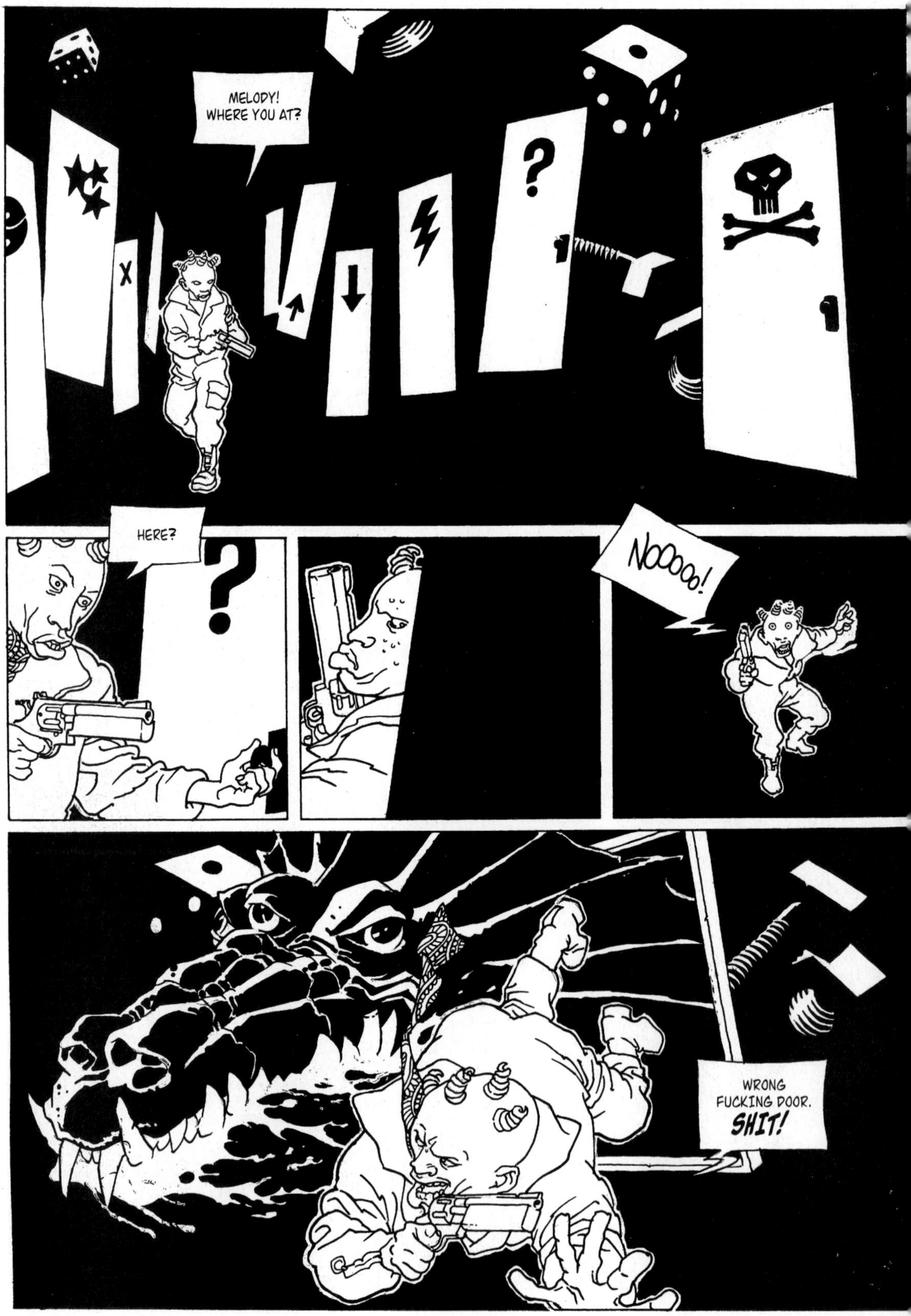
MELODY!
WHERE YOU AT?
HERE?
NOOOOO!
WRONG
FUCKING DOOR.
SHIT!

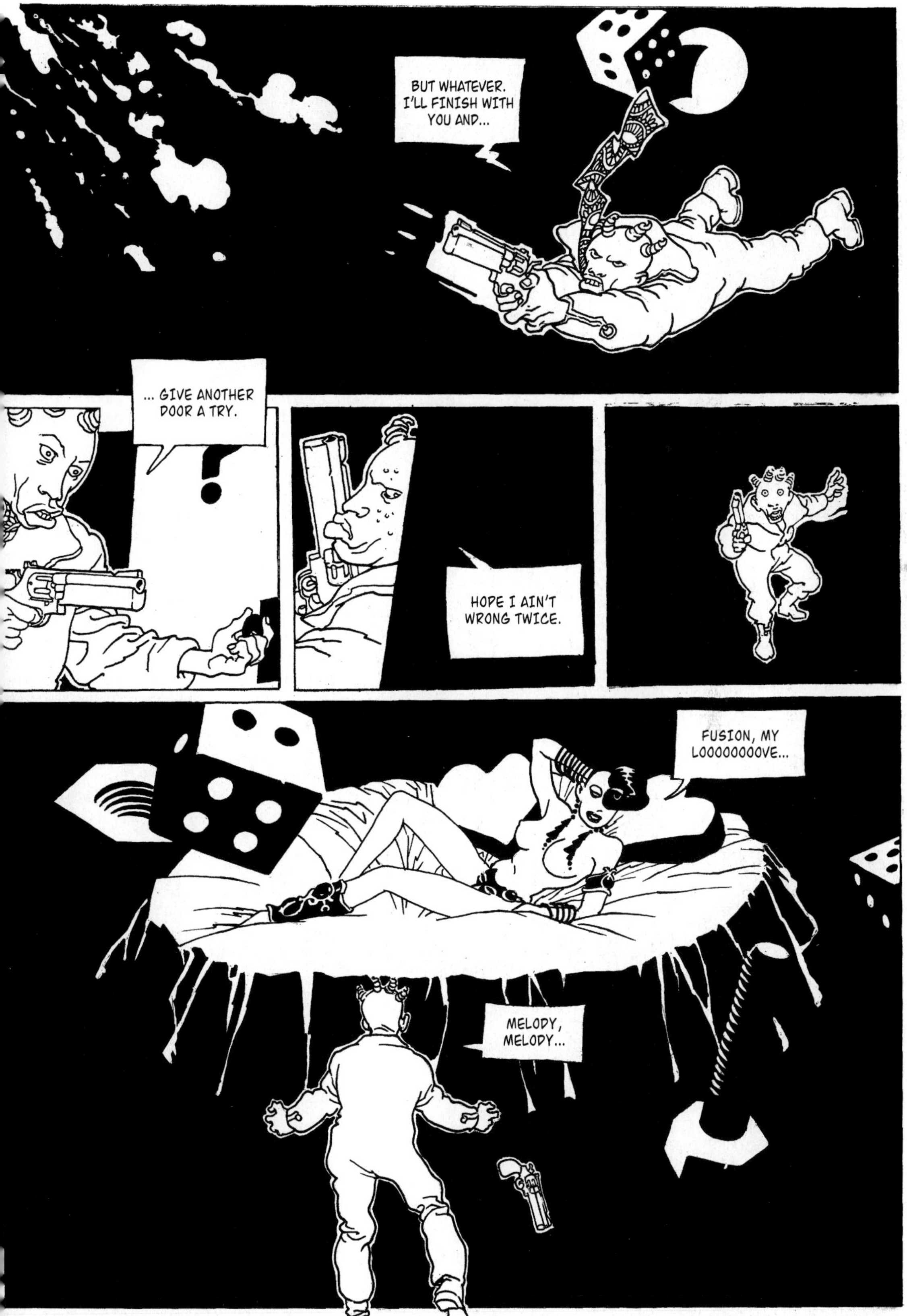
BUT WHATEVER. I'LL FINISH WITH YOU AND...
... GIVE ANOTHER DOOR A TRY.
HOPE I AIN'T WRONG TWICE.
FUSION, MY LOOOOOOOOVE...
MELODY, MELODY...

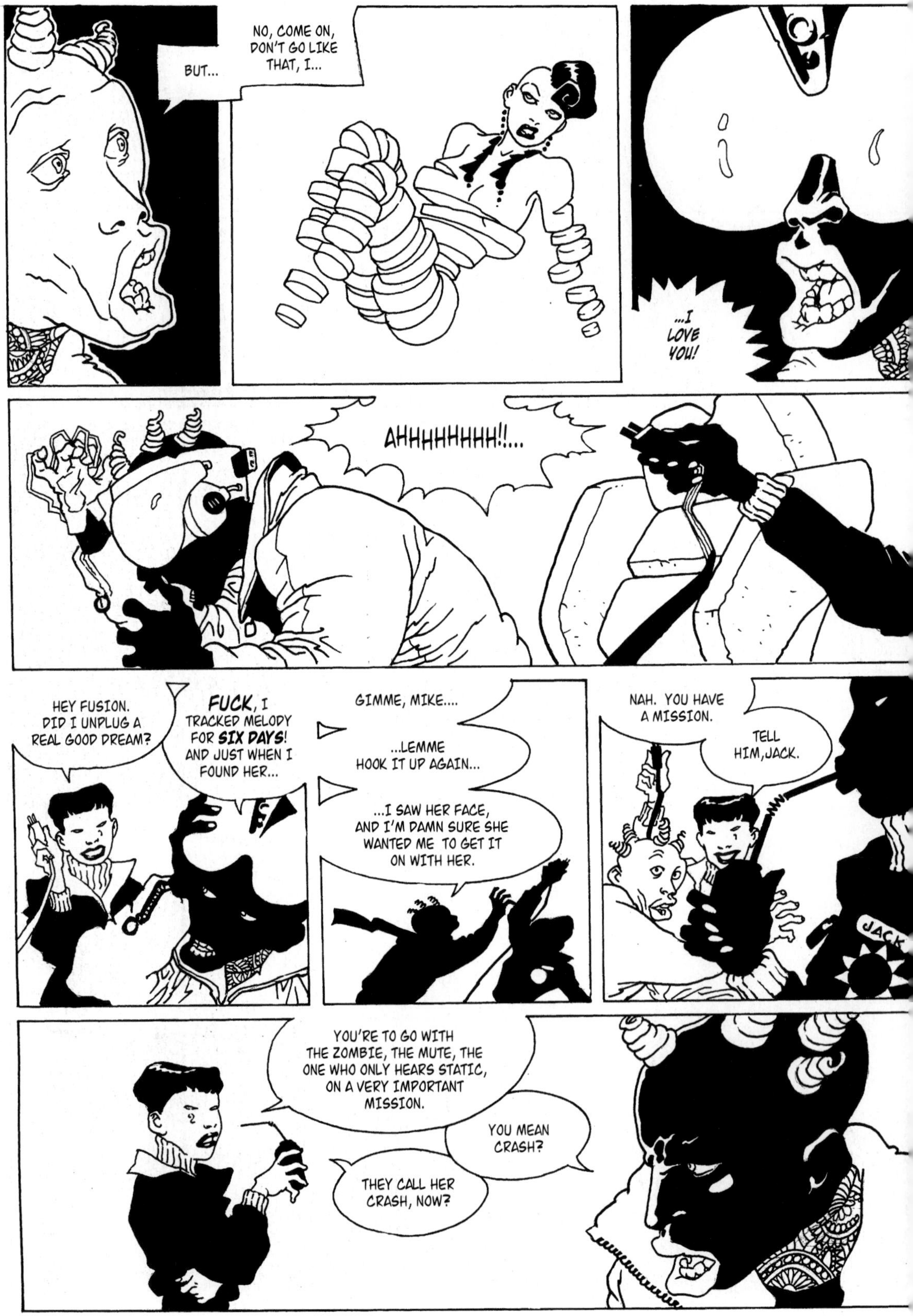
BUT...
NO, COME ON, DON'T GO LIKE THAT, I...
...I LOVE YOU!
AHHHHHHHH!!....
HEY FUSION. DID I UNPLUG A REAL GOOD DREAM?
FUCK, I TRACKED MELODY FOR SIX DAYS! AND JUST WHEN I FOUND HER...
GIMME, MIKE....
...LEMME HOOK IT UP AGAIN...
...I SAW HER FACE, AND I'M DAMN SURE SHE WANTED ME TO GET IT ON WITH HER.
NAH. YOU HAVE A MISSION.
TELL HIM, JACK.
JACK
YOU'RE TO GO WITH THE ZOMBIE, THE MUTE, THE ONE WHO ONLY HEARS STATIC, ON A VERY IMPORTANT MISSION.
YOU MEAN CRASH?
THEY CALL HER CRASH, NOW?

HER WEAPONS DO ALL THE TALKIN'...WHAT OTHER NAME WOULD FIT HER?

TRUE. CRASH IT IS.

JACK

WE HAVE DISCOVERED WHERE THE COUNT HAS HIDDEN THE CLONES HE HAS PRODUCED FROM THE BITS OF HIMSELF.

THE COUNT? THAT OLD FUCK...

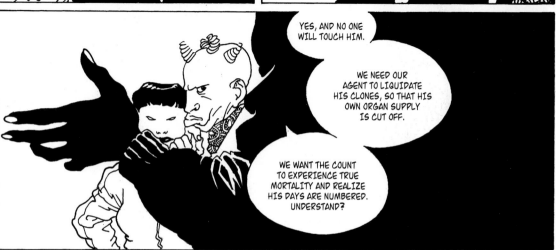

YES, AND NO ONE WILL TOUCH HIM.

WE NEED OUR AGENT TO LIQUIDATE HIS CLONES, SO THAT HIS OWN ORGAN SUPPLY IS CUT OFF.

WE WANT THE COUNT TO EXPERIENCE TRUE MORTALITY AND REALIZE HIS DAYS ARE NUMBERED. UNDERSTAND?

YEAH, BUT WHY NOT SEND CRASH SOLO?

SHE'S A KILLING MACHINE.

SHE COULD TAKE CARE OF THE CLONES ON HER OWN, NO PROBLEM.

WE HAVE OUR DOUBTS.

THAT'S WHY WE NEED YOU.

AND THE SOONER YOU GET MOVING, AND STOP ASKING QUESTIONS, THE SOONER YOU CAN GET BACK TO YOUR MELODY AND THE PLEASURE THAT AWAITS...

OK. WHERE DO I MEET UP WITH CRASH?

SHE IS WAITING FOR YOU. SHE KNOWS THE WAY.

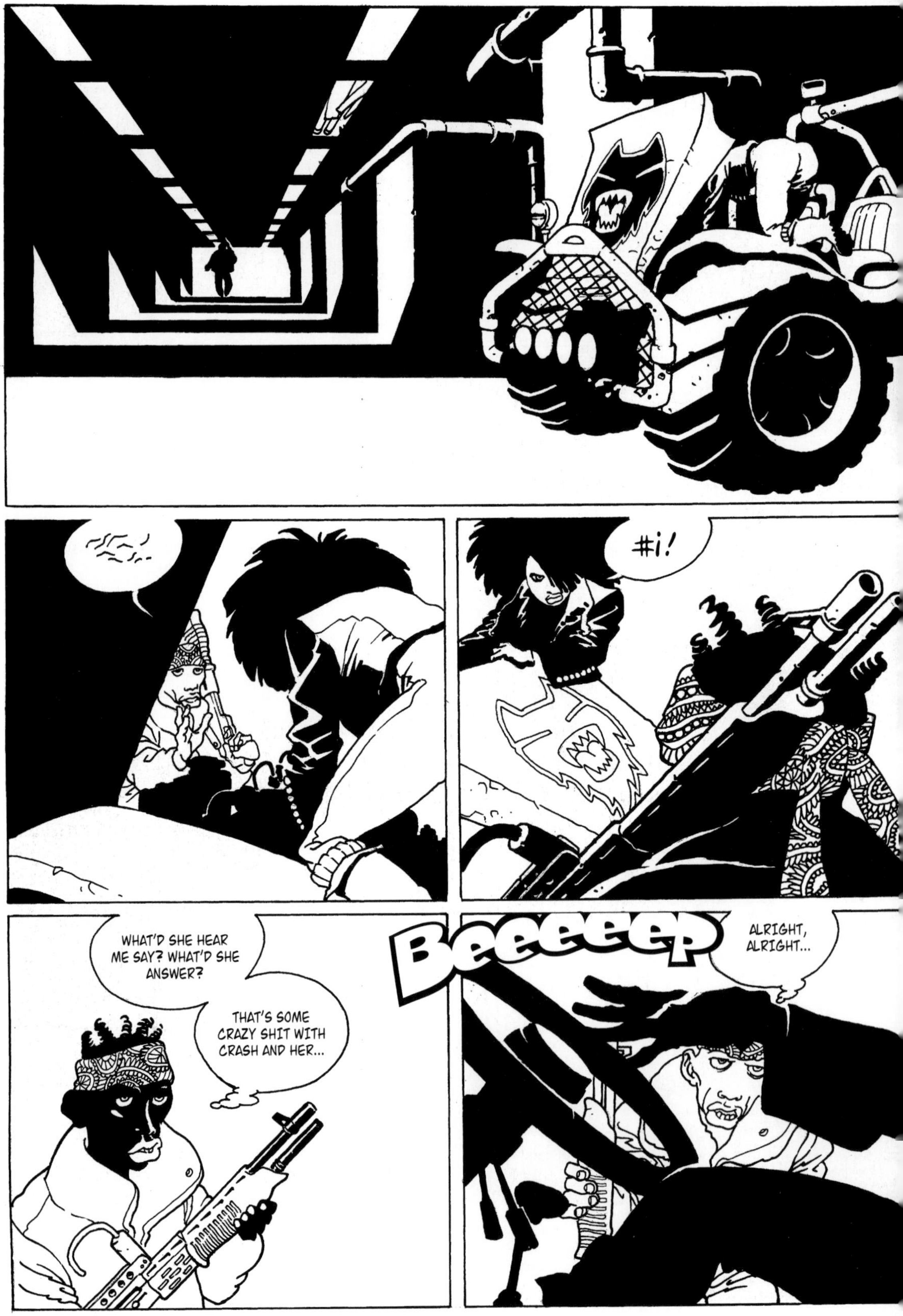
#i!
WHAT'D SHE HEAR ME SAY? WHAT'D SHE ANSWER?
THAT'S SOME CRAZY SHIT WITH CRASH AND HER...
Beeeeep
ALRIGHT, ALRIGHT...

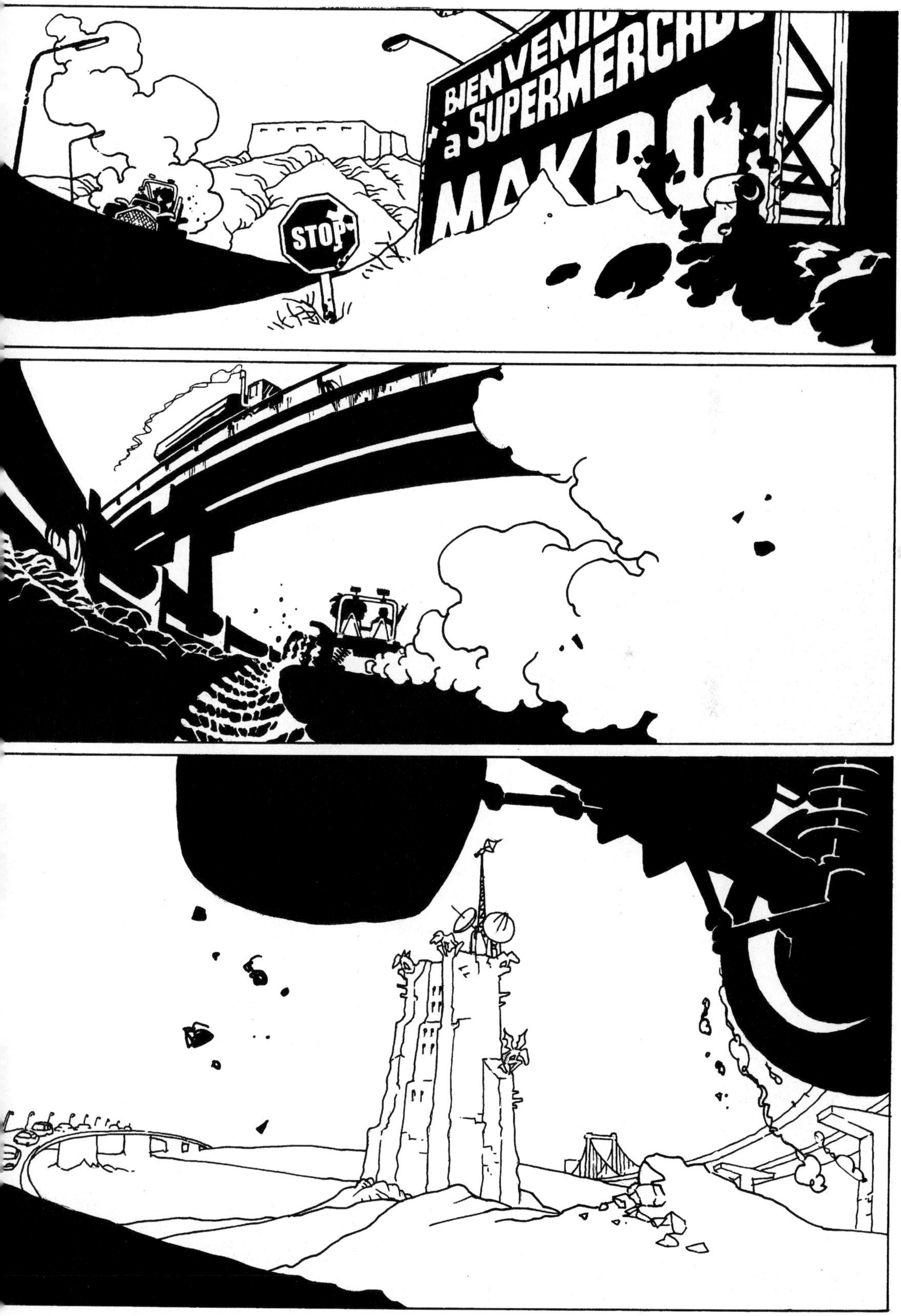
BIENVENID
à SUPERMERCAD
MAKRO
STOP

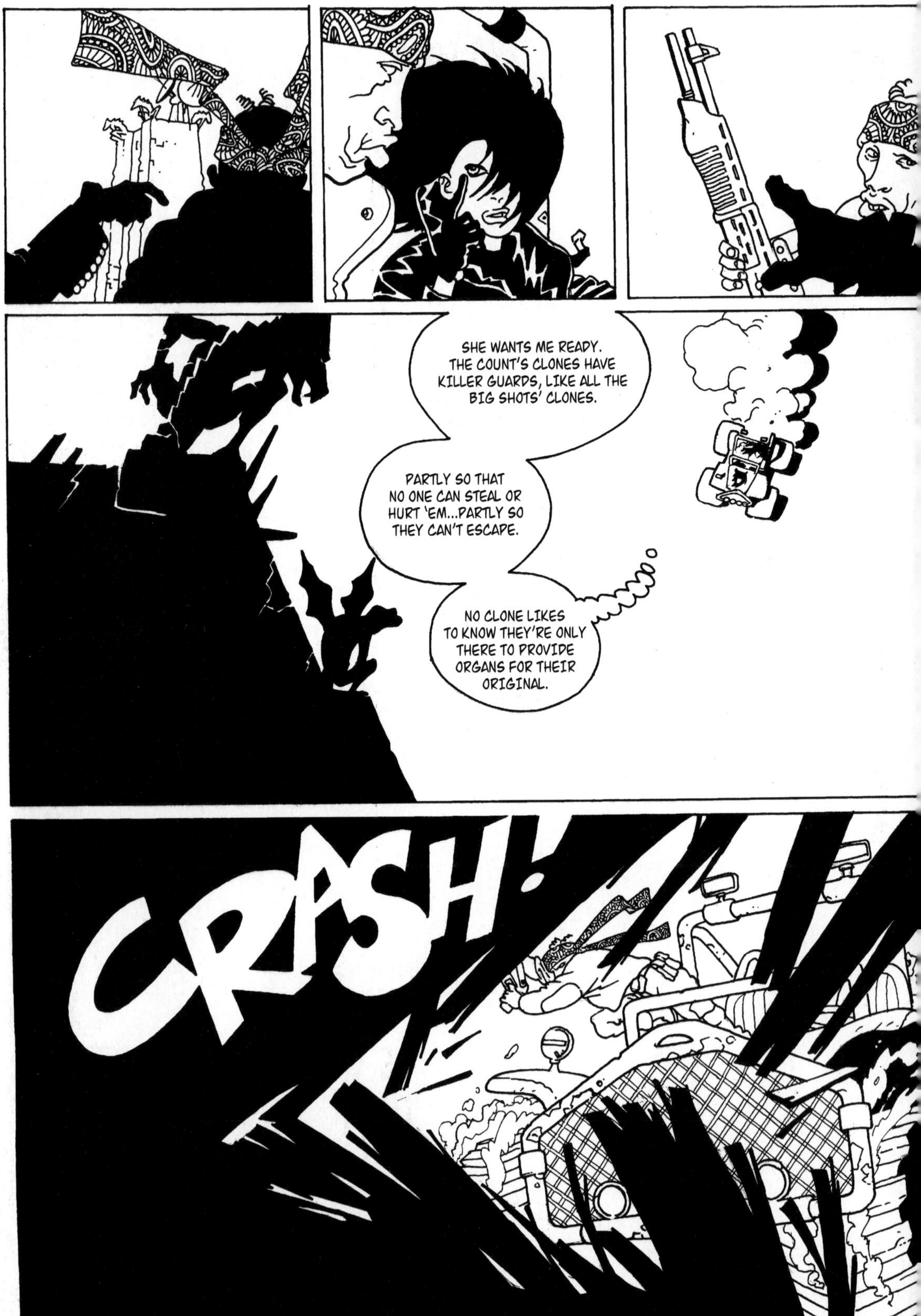
SHE WANTS ME READY. THE COUNT'S CLONES HAVE KILLER GUARDS, LIKE ALL THE BIG SHOTS' CLONES.
PARTLY SO THAT NO ONE CAN STEAL OR HURT 'EM...PARTLY SO THEY CAN'T ESCAPE.
NO CLONE LIKES TO KNOW THEY'RE ONLY THERE TO PROVIDE ORGANS FOR THEIR ORIGINAL.
CRASH!

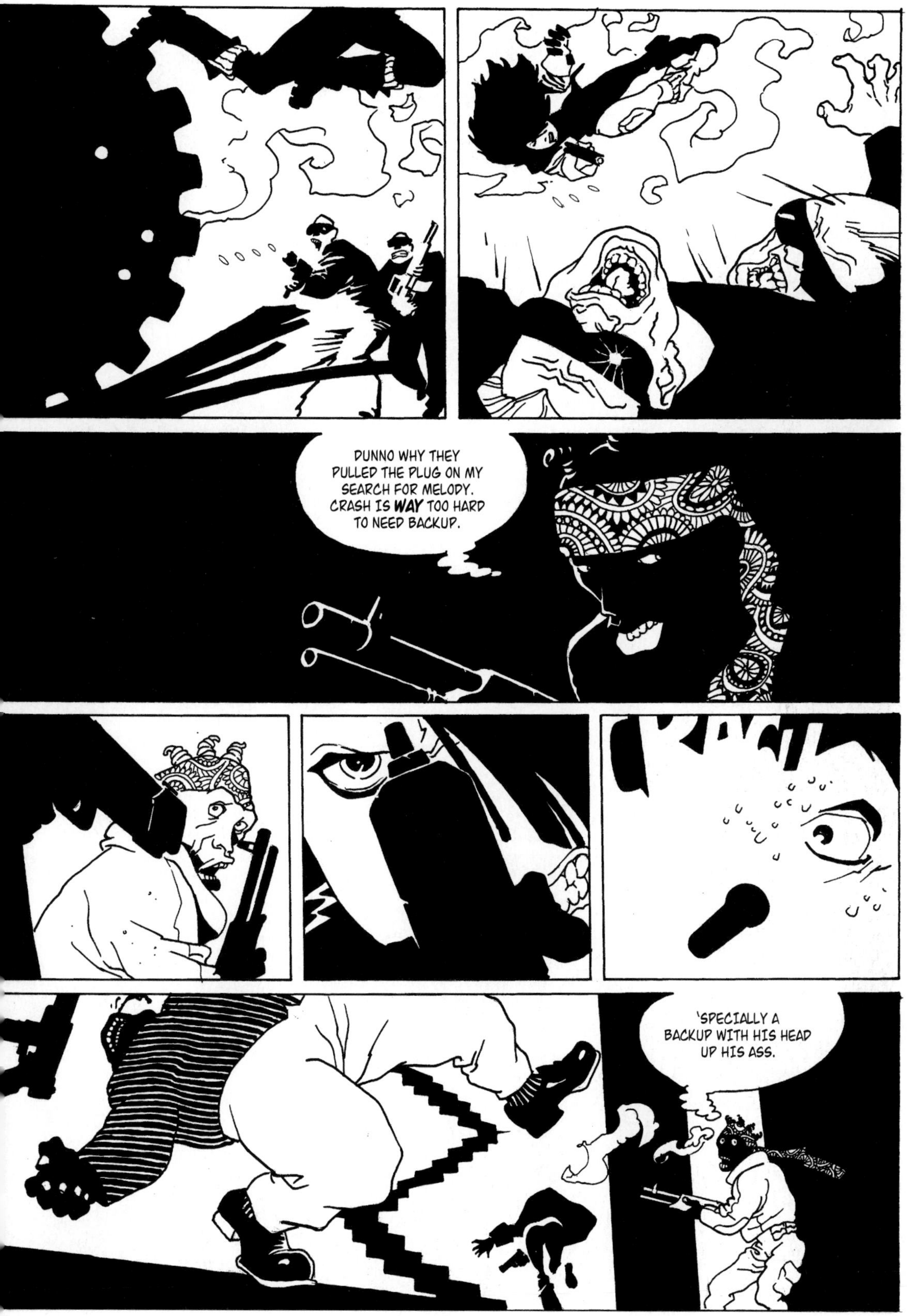
DUNNO WHY THEY PULLED THE PLUG ON MY SEARCH FOR MELODY. CRASH IS WAY TOO HARD TO NEED BACKUP.
'SPECIALLY A BACKUP WITH HIS HEAD UP HIS ASS.

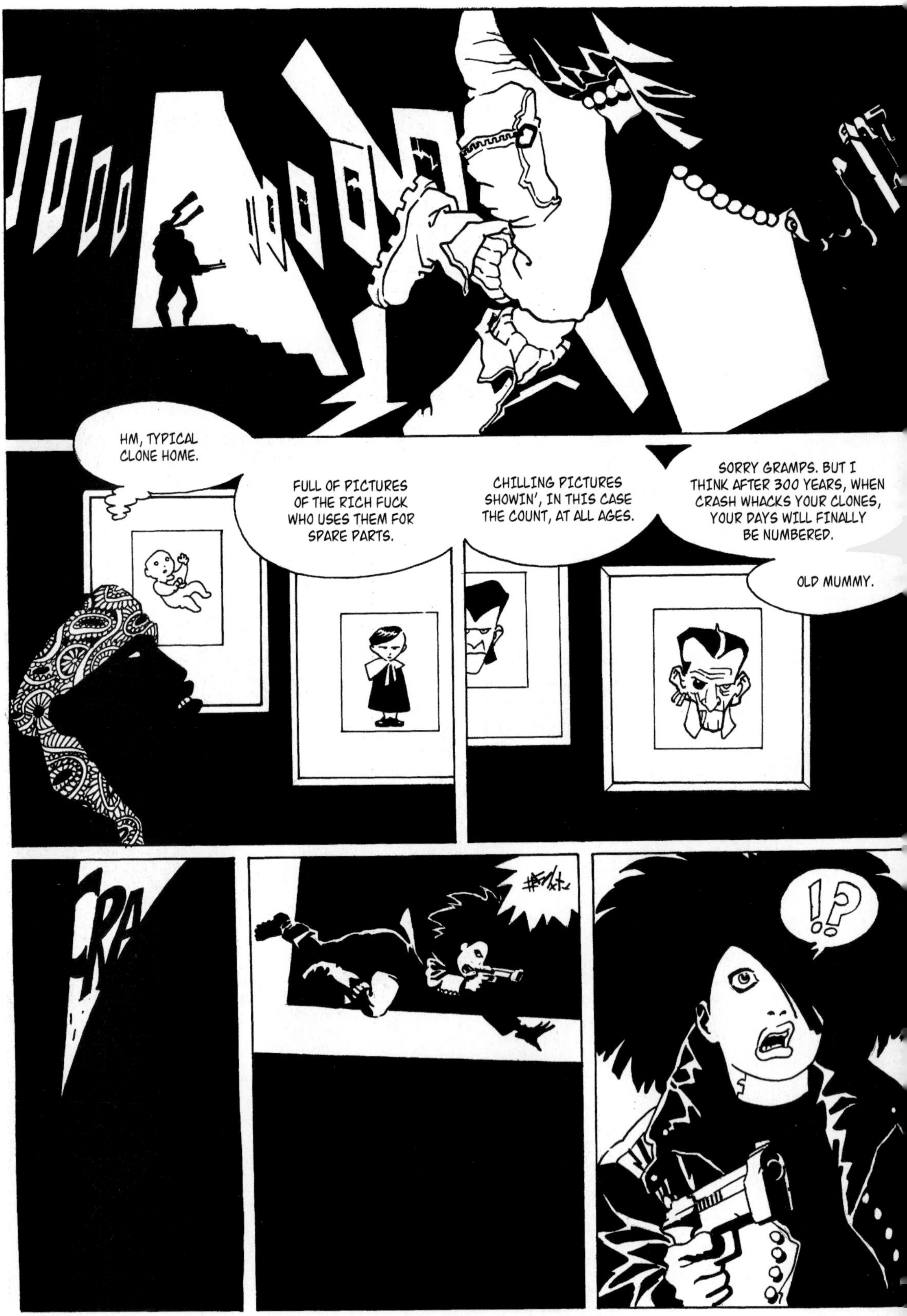
HM, TYPICAL CLONE HOME.
FULL OF PICTURES OF THE RICH FUCK WHO USES THEM FOR SPARE PARTS.
CHILLING PICTURES SHOWIN', IN THIS CASE THE COUNT, AT ALL AGES.
SORRY GRAMPS. BUT I THINK AFTER 300 YEARS, WHEN CRASH WHACKS YOUR CLONES, YOUR DAYS WILL FINALLY BE NUMBERED.
OLD MUMMY.
CRA
!?

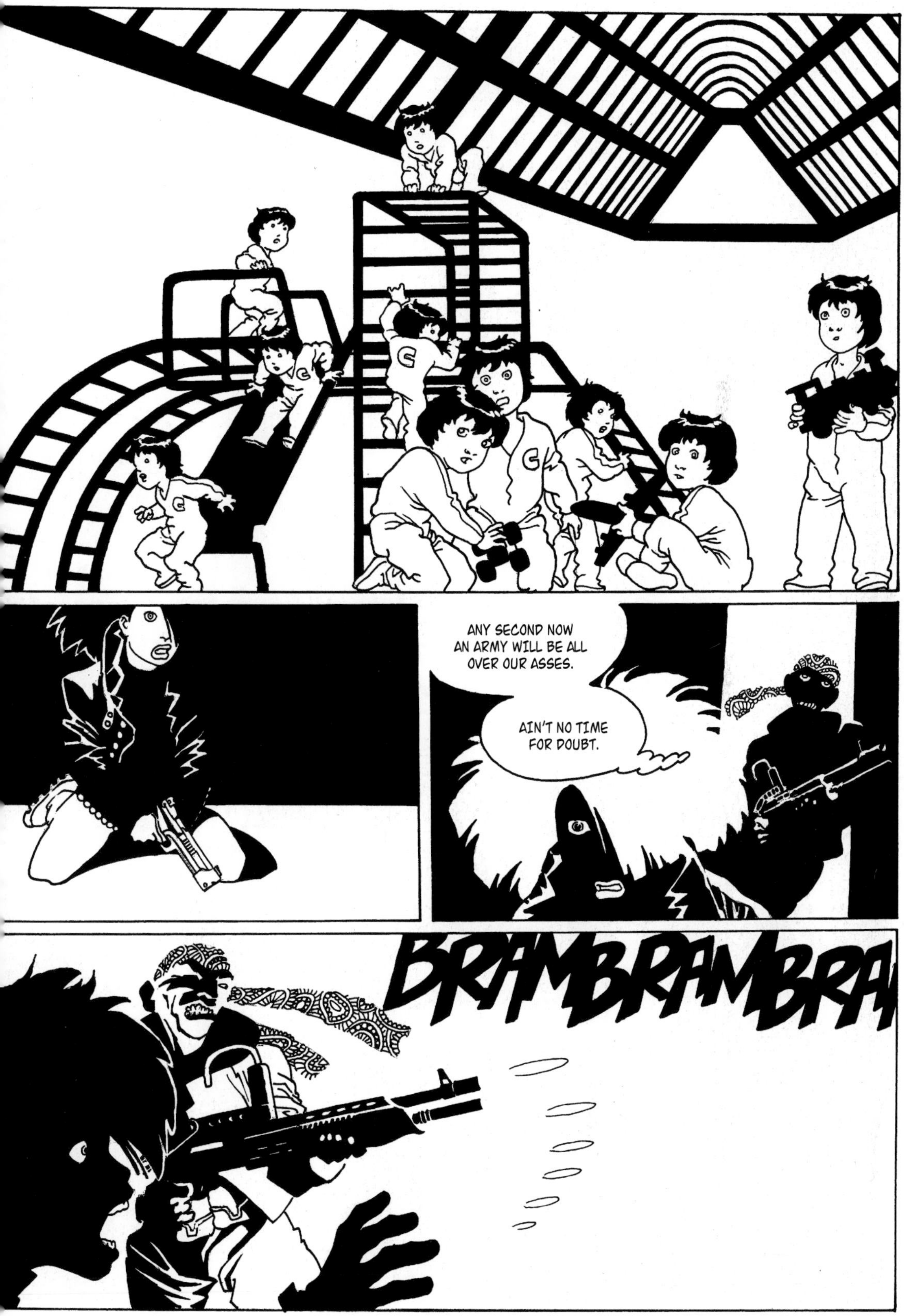
ANY SECOND NOW AN ARMY WILL BE ALL OVER OUR ASSES.
AIN'T NO TIME FOR DOUBT.
BRAMBRAMBRA

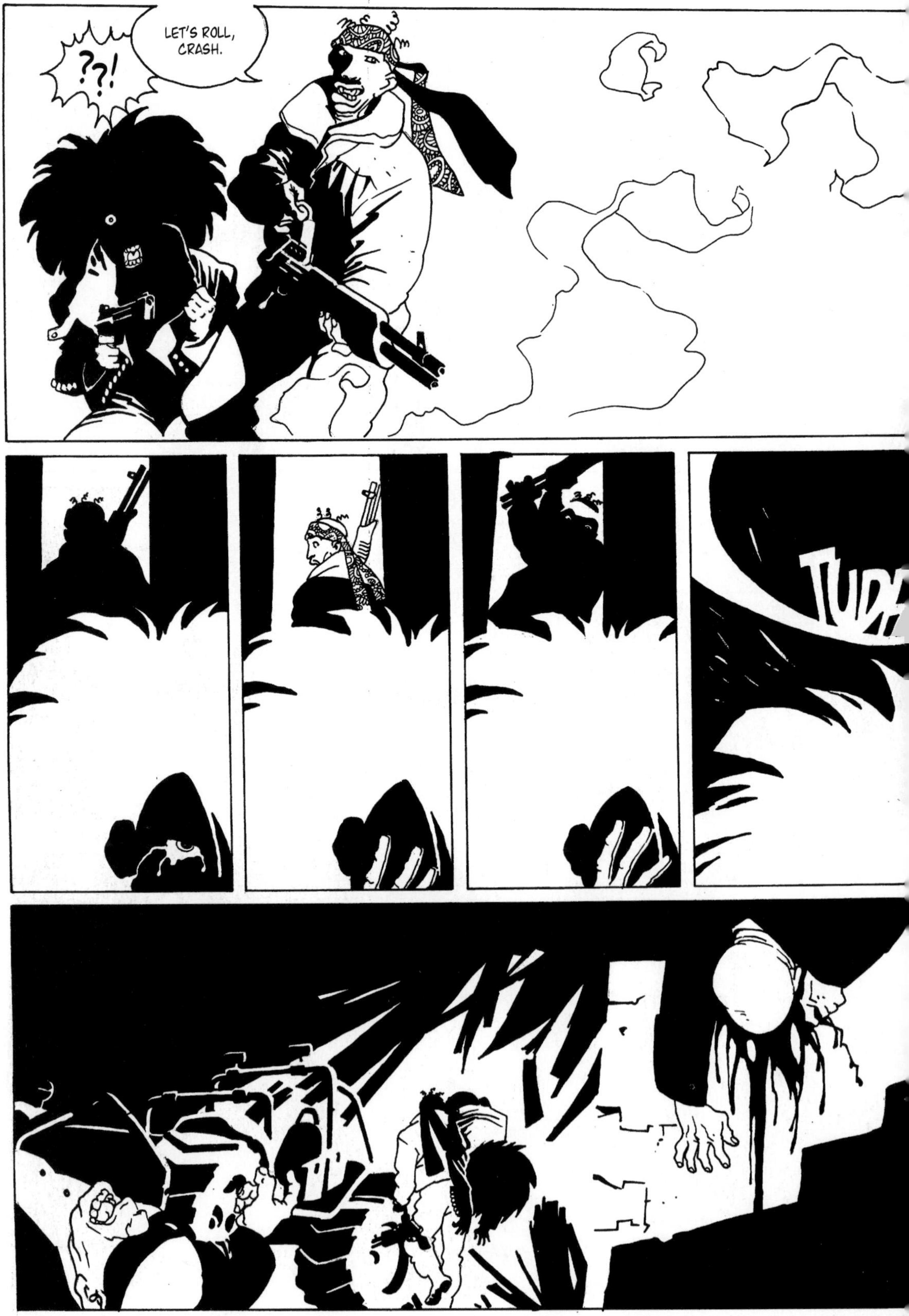
??!
LET'S ROLL, CRASH.
TUD

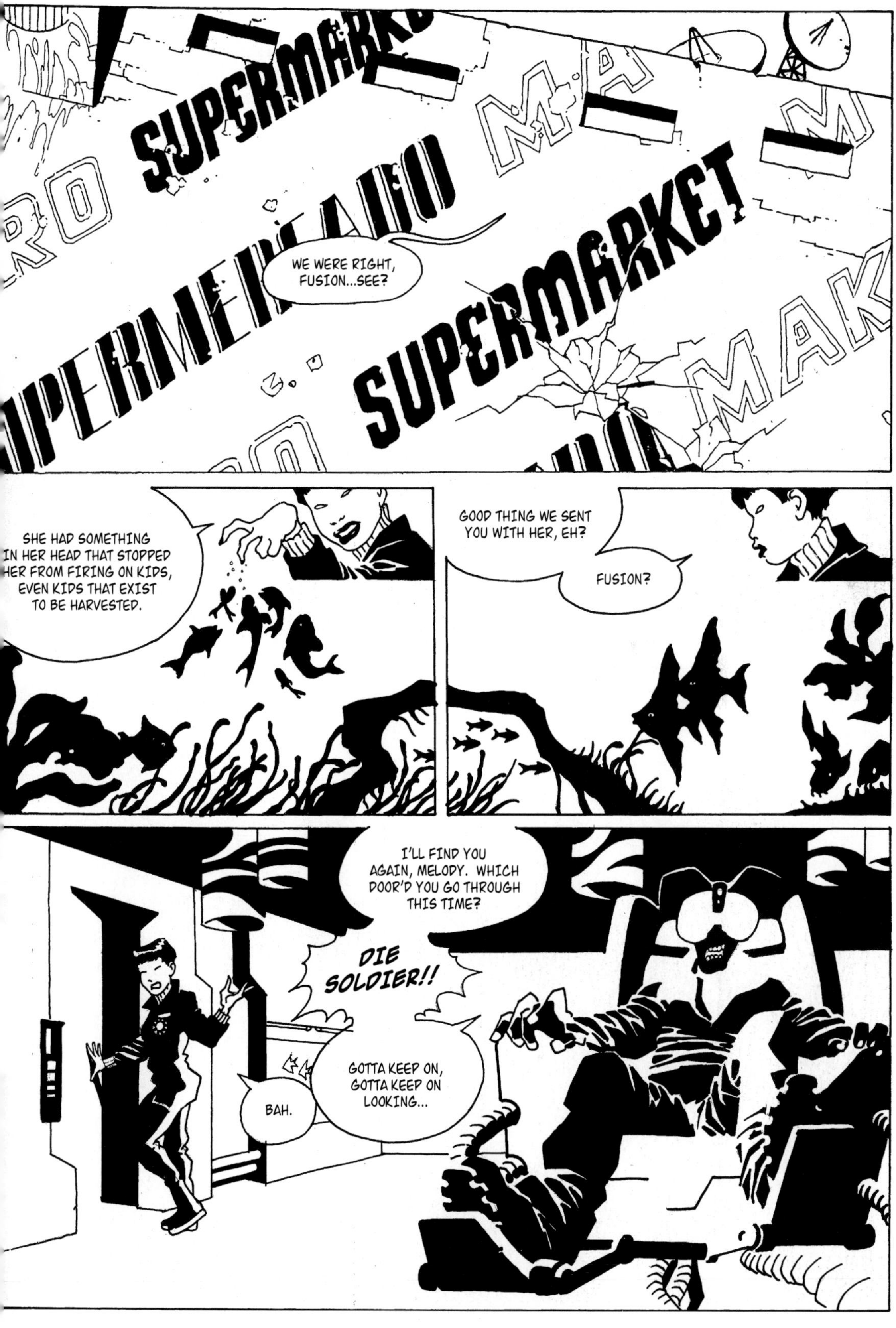
SUPERMARKET
SUPERMARKET
WE WERE RIGHT, FUSION...SEE?
SHE HAD SOMETHING IN HER HEAD THAT STOPPED HER FROM FIRING ON KIDS, EVEN KIDS THAT EXIST TO BE HARVESTED.
GOOD THING WE SENT YOU WITH HER, EH?
FUSION?
I'LL FIND YOU AGAIN, MELODY. WHICH DOOR'D YOU GO THROUGH THIS TIME?
DIE SOLDIER!!
GOTTA KEEP ON, GOTTA KEEP ON LOOKING...
BAH.

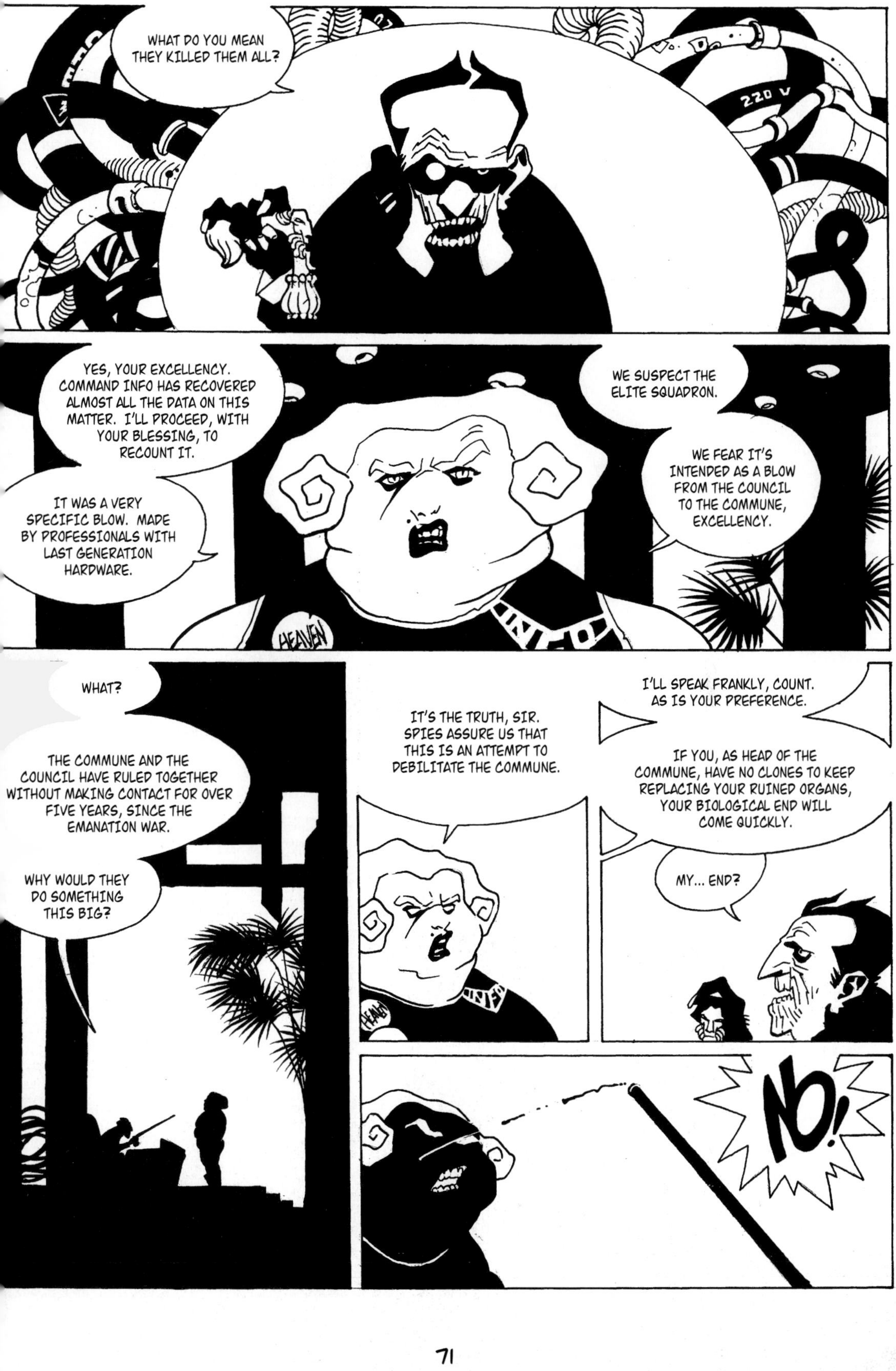
WHAT DO YOU MEAN THEY KILLED THEM ALL?
220 V
YES, YOUR EXCELLENCY. COMMAND INFO HAS RECOVERED ALMOST ALL THE DATA ON THIS MATTER. I'LL PROCEED, WITH YOUR BLESSING, TO RECOUNT IT.
IT WAS A VERY SPECIFIC BLOW. MADE BY PROFESSIONALS WITH LAST GENERATION HARDWARE.
WE SUSPECT THE ELITE SQUADRON.
WE FEAR IT'S INTENDED AS A BLOW FROM THE COUNCIL TO THE COMMUNE, EXCELLENCY.
HEAVEN
WHAT?
THE COMMUNE AND THE COUNCIL HAVE RULED TOGETHER WITHOUT MAKING CONTACT FOR OVER FIVE YEARS, SINCE THE EMANATION WAR.
WHY WOULD THEY DO SOMETHING THIS BIG?
IT'S THE TRUTH, SIR. SPIES ASSURE US THAT THIS IS AN ATTEMPT TO DEBILITATE THE COMMUNE.
I'LL SPEAK FRANKLY, COUNT. AS IS YOUR PREFERENCE.
IF YOU, AS HEAD OF THE COMMUNE, HAVE NO CLONES TO KEEP REPLACING YOUR RUINED ORGANS, YOUR BIOLOGICAL END WILL COME QUICKLY.
MY... END?
NO!

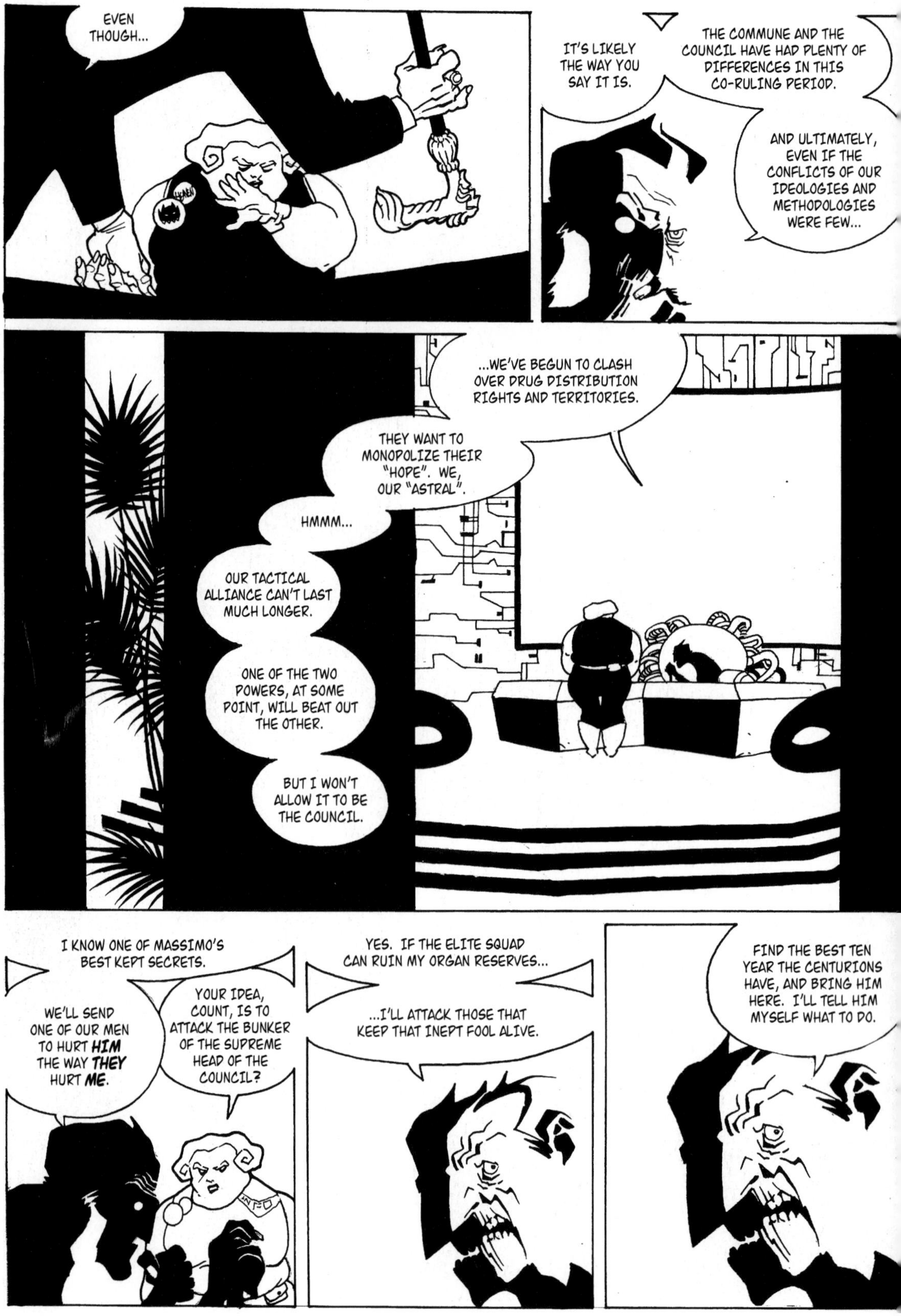
EVEN THOUGH...
IT'S LIKELY THE WAY YOU SAY IT IS.
THE COMMUNE AND THE COUNCIL HAVE HAD PLENTY OF DIFFERENCES IN THIS CO-RULING PERIOD.
AND ULTIMATELY, EVEN IF THE CONFLICTS OF OUR IDEOLOGIES AND METHODOLOGIES WERE FEW...
...WE'VE BEGUN TO CLASH OVER DRUG DISTRIBUTION RIGHTS AND TERRITORIES.
THEY WANT TO MONOPOLIZE THEIR "HOPE". WE, OUR "ASTRAL".
HMMM...
OUR TACTICAL ALLIANCE CAN'T LAST MUCH LONGER.
ONE OF THE TWO POWERS, AT SOME POINT, WILL BEAT OUT THE OTHER.
BUT I WON'T ALLOW IT TO BE THE COUNCIL.
I KNOW ONE OF MASSIMO'S BEST KEPT SECRETS.
WE'LL SEND ONE OF OUR MEN TO HURT **HIM** THE WAY **THEY** HURT **ME**.
YOUR IDEA, COUNT, IS TO ATTACK THE BUNKER OF THE SUPREME HEAD OF THE COUNCIL?
YES. IF THE ELITE SQUAD CAN RUIN MY ORGAN RESERVES...
...I'LL ATTACK THOSE THAT KEEP THAT INEPT FOOL ALIVE.
FIND THE BEST TEN YEAR THE CENTURIONS HAVE, AND BRING HIM HERE. I'LL TELL HIM MYSELF WHAT TO DO.

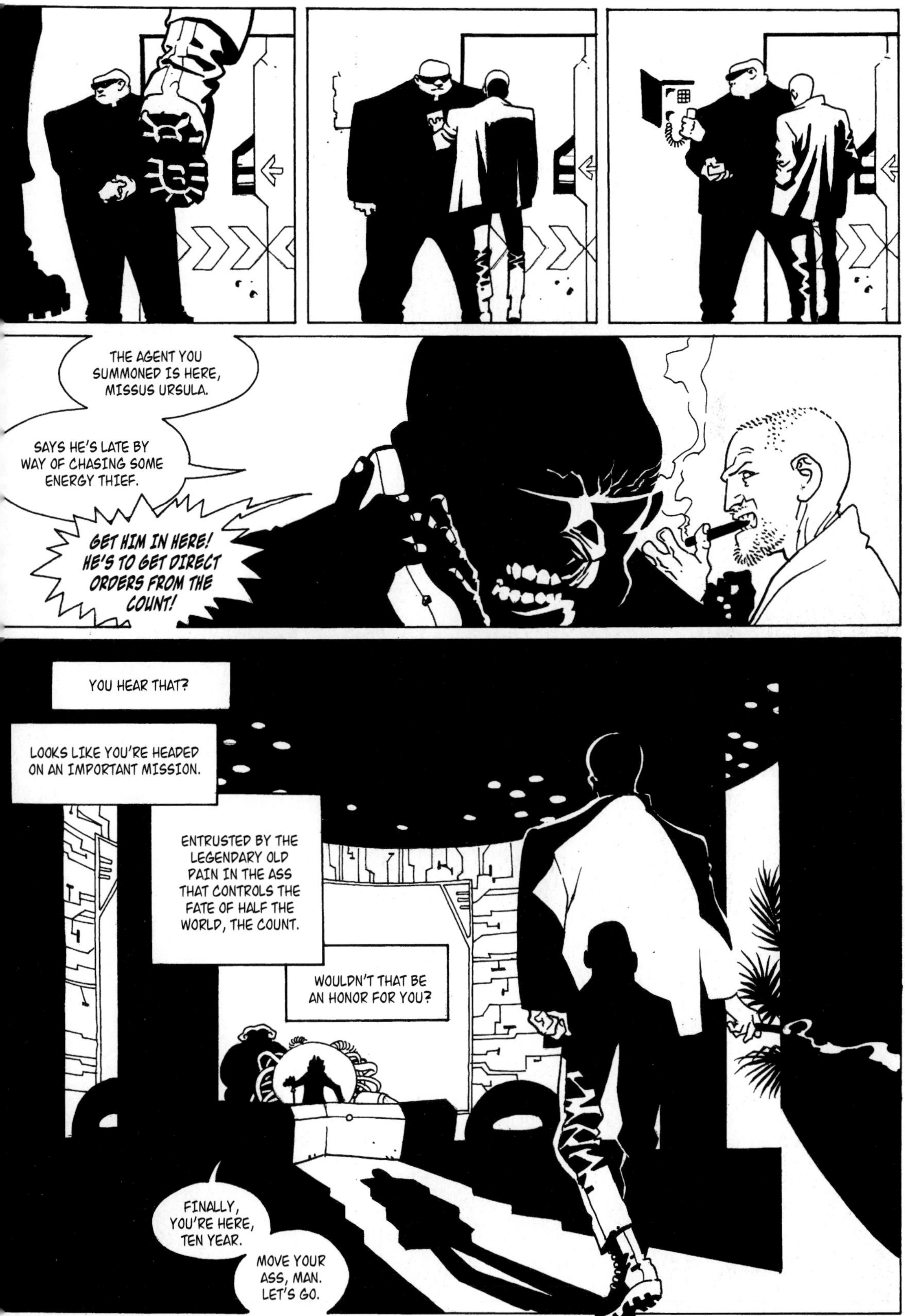
THE AGENT YOU SUMMONED IS HERE, MISSUS URSULA.
SAYS HE'S LATE BY WAY OF CHASING SOME ENERGY THIEF.
GET HIM IN HERE! HE'S TO GET DIRECT ORDERS FROM THE COUNT!
YOU HEAR THAT?
LOOKS LIKE YOU'RE HEADED ON AN IMPORTANT MISSION.
ENTRUSTED BY THE LEGENDARY OLD PAIN IN THE ASS THAT CONTROLS THE FATE OF HALF THE WORLD, THE COUNT.
WOULDN'T THAT BE AN HONOR FOR YOU?
FINALLY, YOU'RE HERE, TEN YEAR.
MOVE YOUR ASS, MAN. LET'S GO.

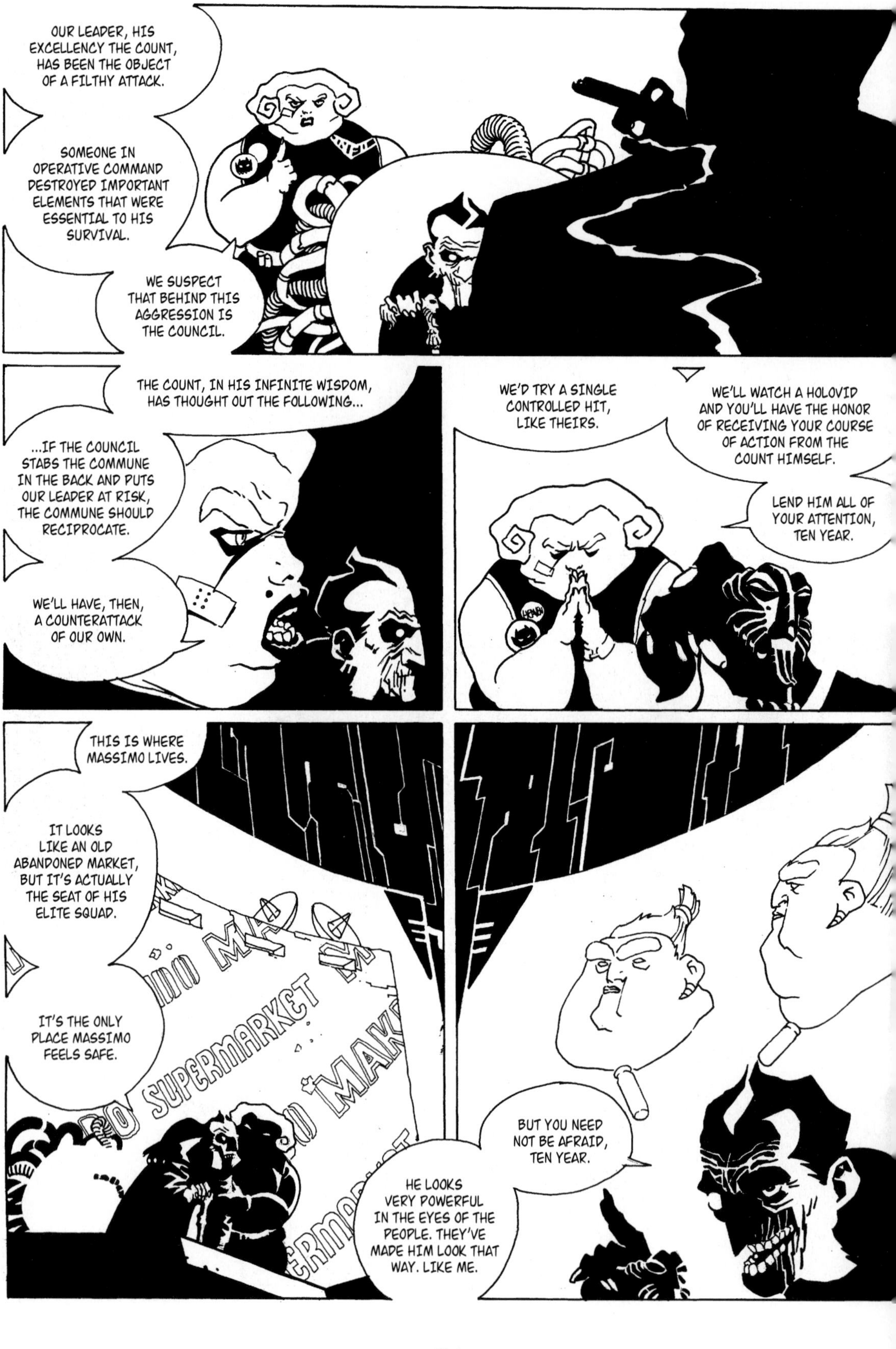
OUR LEADER, HIS EXCELLENCY THE COUNT, HAS BEEN THE OBJECT OF A FILTHY ATTACK.
SOMEONE IN OPERATIVE COMMAND DESTROYED IMPORTANT ELEMENTS THAT WERE ESSENTIAL TO HIS SURVIVAL.
WE SUSPECT THAT BEHIND THIS AGGRESSION IS THE COUNCIL.
THE COUNT, IN HIS INFINITE WISDOM, HAS THOUGHT OUT THE FOLLOWING...
...IF THE COUNCIL STABS THE COMMUNE IN THE BACK AND PUTS OUR LEADER AT RISK, THE COMMUNE SHOULD RECIPROCATE.
WE'LL HAVE, THEN, A COUNTERATTACK OF OUR OWN.
WE'D TRY A SINGLE CONTROLLED HIT, LIKE THEIRS.
WE'LL WATCH A HOLOVID AND YOU'LL HAVE THE HONOR OF RECEIVING YOUR COURSE OF ACTION FROM THE COUNT HIMSELF.
LEND HIM ALL OF YOUR ATTENTION, TEN YEAR.
THIS IS WHERE MASSIMO LIVES.
IT LOOKS LIKE AN OLD ABANDONED MARKET, BUT IT'S ACTUALLY THE SEAT OF HIS ELITE SQUAD.
IT'S THE ONLY PLACE MASSIMO FEELS SAFE.
SUPERMARKCT
BUT YOU NEED NOT BE AFRAID, TEN YEAR.
HE LOOKS VERY POWERFUL IN THE EYES OF THE PEOPLE. THEY'VE MADE HIM LOOK THAT WAY. LIKE ME.

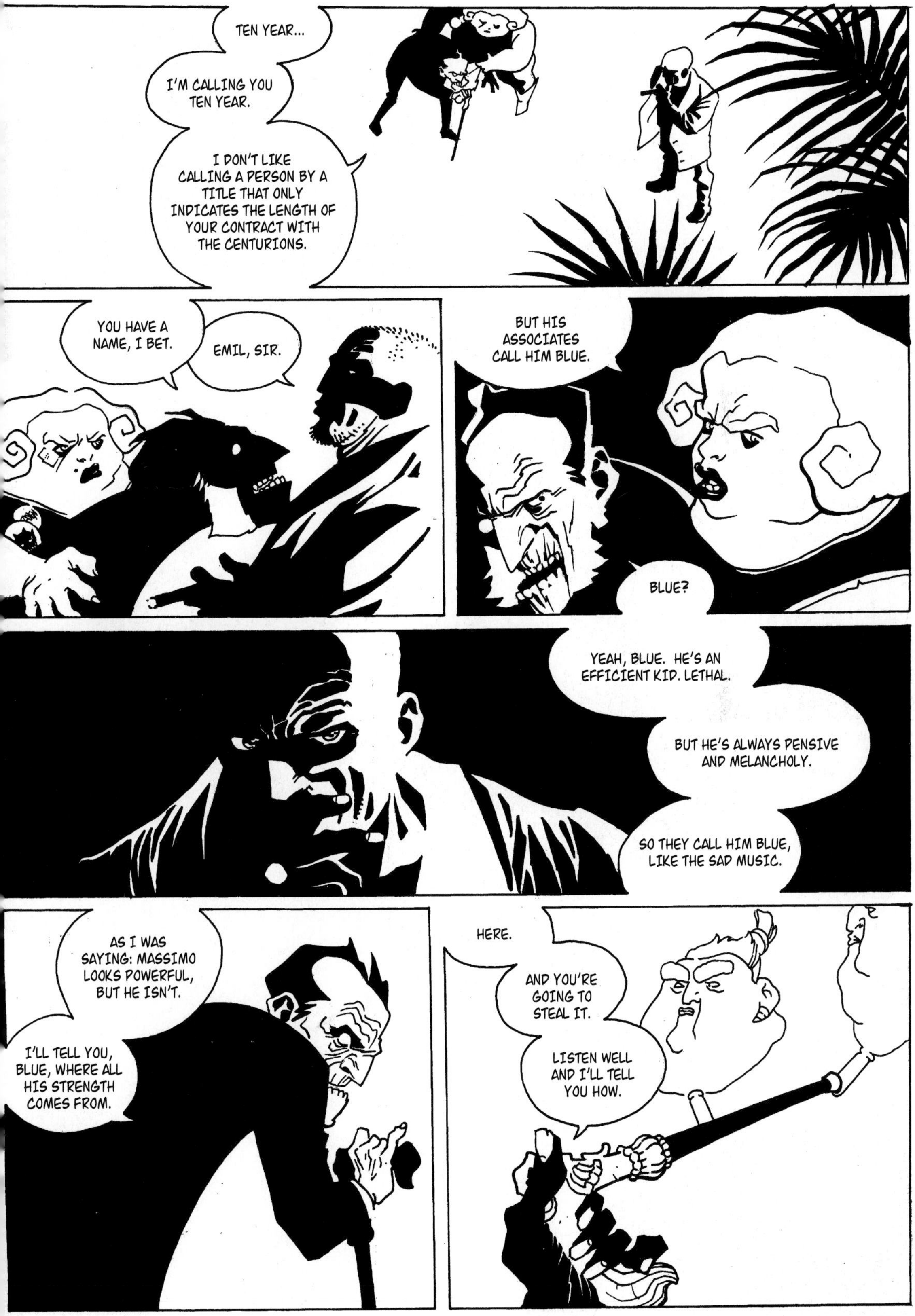
TEN YEAR...
I'M CALLING YOU TEN YEAR.
I DON'T LIKE CALLING A PERSON BY A TITLE THAT ONLY INDICATES THE LENGTH OF YOUR CONTRACT WITH THE CENTURIONS.
YOU HAVE A NAME, I BET.
EMIL, SIR.
BUT HIS ASSOCIATES CALL HIM BLUE.
BLUE?
YEAH, BLUE. HE'S AN EFFICIENT KID. LETHAL.
BUT HE'S ALWAYS PENSIVE AND MELANCHOLY.
SO THEY CALL HIM BLUE, LIKE THE SAD MUSIC.
AS I WAS SAYING: MASSIMO LOOKS POWERFUL, BUT HE ISN'T.
I'LL TELL YOU, BLUE, WHERE ALL HIS STRENGTH COMES FROM.
HERE.
AND YOU'RE GOING TO STEAL IT.
LISTEN WELL AND I'LL TELL YOU HOW.

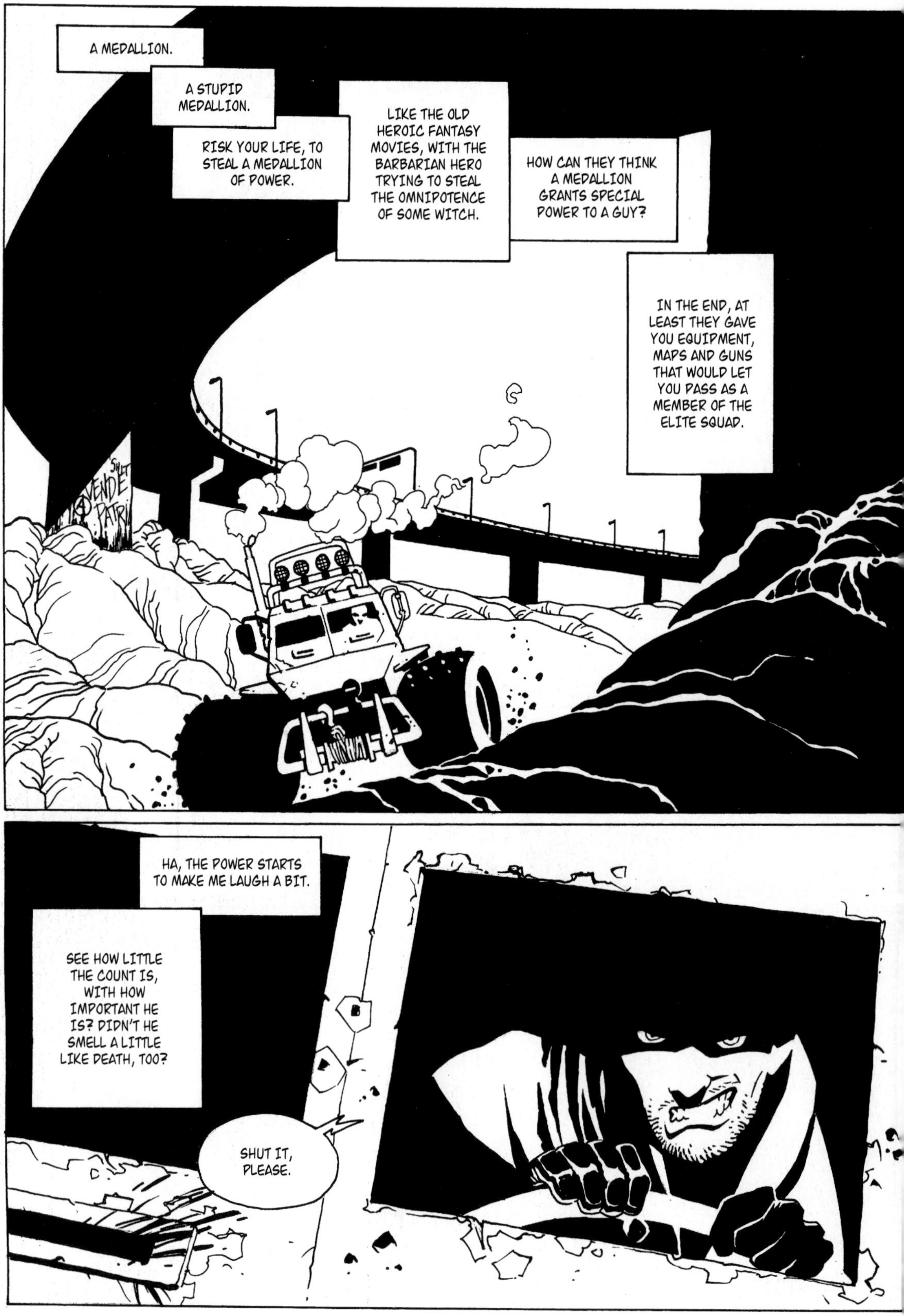
A MEDALLION.
A STUPID MEDALLION.
RISK YOUR LIFE, TO STEAL A MEDALLION OF POWER.
LIKE THE OLD HEROIC FANTASY MOVIES, WITH THE BARBARIAN HERO TRYING TO STEAL THE OMNIPOTENCE OF SOME WITCH.
HOW CAN THEY THINK A MEDALLION GRANTS SPECIAL POWER TO A GUY?
IN THE END, AT LEAST THEY GAVE YOU EQUIPMENT, MAPS AND GUNS THAT WOULD LET YOU PASS AS A MEMBER OF THE ELITE SQUAD.
HA, THE POWER STARTS TO MAKE ME LAUGH A BIT.
SEE HOW LITTLE THE COUNT IS, WITH HOW IMPORTANT HE IS? DIDN'T HE SMELL A LITTLE LIKE DEATH, TOO?
SHUT IT, PLEASE.

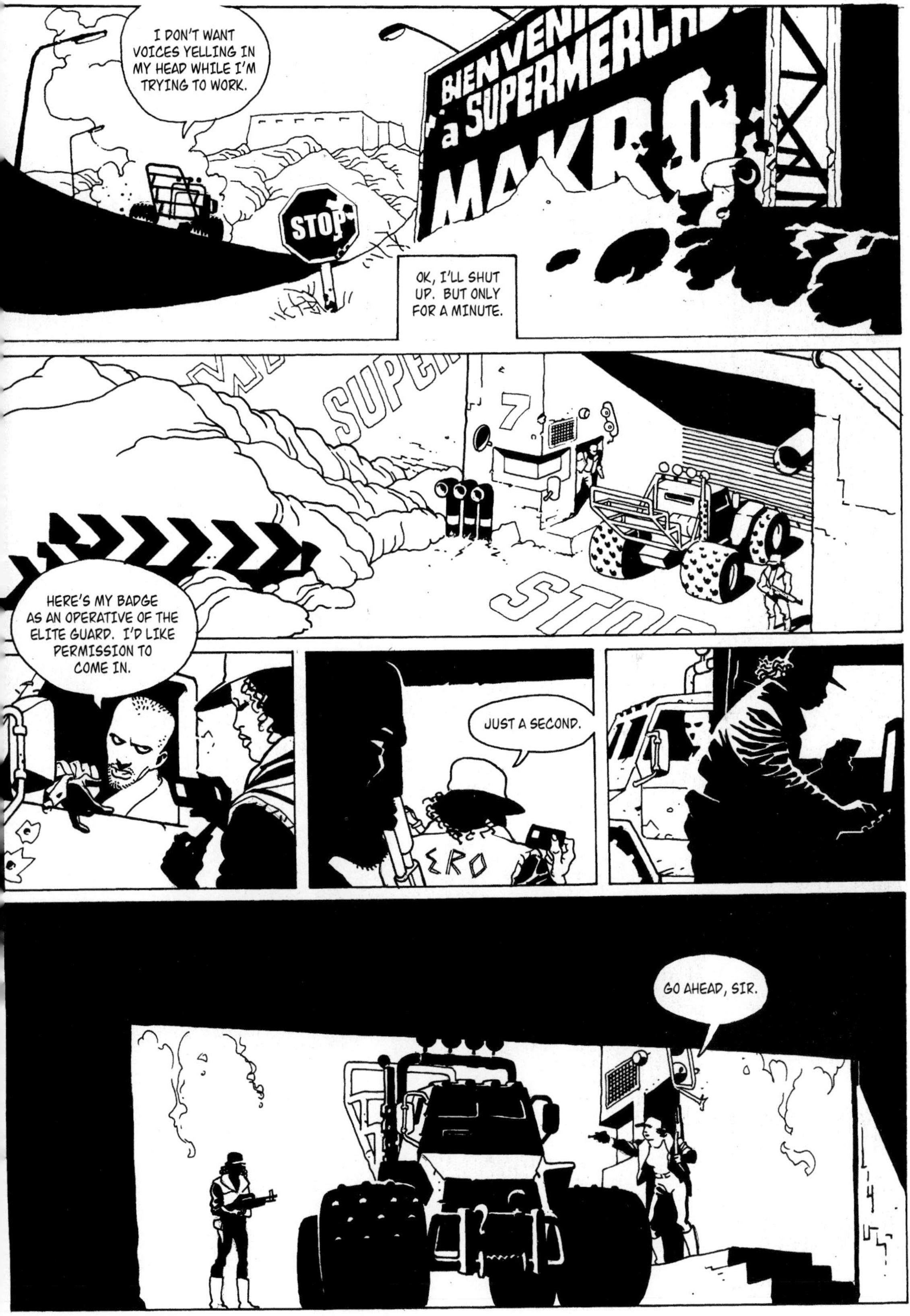

I DON'T WANT VOICES YELLING IN MY HEAD WHILE I'M TRYING TO WORK.
BIENVENI
a SUPERMERCAD
MAKRO
STOP
OK, I'LL SHUT UP. BUT ONLY FOR A MINUTE.
SUPER
STOP
HERE'S MY BADGE AS AN OPERATIVE OF THE ELITE GUARD. I'D LIKE PERMISSION TO COME IN.
JUST A SECOND.
GO AHEAD, SIR.

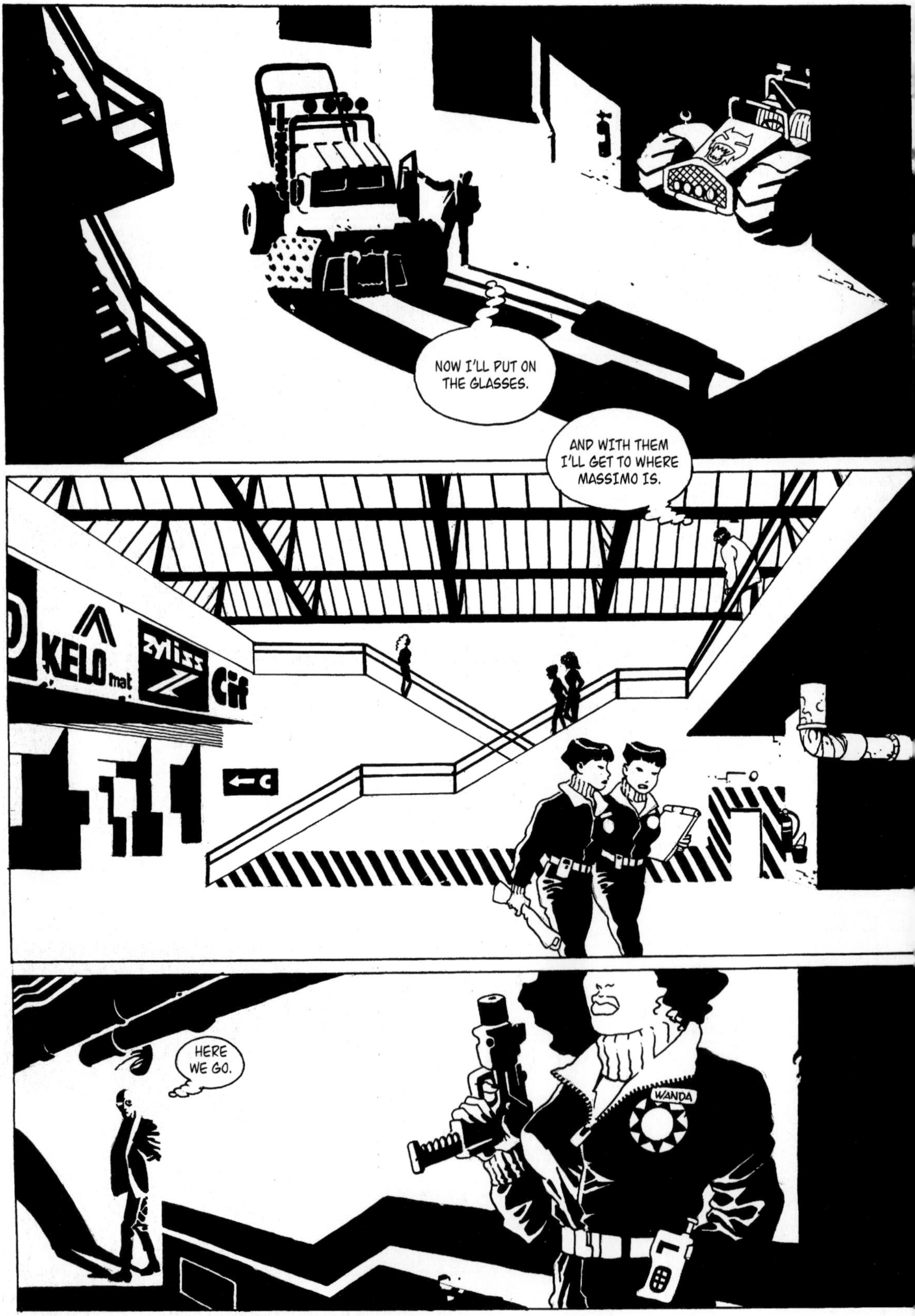
NOW I'LL PUT ON THE GLASSES.
AND WITH THEM I'LL GET TO WHERE MASSIMO IS.
KELO mat
zyliss
Cif
HERE WE GO.
WANDA

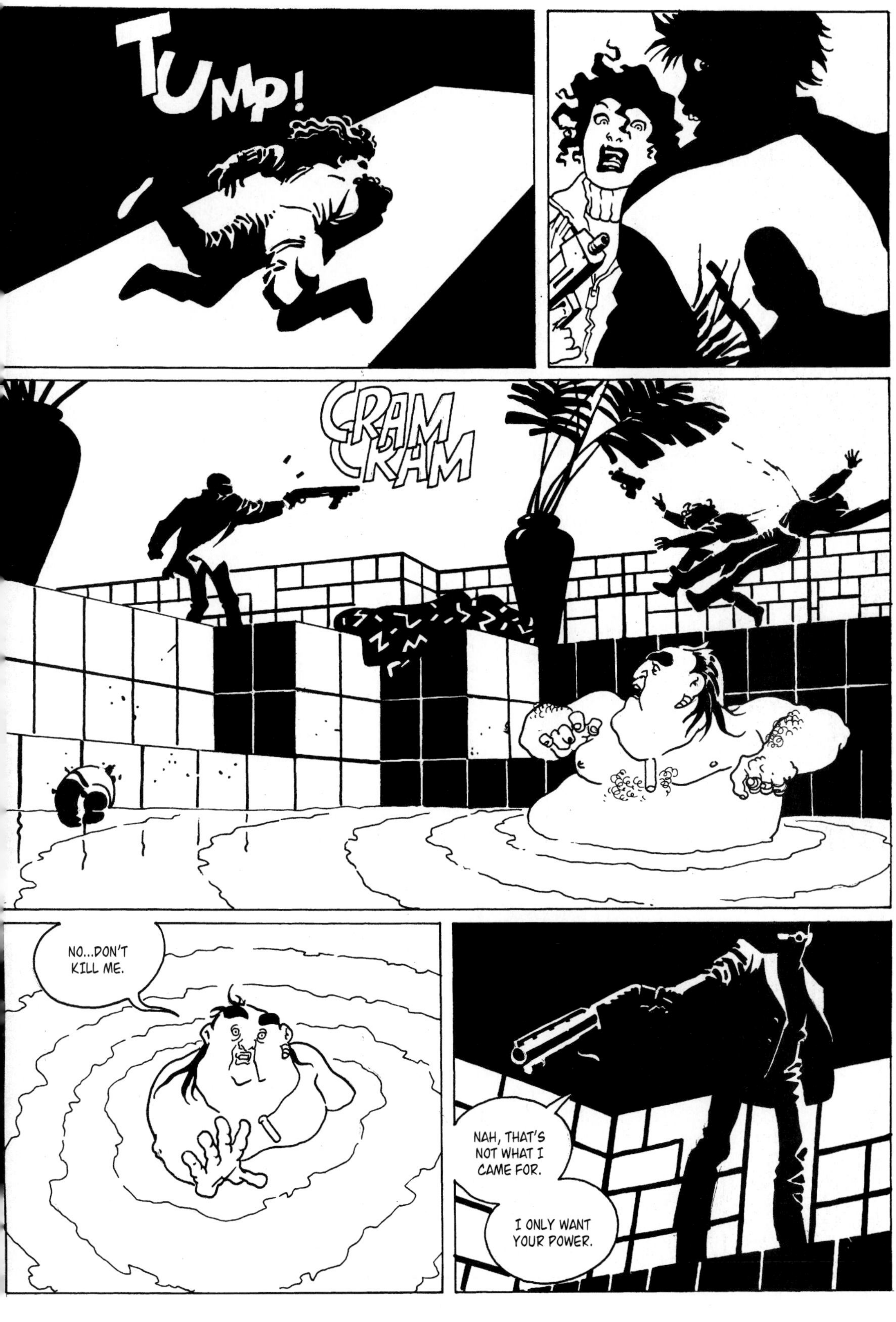
TUMP!
CRAM
CRAM
NO...DON'T
KILL ME.
NAH, THAT'S
NOT WHAT I
CAME FOR.
I ONLY WANT
YOUR POWER.

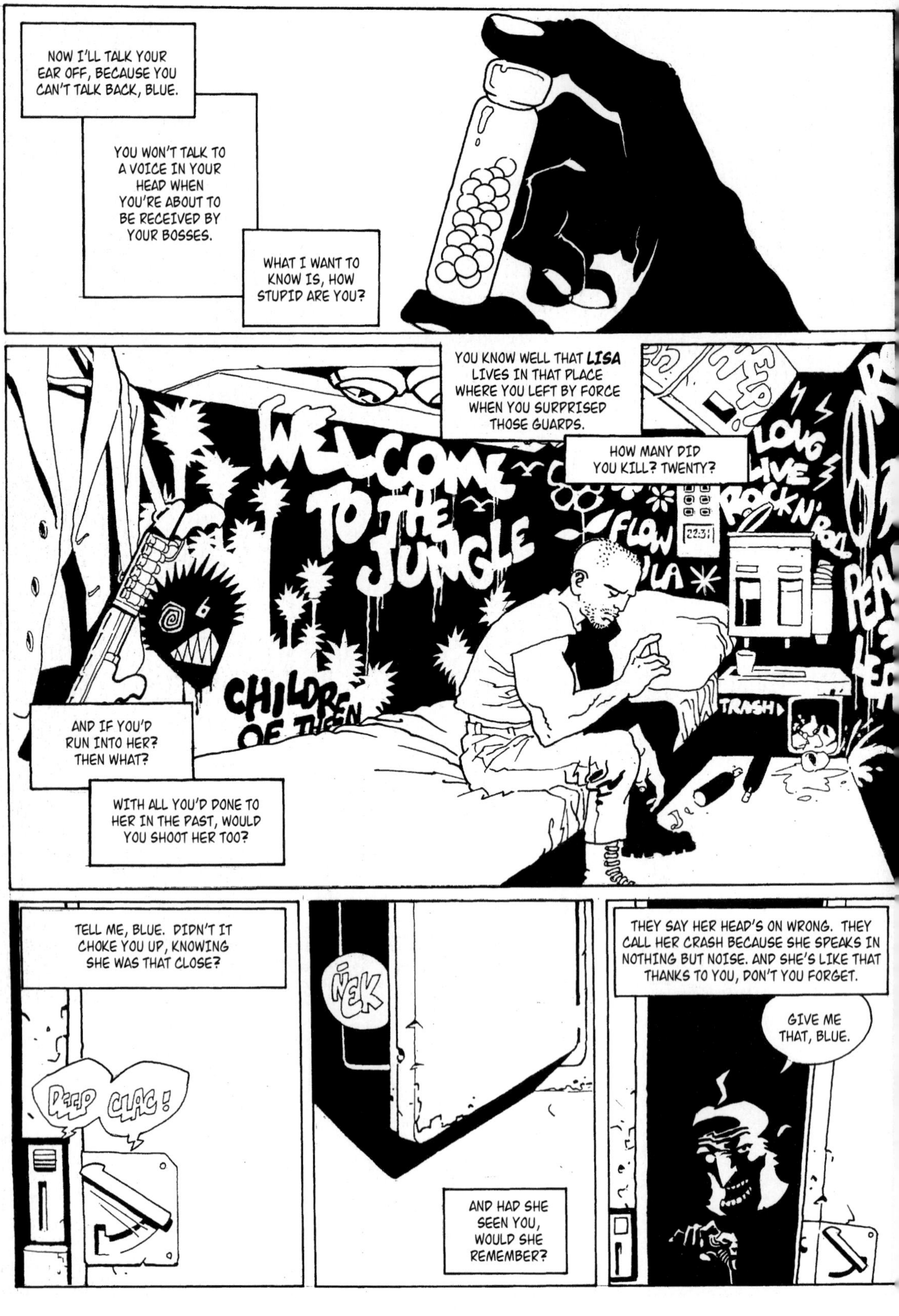
NOW I'LL TALK YOUR EAR OFF, BECAUSE YOU CAN'T TALK BACK, BLUE.
YOU WON'T TALK TO A VOICE IN YOUR HEAD WHEN YOU'RE ABOUT TO BE RECEIVED BY YOUR BOSSES.
WHAT I WANT TO KNOW IS, HOW STUPID ARE YOU?
YOU KNOW WELL THAT LISA LIVES IN THAT PLACE WHERE YOU LEFT BY FORCE WHEN YOU SURPRISED THOSE GUARDS.
HOW MANY DID YOU KILL? TWENTY?
WELCOME TO THE JUNGLE
LONG LIVE ROCK'N'ROLL
22:31
TRASH
AND IF YOU'D RUN INTO HER? THEN WHAT?
WITH ALL YOU'D DONE TO HER IN THE PAST, WOULD YOU SHOOT HER TOO?
TELL ME, BLUE. DIDN'T IT CHOKE YOU UP, KNOWING SHE WAS THAT CLOSE?
DEEP
CLAC!
ÑEK
AND HAD SHE SEEN YOU, WOULD SHE REMEMBER?
THEY SAY HER HEAD'S ON WRONG. THEY CALL HER CRASH BECAUSE SHE SPEAKS IN NOTHING BUT NOISE. AND SHE'S LIKE THAT THANKS TO YOU, DON'T YOU FORGET.
GIVE ME THAT, BLUE.

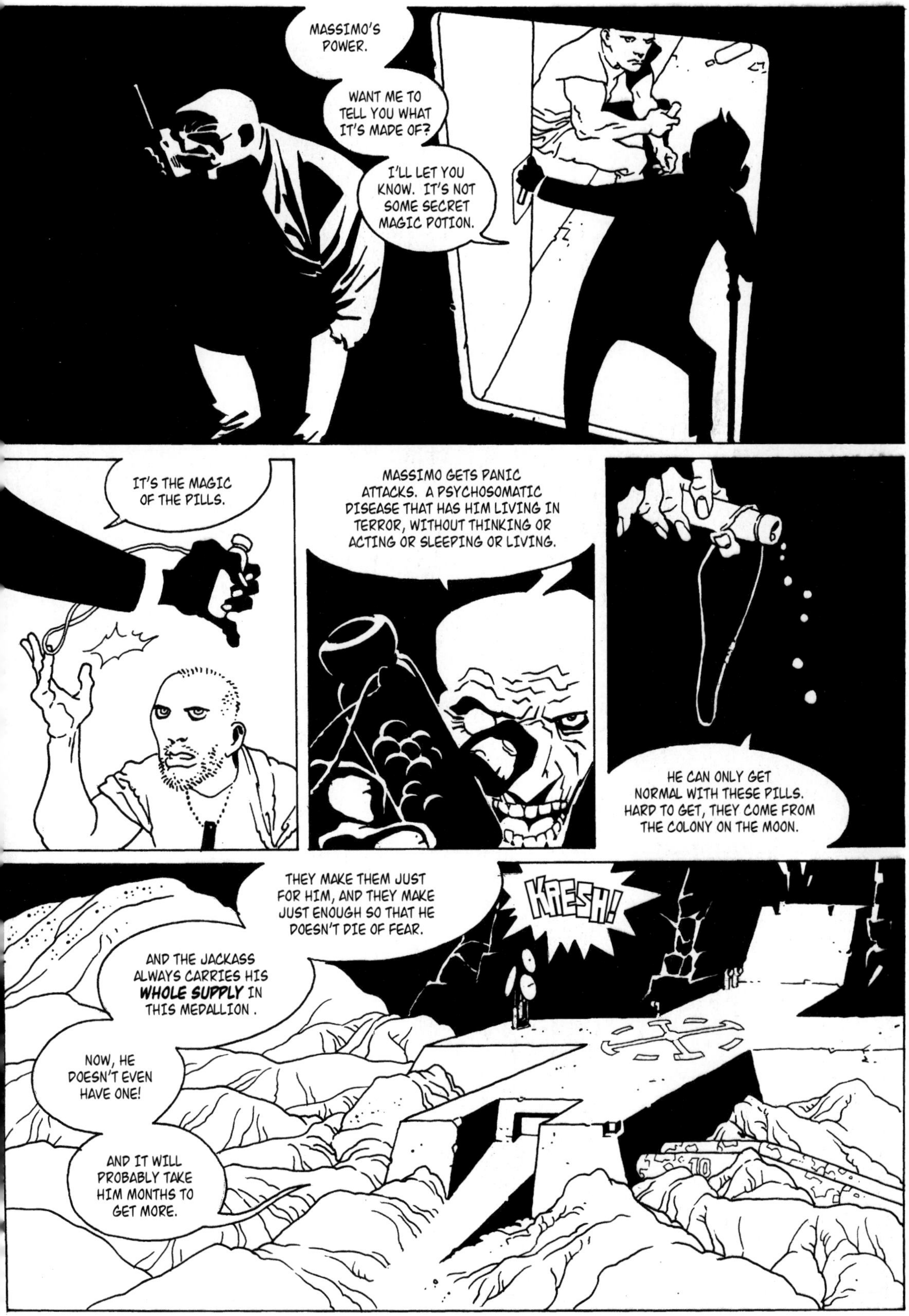
MASSIMO'S POWER.
WANT ME TO TELL YOU WHAT IT'S MADE OF?
I'LL LET YOU KNOW. IT'S NOT SOME SECRET MAGIC POTION.
IT'S THE MAGIC OF THE PILLS.
MASSIMO GETS PANIC ATTACKS. A PSYCHOSOMATIC DISEASE THAT HAS HIM LIVING IN TERROR, WITHOUT THINKING OR ACTING OR SLEEPING OR LIVING.
HE CAN ONLY GET NORMAL WITH THESE PILLS. HARD TO GET, THEY COME FROM THE COLONY ON THE MOON.
THEY MAKE THEM JUST FOR HIM, AND THEY MAKE JUST ENOUGH SO THAT HE DOESN'T DIE OF FEAR.
KRESH!
AND THE JACKASS ALWAYS CARRIES HIS **WHOLE SUPPLY** IN THIS MEDALLION.
NOW, HE DOESN'T EVEN HAVE ONE!
AND IT WILL PROBABLY TAKE HIM MONTHS TO GET MORE.

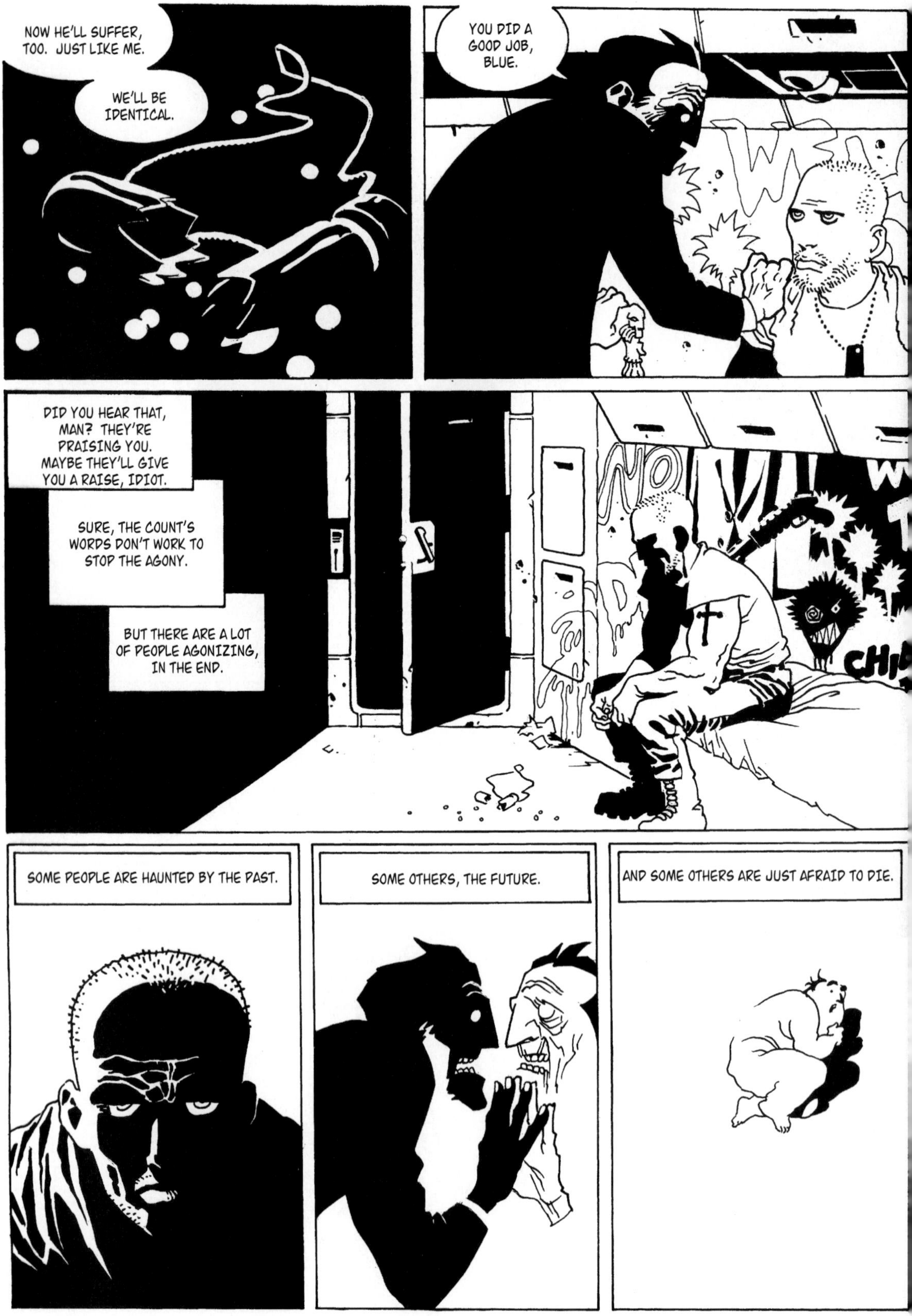
NOW HE'LL SUFFER, TOO. JUST LIKE ME.
WE'LL BE IDENTICAL.
YOU DID A GOOD JOB, BLUE.
DID YOU HEAR THAT, MAN? THEY'RE PRAISING YOU. MAYBE THEY'LL GIVE YOU A RAISE, IDIOT.
SURE, THE COUNT'S WORDS DON'T WORK TO STOP THE AGONY.
BUT THERE ARE A LOT OF PEOPLE AGONIZING, IN THE END.
SOME PEOPLE ARE HAUNTED BY THE PAST.
SOME OTHERS, THE FUTURE.
AND SOME OTHERS ARE JUST AFRAID TO DIE.

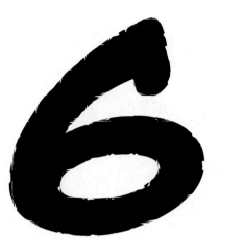

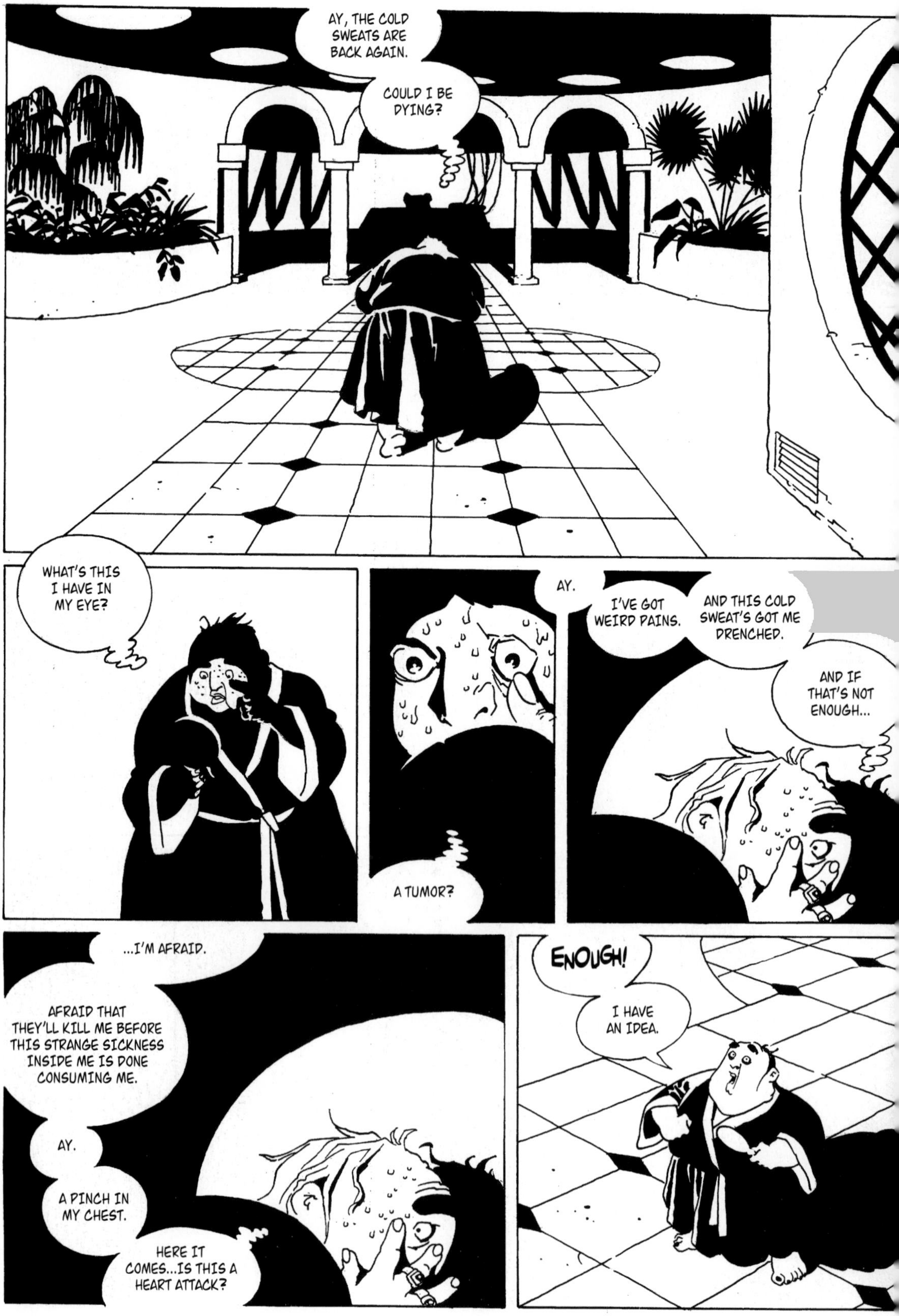

AY, THE COLD SWEATS ARE BACK AGAIN.
COULD I BE DYING?
WHAT'S THIS I HAVE IN MY EYE?
AY.
A TUMOR?
I'VE GOT WEIRD PAINS.
AND THIS COLD SWEAT'S GOT ME DRENCHED.
AND IF THAT'S NOT ENOUGH...
...I'M AFRAID.
AFRAID THAT THEY'LL KILL ME BEFORE THIS STRANGE SICKNESS INSIDE ME IS DONE CONSUMING ME.
AY.
A PINCH IN MY CHEST.
HERE IT COMES...IS THIS A HEART ATTACK?
ENOUGH!
I HAVE AN IDEA.

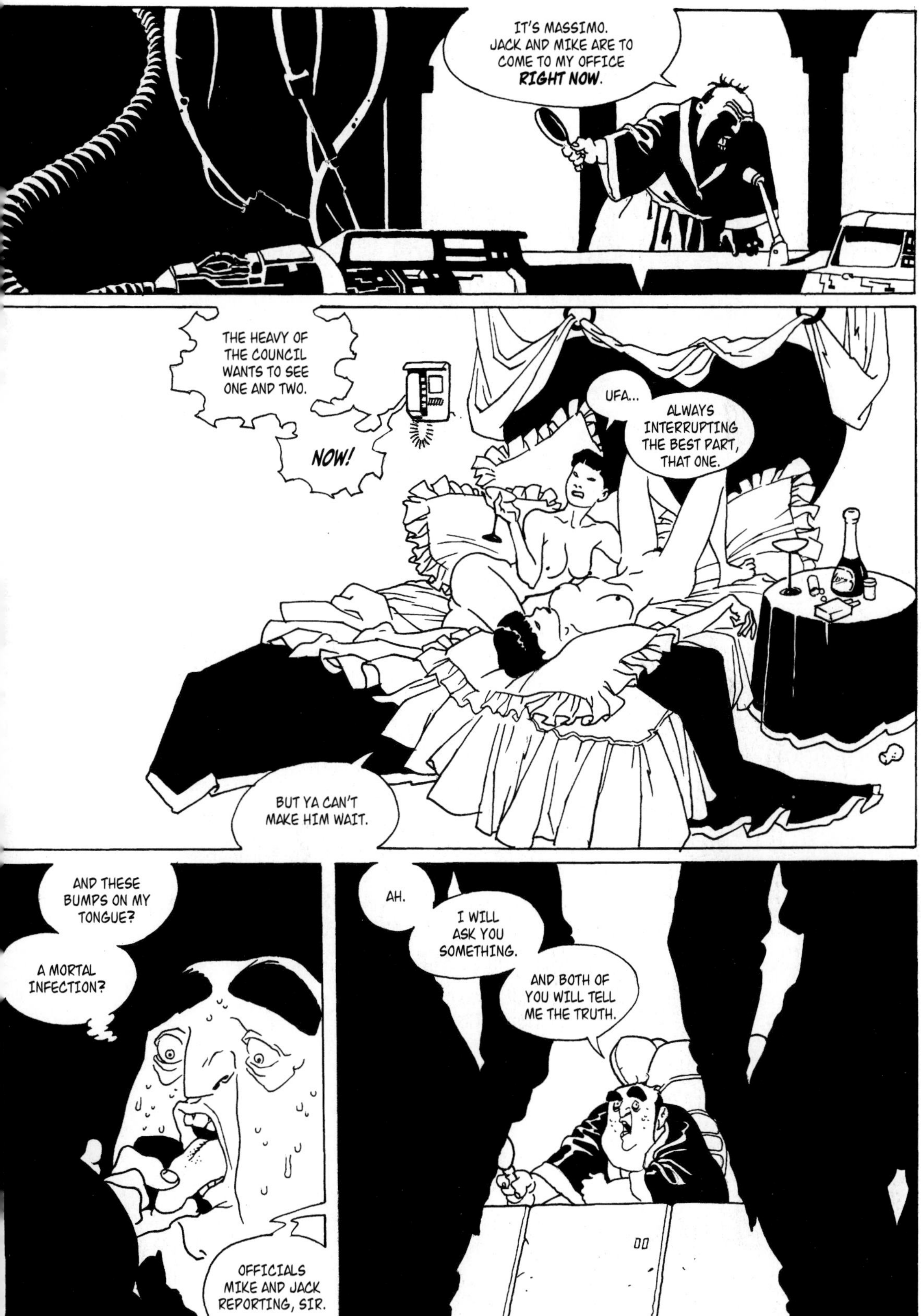
IT'S MASSIMO. JACK AND MIKE ARE TO COME TO MY OFFICE RIGHT NOW.
THE HEAVY OF THE COUNCIL WANTS TO SEE ONE AND TWO.
NOW!
UFA...
ALWAYS INTERRUPTING THE BEST PART, THAT ONE.
BUT YA CAN'T MAKE HIM WAIT.
AND THESE BUMPS ON MY TONGUE?
A MORTAL INFECTION?
OFFICIALS MIKE AND JACK REPORTING, SIR.
AH.
I WILL ASK YOU SOMETHING.
AND BOTH OF YOU WILL TELL ME THE TRUTH.

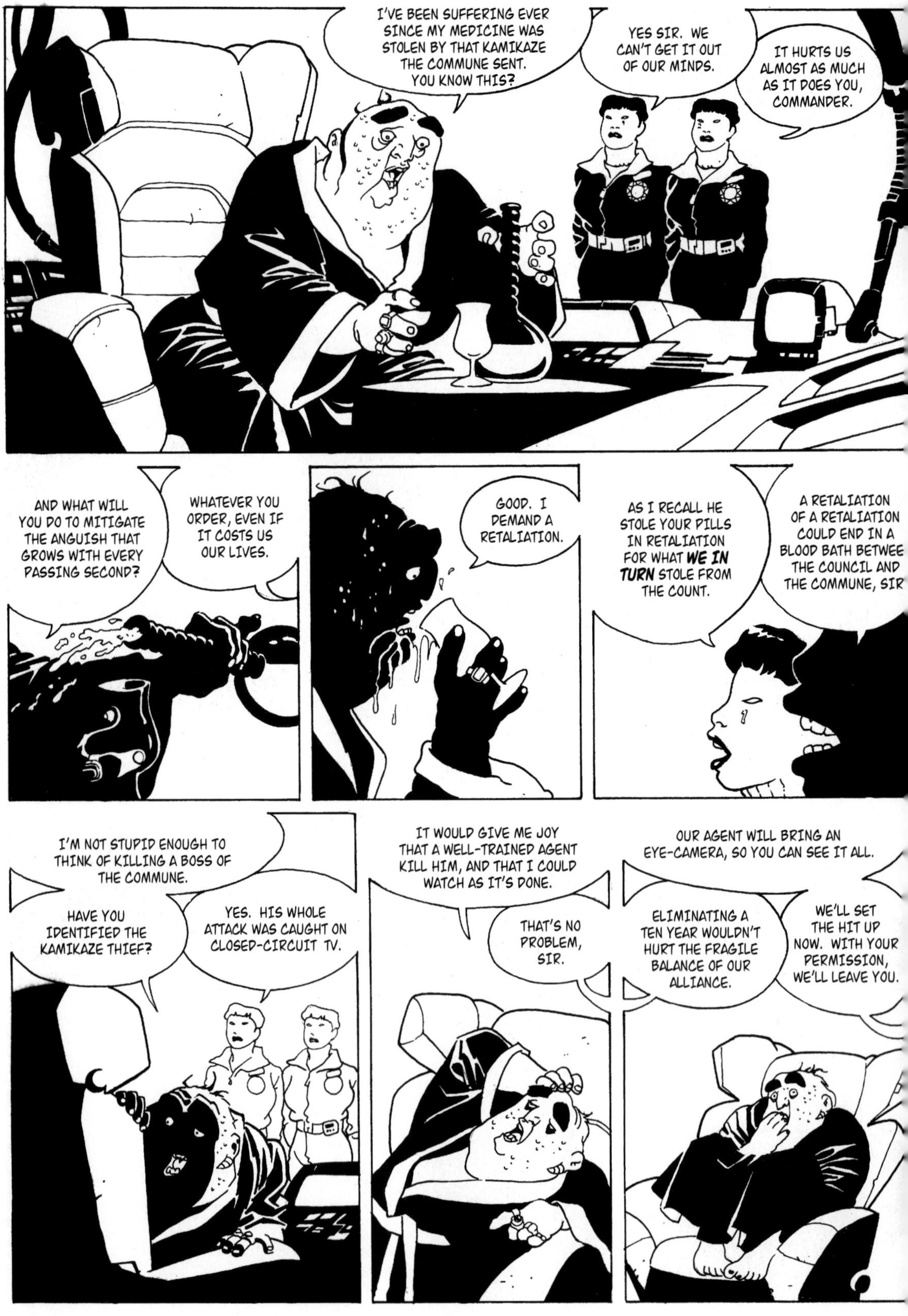
I'VE BEEN SUFFERING EVER SINCE MY MEDICINE WAS STOLEN BY THAT KAMIKAZE THE COMMUNE SENT. YOU KNOW THIS?
YES SIR. WE CAN'T GET IT OUT OF OUR MINDS.
IT HURTS US ALMOST AS MUCH AS IT DOES YOU, COMMANDER.
AND WHAT WILL YOU DO TO MITIGATE THE ANGUISH THAT GROWS WITH EVERY PASSING SECOND?
WHATEVER YOU ORDER, EVEN IF IT COSTS US OUR LIVES.
GOOD. I DEMAND A RETALIATION.
AS I RECALL HE STOLE YOUR PILLS IN RETALIATION FOR WHAT **WE IN TURN** STOLE FROM THE COUNT.
A RETALIATION OF A RETALIATION COULD END IN A BLOOD BATH BETWEE THE COUNCIL AND THE COMMUNE, SIR
I'M NOT STUPID ENOUGH TO THINK OF KILLING A BOSS OF THE COMMUNE.
HAVE YOU IDENTIFIED THE KAMIKAZE THIEF?
YES. HIS WHOLE ATTACK WAS CAUGHT ON CLOSED-CIRCUIT TV.
IT WOULD GIVE ME JOY THAT A WELL-TRAINED AGENT KILL HIM, AND THAT I COULD WATCH AS IT'S DONE.
THAT'S NO PROBLEM, SIR.
OUR AGENT WILL BRING AN EYE-CAMERA, SO YOU CAN SEE IT ALL.
ELIMINATING A TEN YEAR WOULDN'T HURT THE FRAGILE BALANCE OF OUR ALLIANCE.
WE'LL SET THE HIT UP NOW. WITH YOUR PERMISSION, WE'LL LEAVE YOU.

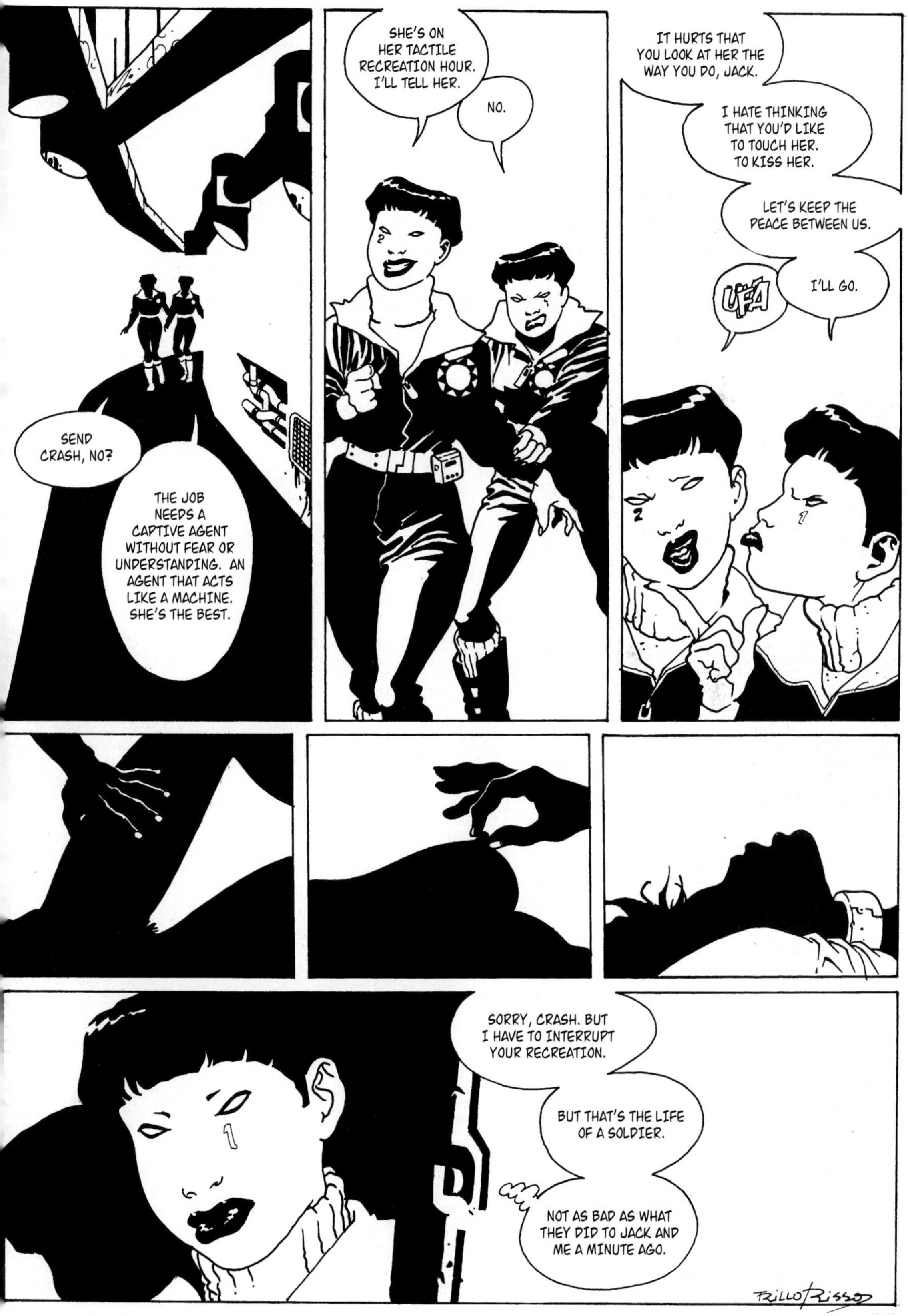

SEND CRASH, NO?
THE JOB NEEDS A CAPTIVE AGENT WITHOUT FEAR OR UNDERSTANDING. AN AGENT THAT ACTS LIKE A MACHINE. SHE'S THE BEST.
SHE'S ON HER TACTILE RECREATION HOUR. I'LL TELL HER.
NO.
IT HURTS THAT YOU LOOK AT HER THE WAY YOU DO, JACK.
I HATE THINKING THAT YOU'D LIKE TO TOUCH HER. TO KISS HER.
LET'S KEEP THE PEACE BETWEEN US.
UFA
I'LL GO.
SORRY, CRASH. BUT I HAVE TO INTERRUPT YOUR RECREATION.
BUT THAT'S THE LIFE OF A SOLDIER.
NOT AS BAD AS WHAT THEY DID TO JACK AND ME A MINUTE AGO.
TRILLO RISSO

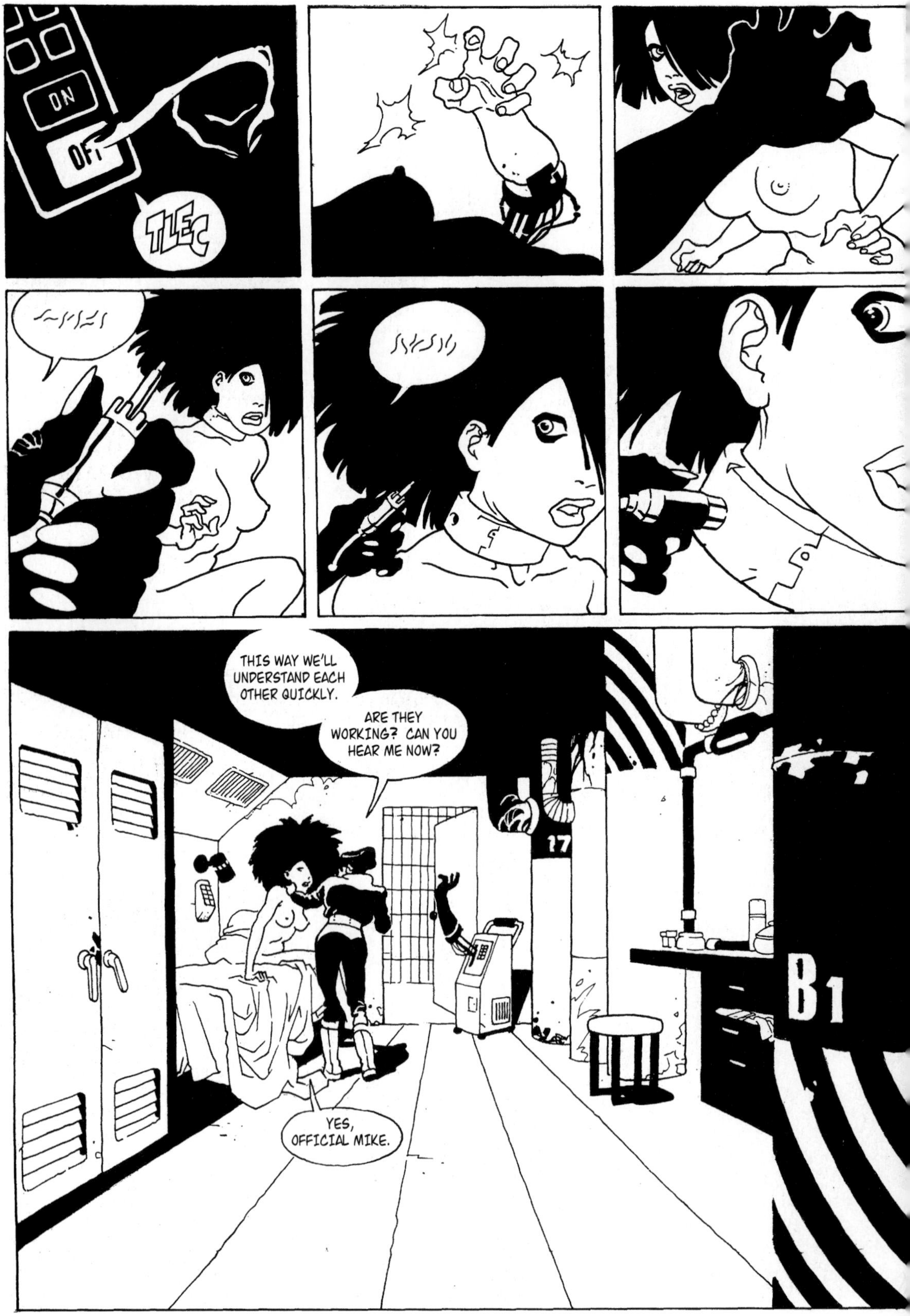
ON
OFF
TLEC
THIS WAY WE'LL UNDERSTAND EACH OTHER QUICKLY.
ARE THEY WORKING? CAN YOU HEAR ME NOW?
YES, OFFICIAL MIKE.
17
B1

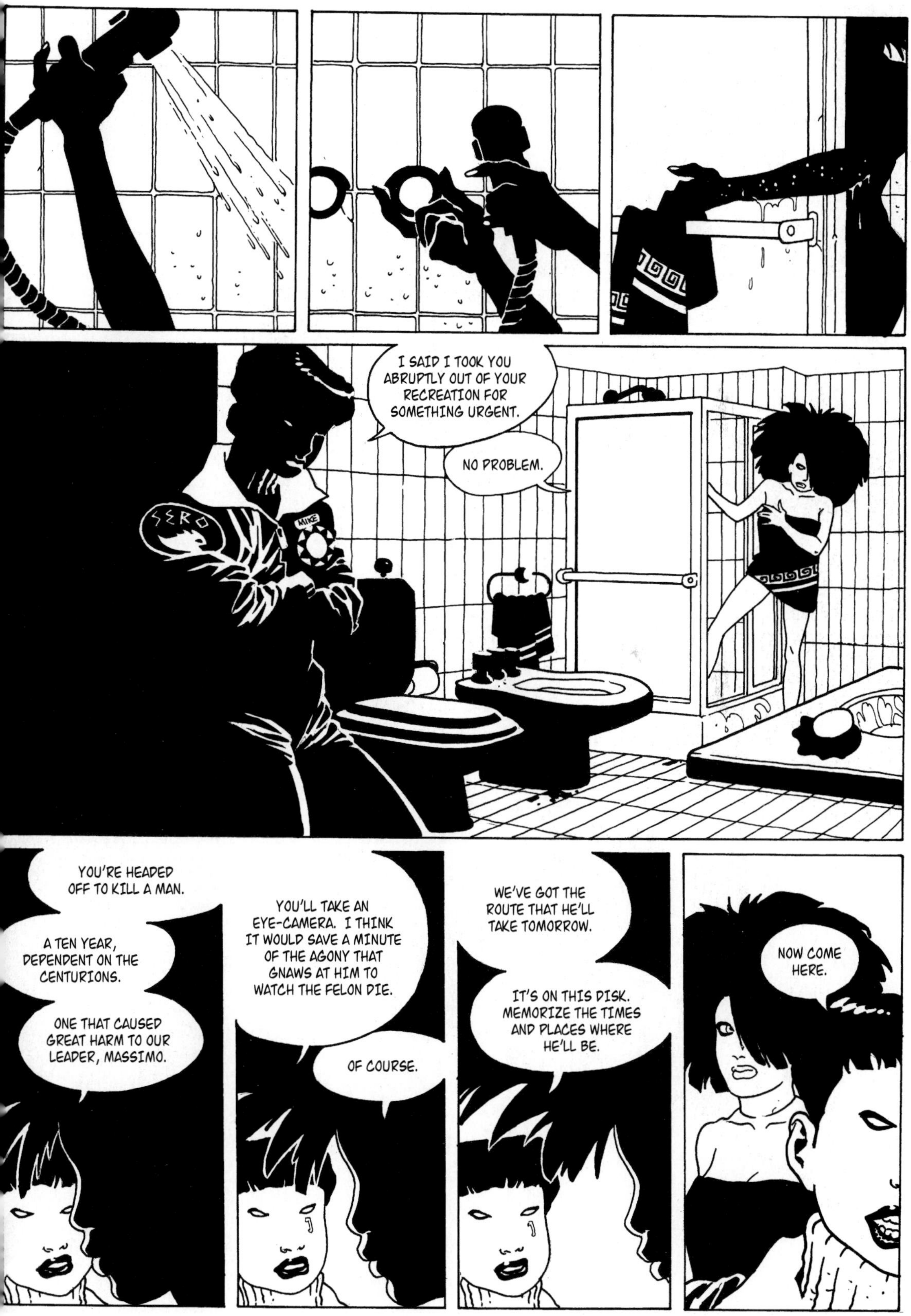

I SAID I TOOK YOU ABRUPTLY OUT OF YOUR RECREATION FOR SOMETHING URGENT.
NO PROBLEM.
YOU'RE HEADED OFF TO KILL A MAN.
A TEN YEAR, DEPENDENT ON THE CENTURIONS.
ONE THAT CAUSED GREAT HARM TO OUR LEADER, MASSIMO.
YOU'LL TAKE AN EYE-CAMERA. I THINK IT WOULD SAVE A MINUTE OF THE AGONY THAT GNAWS AT HIM TO WATCH THE FELON DIE.
OF COURSE.
WE'VE GOT THE ROUTE THAT HE'LL TAKE TOMORROW.
IT'S ON THIS DISK. MEMORIZE THE TIMES AND PLACES WHERE HE'LL BE.
NOW COME HERE.

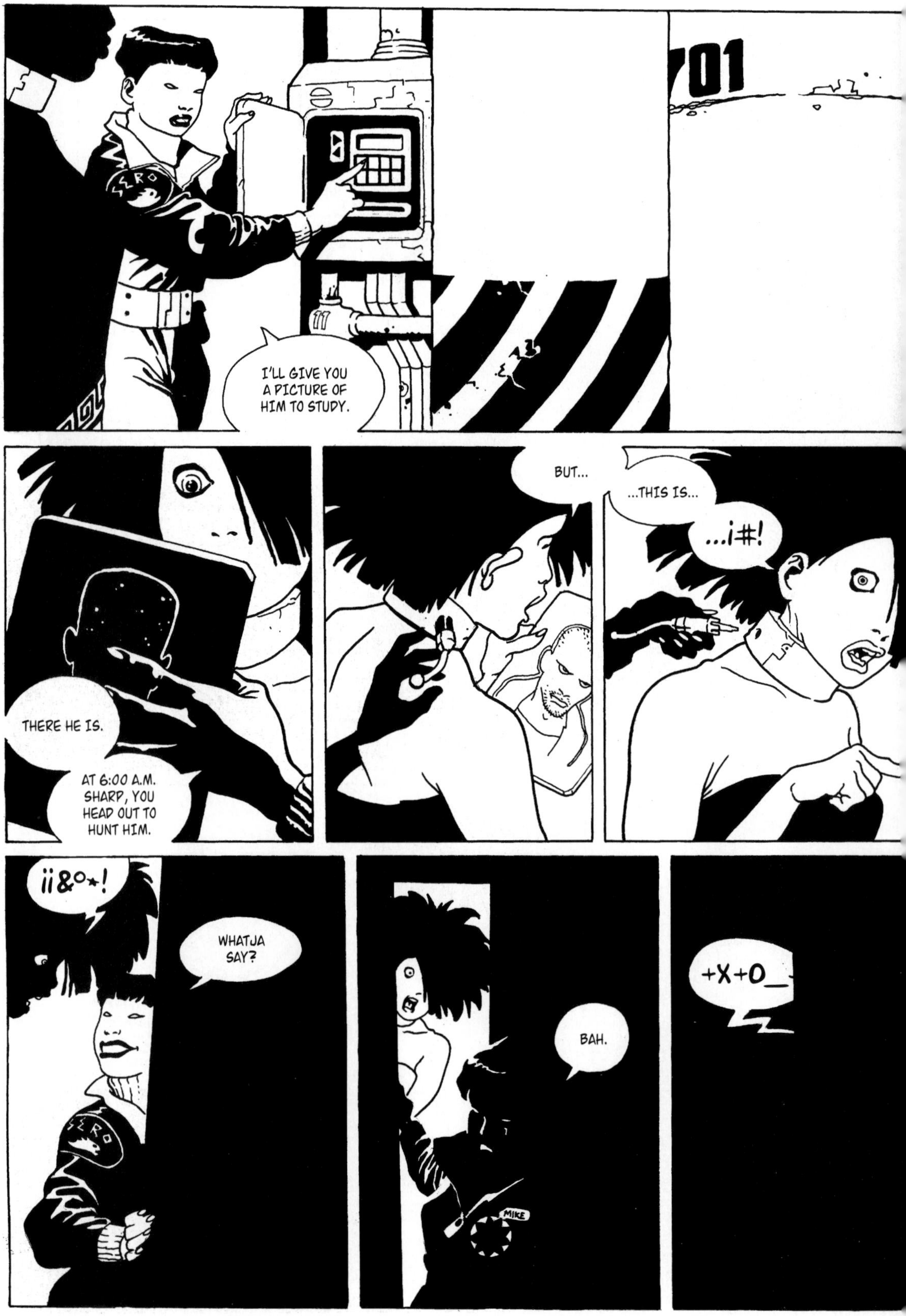

I'LL GIVE YOU A PICTURE OF HIM TO STUDY.
701
THERE HE IS.
AT 6:00 A.M. SHARP, YOU HEAD OUT TO HUNT HIM.
BUT...
...THIS IS...
...¡#!
¡¡&º*!
WHATJA SAY?
BAH.
+X+O_

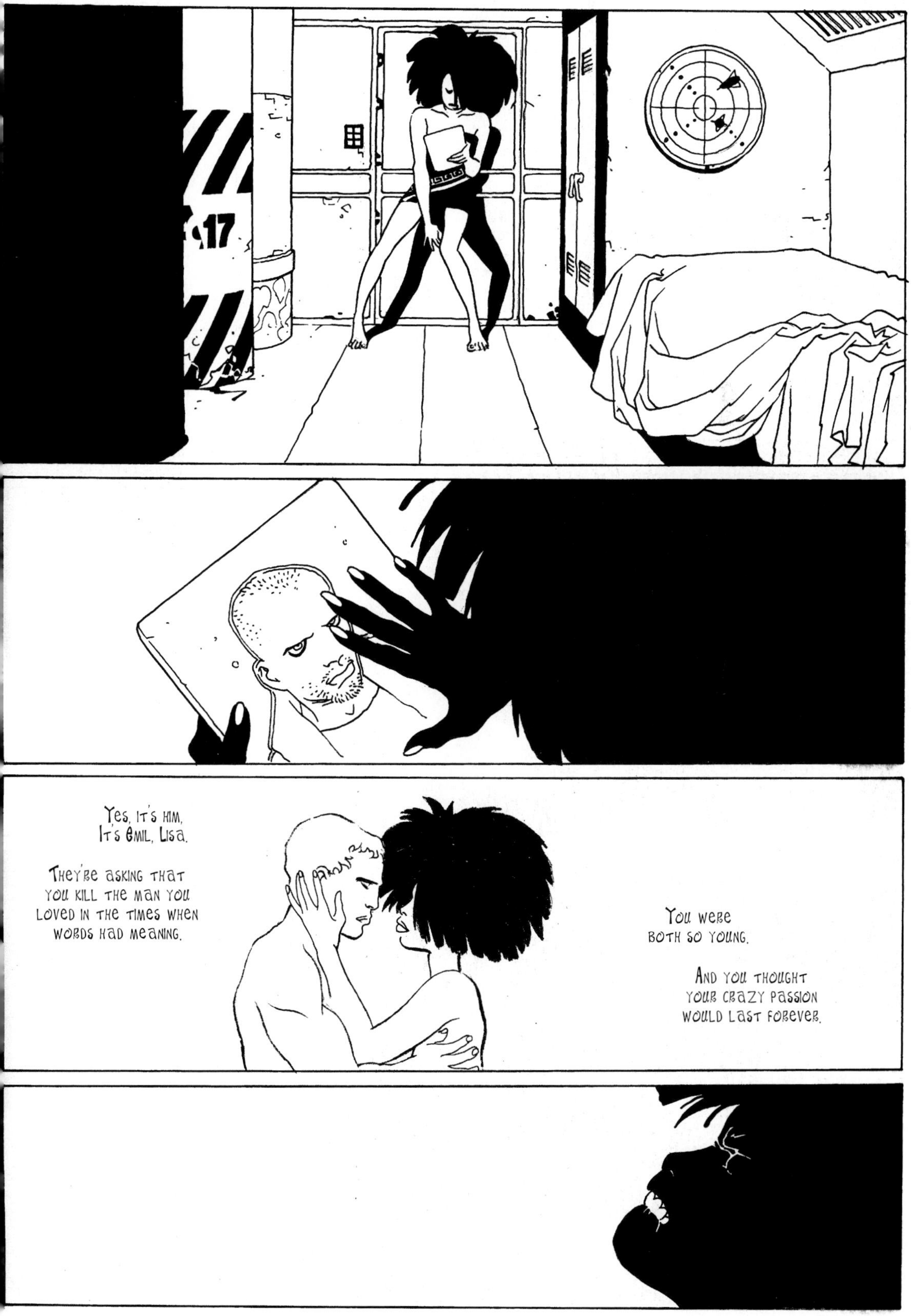
Yes, it's him, It's Emil, Lisa.
They're asking that you kill the man you loved in the times when words had meaning.
You were both so young.
And you thought your crazy passion would last forever.

BETTER YOU REMEMBER
THE BAD PARTS, NOW THAT
LISA'S NOT WHO YOU ARE.

THE BAD PARTS, CRASH.

THAT DRUG HE
USED TO SHOOT.
THAT HOPE.

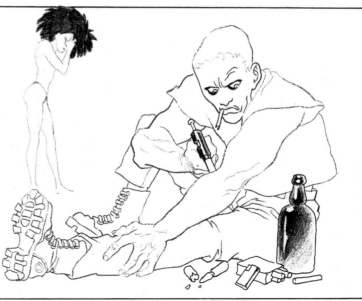

A DRUG CALLED
HOPE (WHICH YOU
KNOW SO WELL).

HE NEEDED IT
MORE THAN YOU.

HE'D GO BAD WITHOUT
IT IN HIS VEINS.

LIKE THAT DAY, DESPERATE
FOR A LITTLE SCRATCH TO
BUY THAT ELUSIVE AND
EPHEMERAL HOPE, HE
HANDED YOU OVER TO TWO
HORRIBLE BEINGS.

HE SOLD YOU.

BETRAYED YOUR
LOVE AND SOLD YOU.

KILLED THE BEATING
OF YOUR HEART AND
SOLD YOU.

FIRST THE HORRIBLE BEINGS WHORED YOU OUT TO RECOUP THEIR INVESTMENT.

LATER WHEN THEY KNEW YOUR MENTAL AND PHYSICAL HEALTH WOULDN'T TAKE TOO MUCH OF THAT...

THEY SENT YOU TO A SECRET SANITARIUM.

...WHERE THEY WENT ABOUT REMOVING YOUR ORGANS, ONE BY ONE, WITHOUT LETTING YOU DIE.

A LUNG TODAY...

...A KIDNEY TOMORROW...

...A PIECE OF LIVER NEXT WEEK.

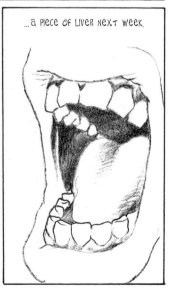

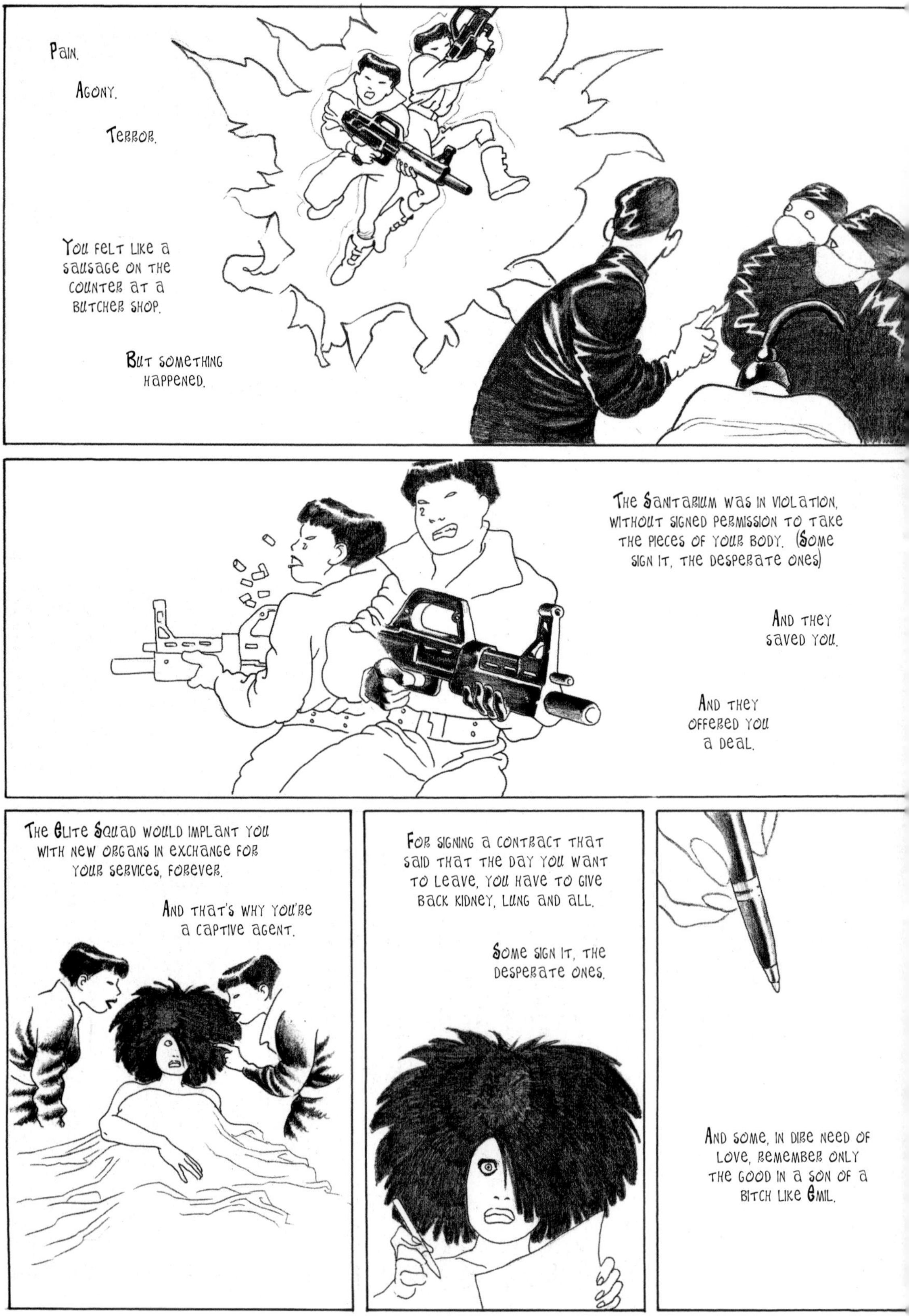
Pain.
Agony.
Terror.
You felt like a sausage on the counter at a butcher shop.
But something happened.
The Sanitarium was in violation, without signed permission to take the pieces of your body. (Some sign it, the desperate ones)
And they saved you.
And they offered you a deal.
The Elite Squad would implant you with new organs in exchange for your services, forever.
And that's why you're a captive agent.
For signing a contract that said that the day you want to leave, you have to give back kidney, lung and all.
Some sign it, the desperate ones.
And some, in dire need of love, remember only the good in a son of a bitch like Emil.

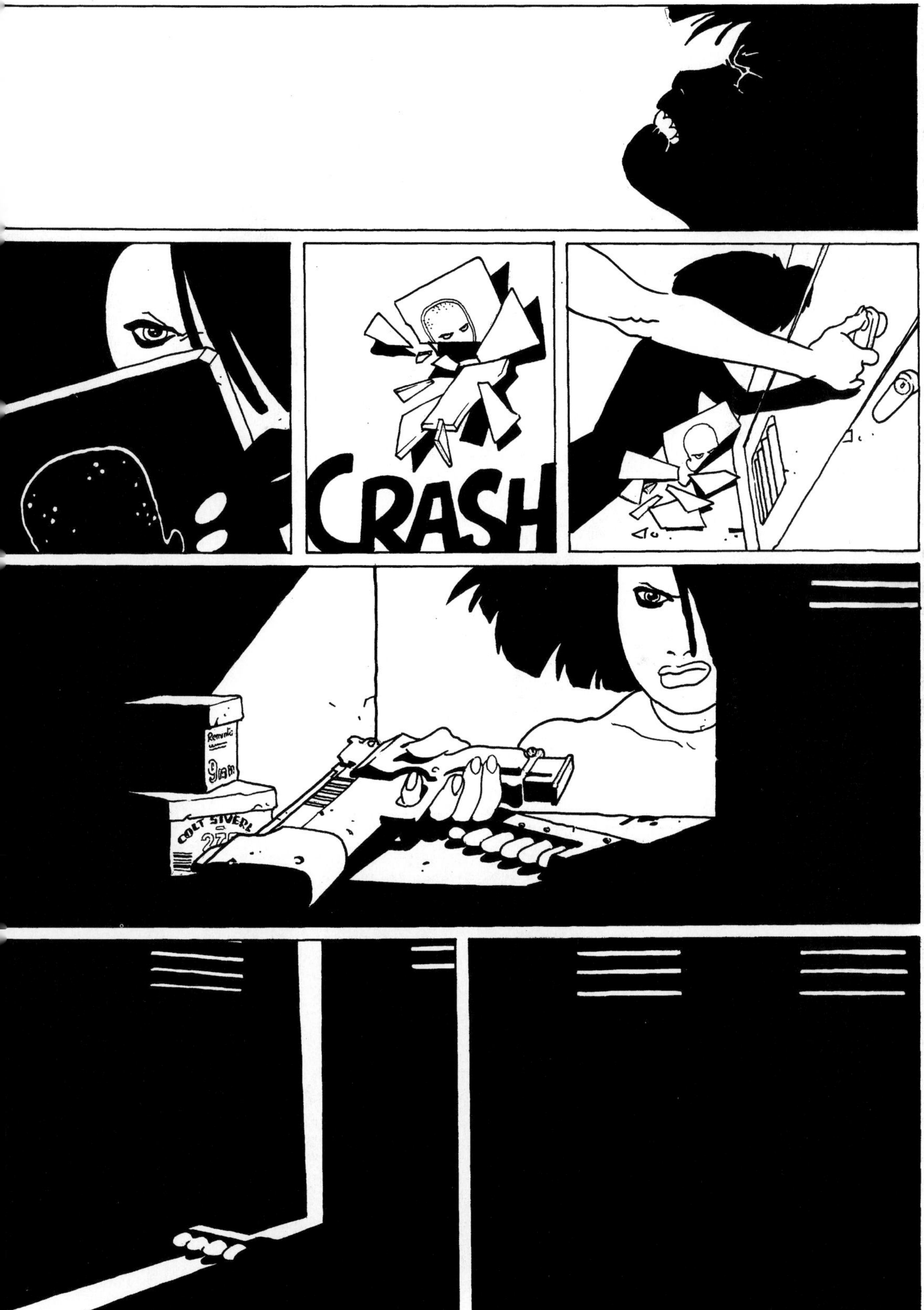
CRASH

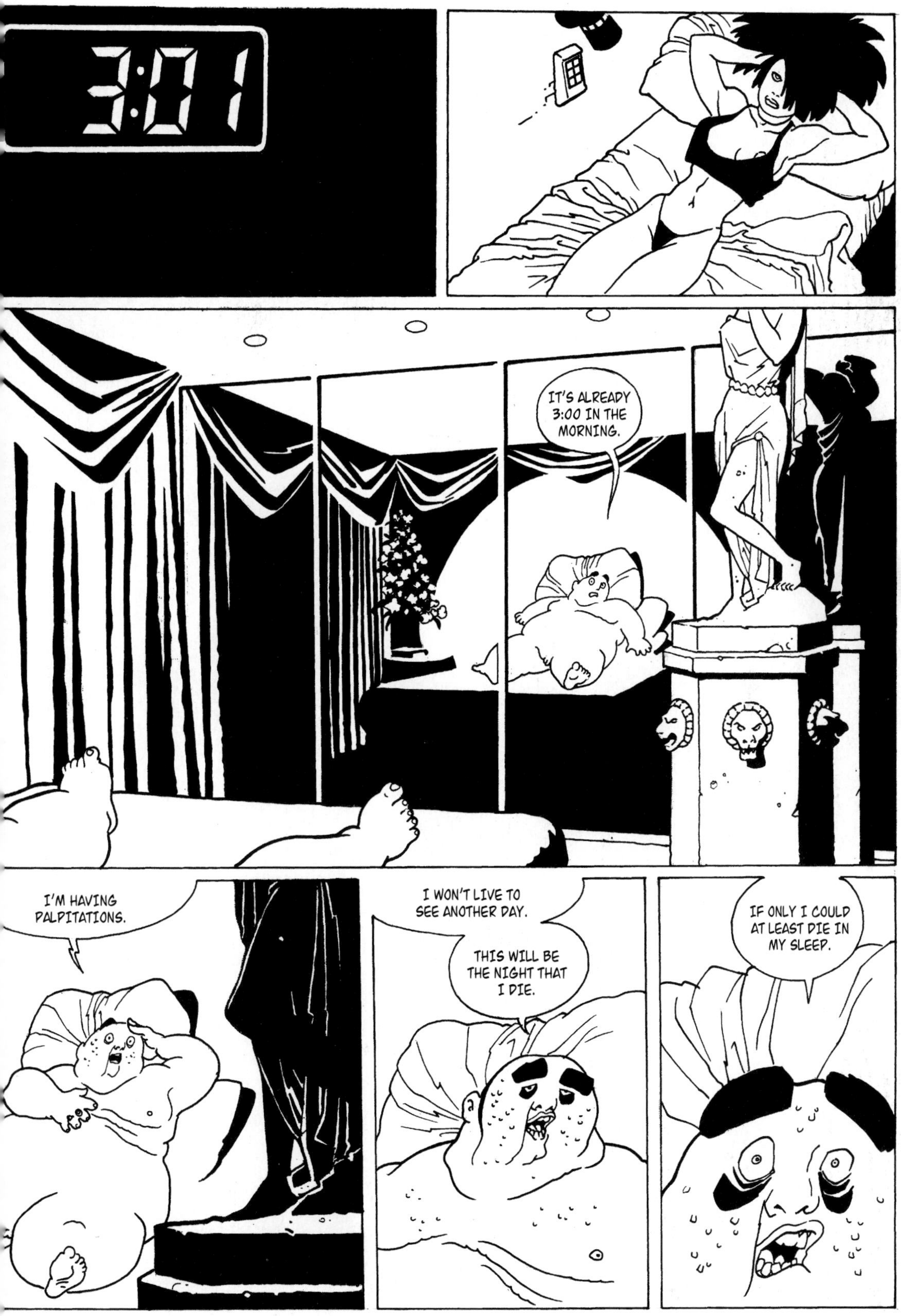
3:01
IT'S ALREADY 3:00 IN THE MORNING.
I'M HAVING PALPITATIONS.
I WON'T LIVE TO SEE ANOTHER DAY.
THIS WILL BE THE NIGHT THAT I DIE.
IF ONLY I COULD AT LEAST DIE IN MY SLEEP.

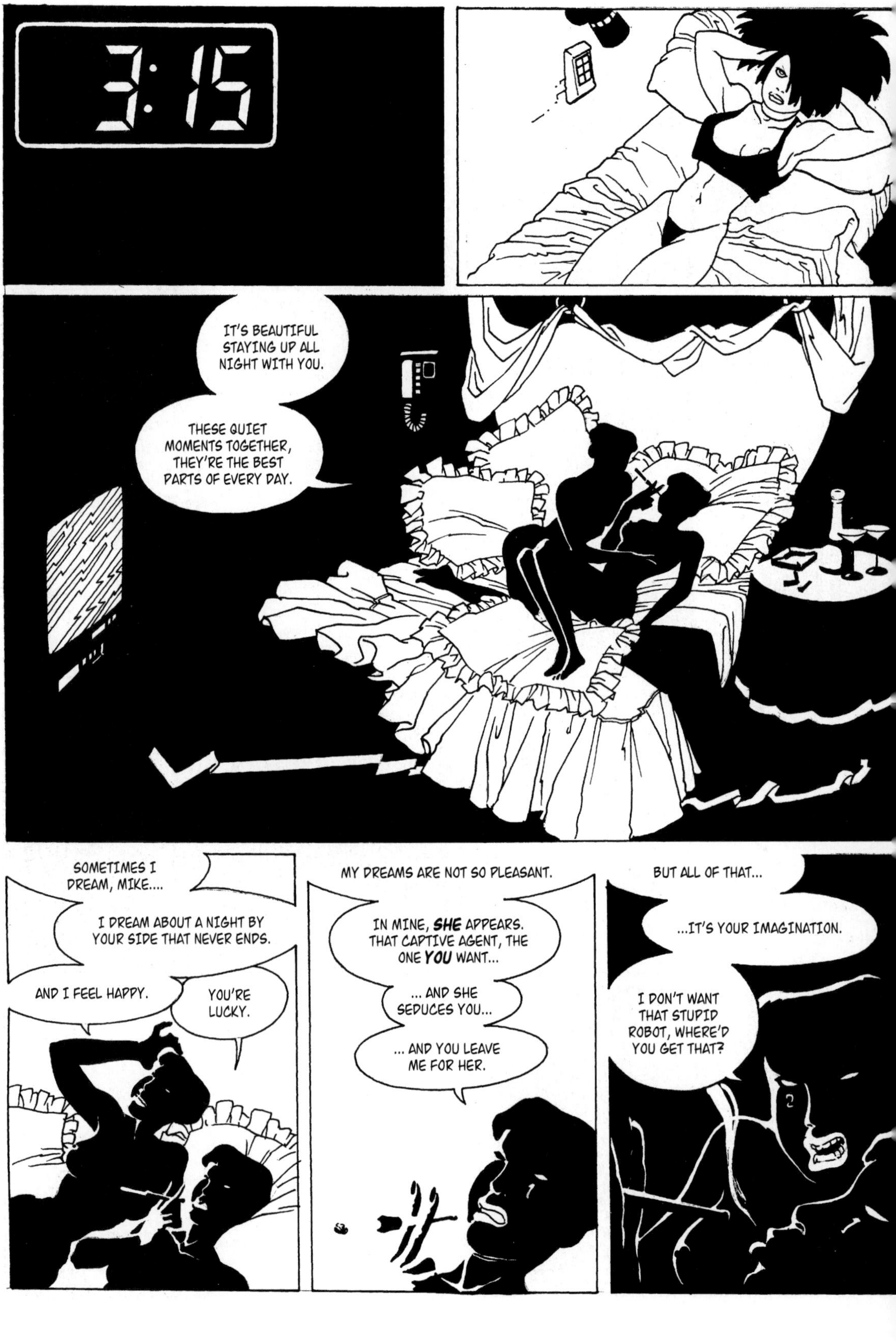
3:15
IT'S BEAUTIFUL STAYING UP ALL NIGHT WITH YOU.
THESE QUIET MOMENTS TOGETHER, THEY'RE THE BEST PARTS OF EVERY DAY.
SOMETIMES I DREAM, MIKE....
I DREAM ABOUT A NIGHT BY YOUR SIDE THAT NEVER ENDS.
AND I FEEL HAPPY.
YOU'RE LUCKY.
MY DREAMS ARE NOT SO PLEASANT.
IN MINE, SHE APPEARS. THAT CAPTIVE AGENT, THE ONE YOU WANT...
... AND SHE SEDUCES YOU...
... AND YOU LEAVE ME FOR HER.
BUT ALL OF THAT...
...IT'S YOUR IMAGINATION.
I DON'T WANT THAT STUPID ROBOT, WHERE'D YOU GET THAT?

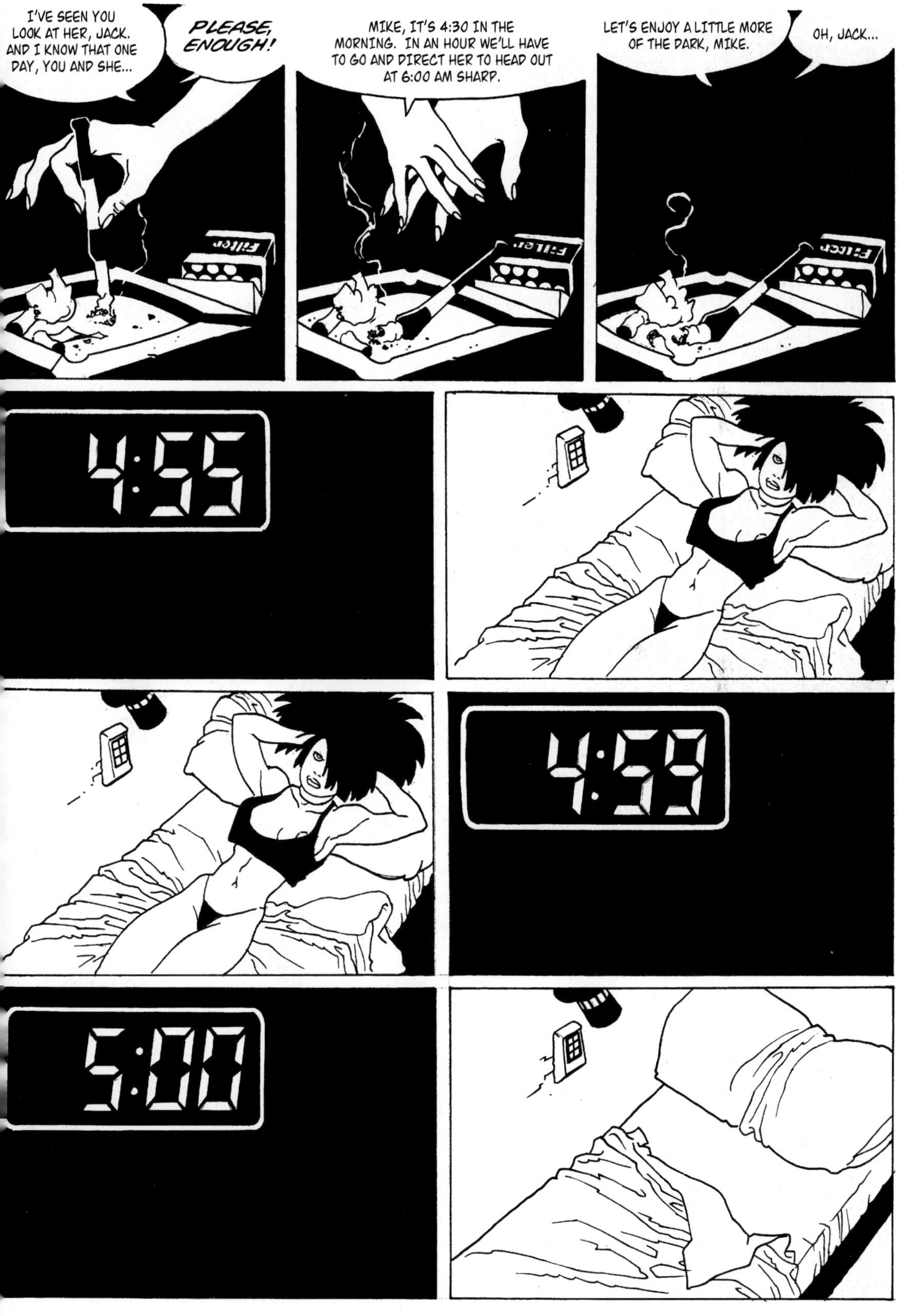

I'VE SEEN YOU LOOK AT HER, JACK. AND I KNOW THAT ONE DAY, YOU AND SHE...
PLEASE, ENOUGH!
MIKE, IT'S 4:30 IN THE MORNING. IN AN HOUR WE'LL HAVE TO GO AND DIRECT HER TO HEAD OUT AT 6:00 AM SHARP.
LET'S ENJOY A LITTLE MORE OF THE DARK, MIKE.
OH, JACK...
Filter
Filter
Filter
4:55
4:59
5:00

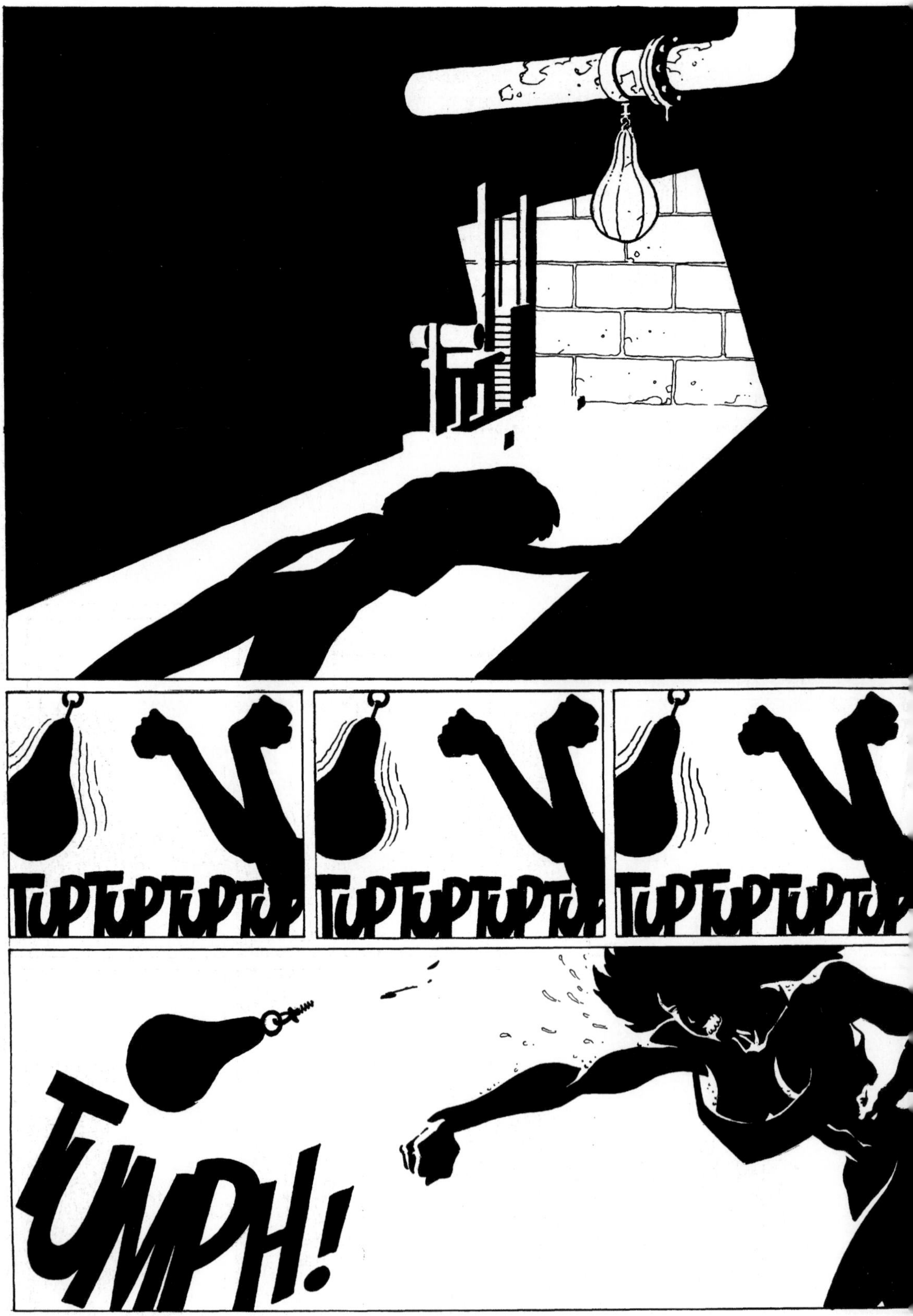
TUPTUPTUPTUP
TUPTUPTUPTUP
TUPTUPTUPTUP
THUMPH!

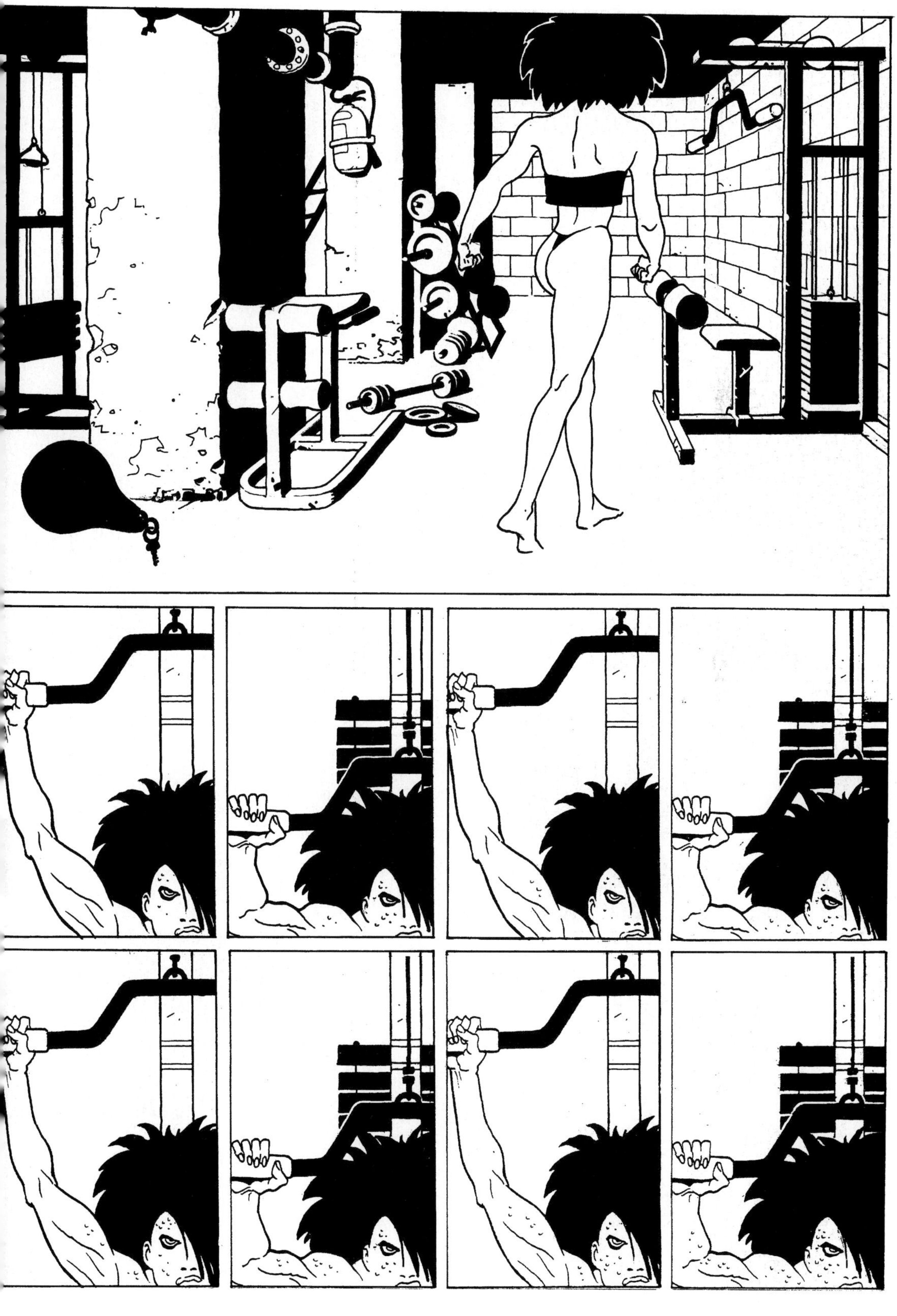

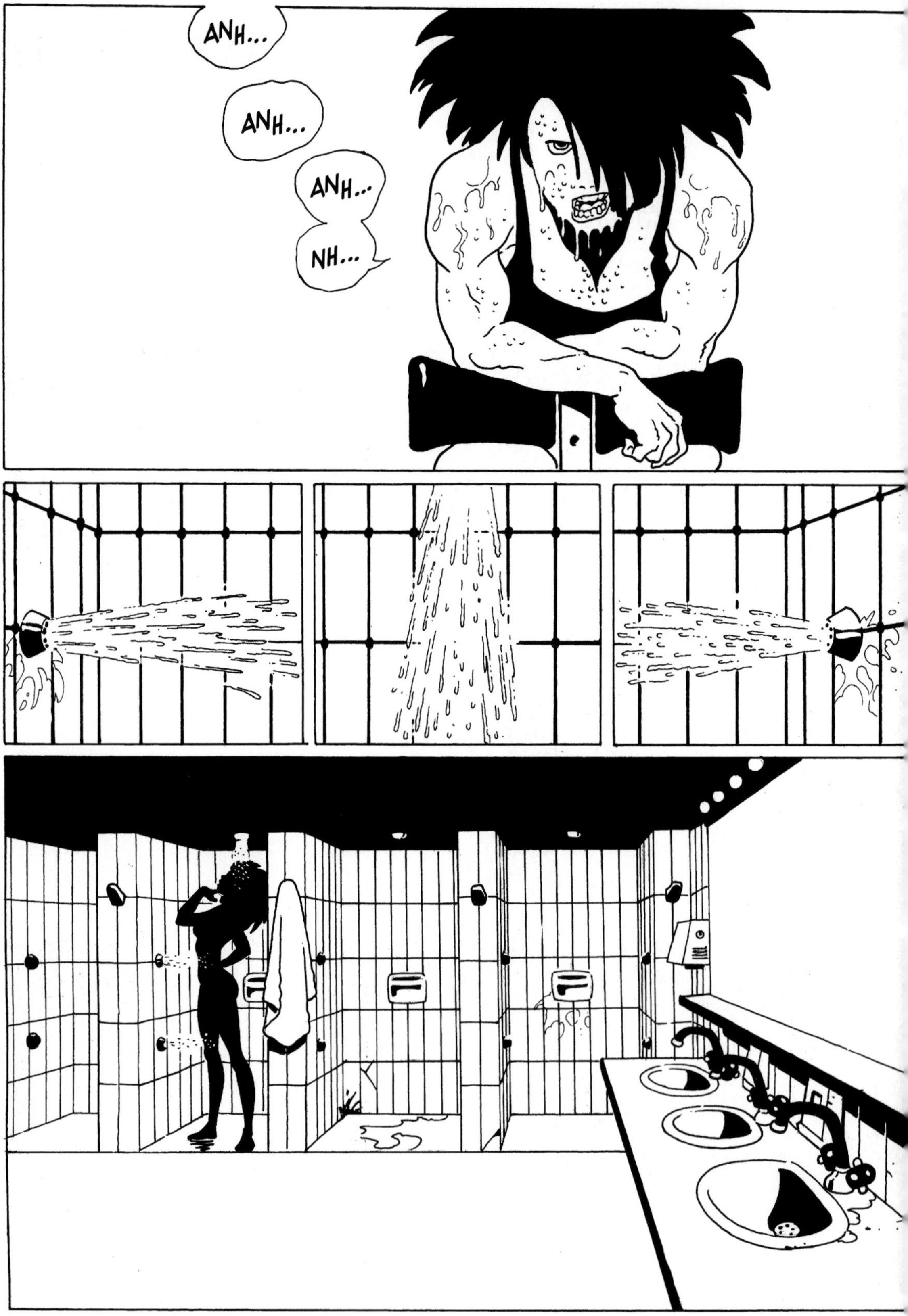
ANH...
ANH...
ANH...
NH...

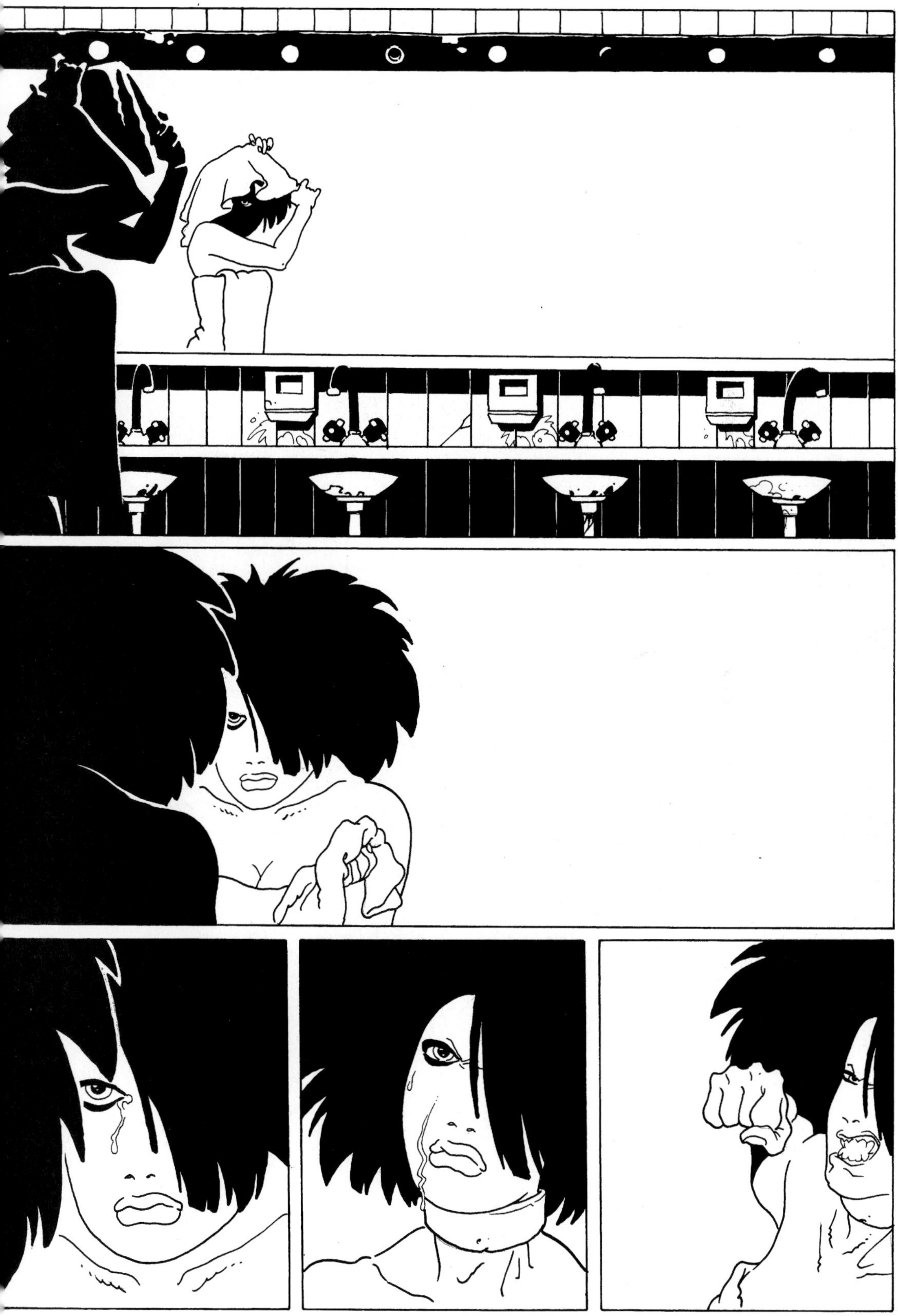

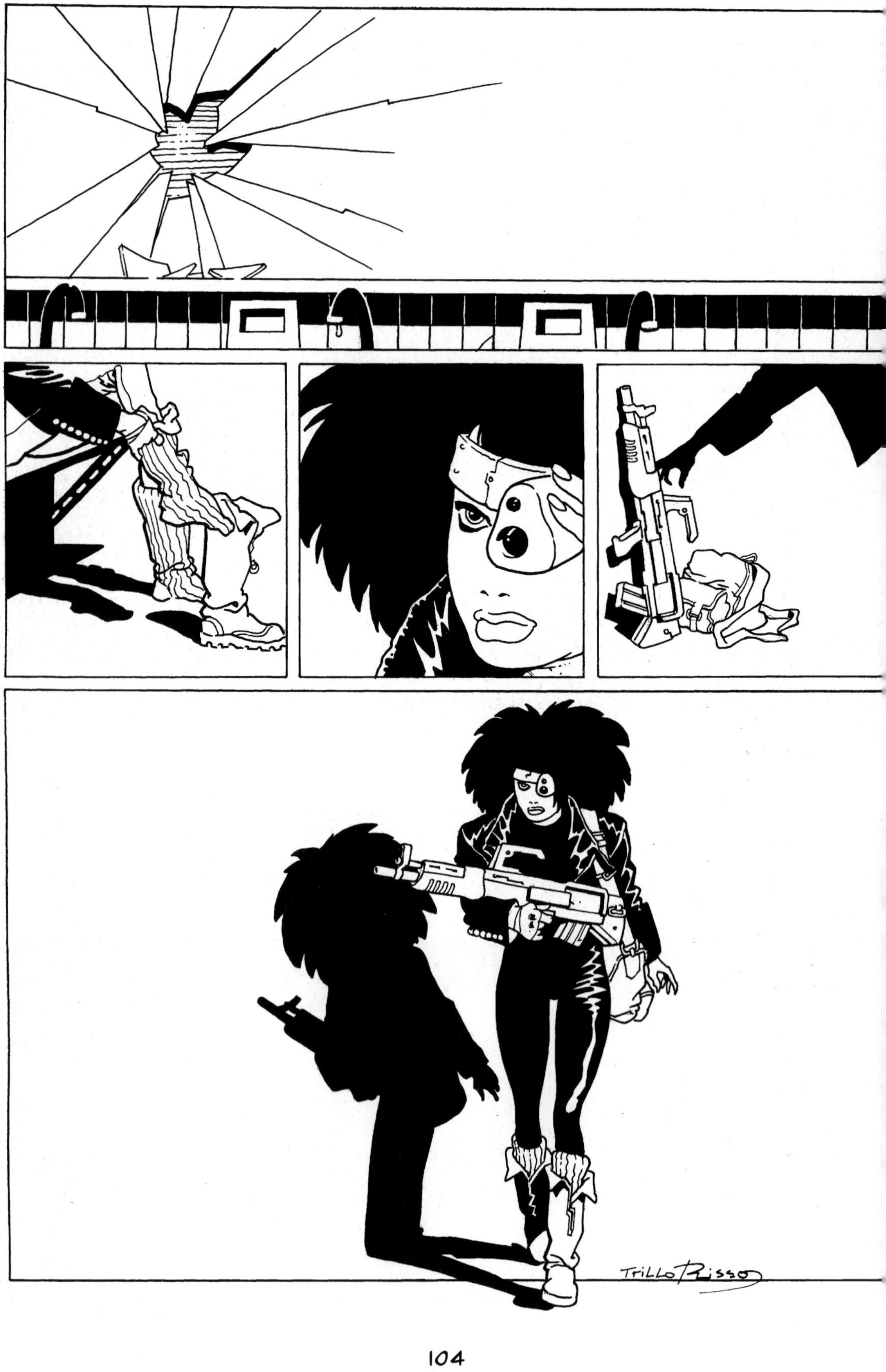
Trillo Risso

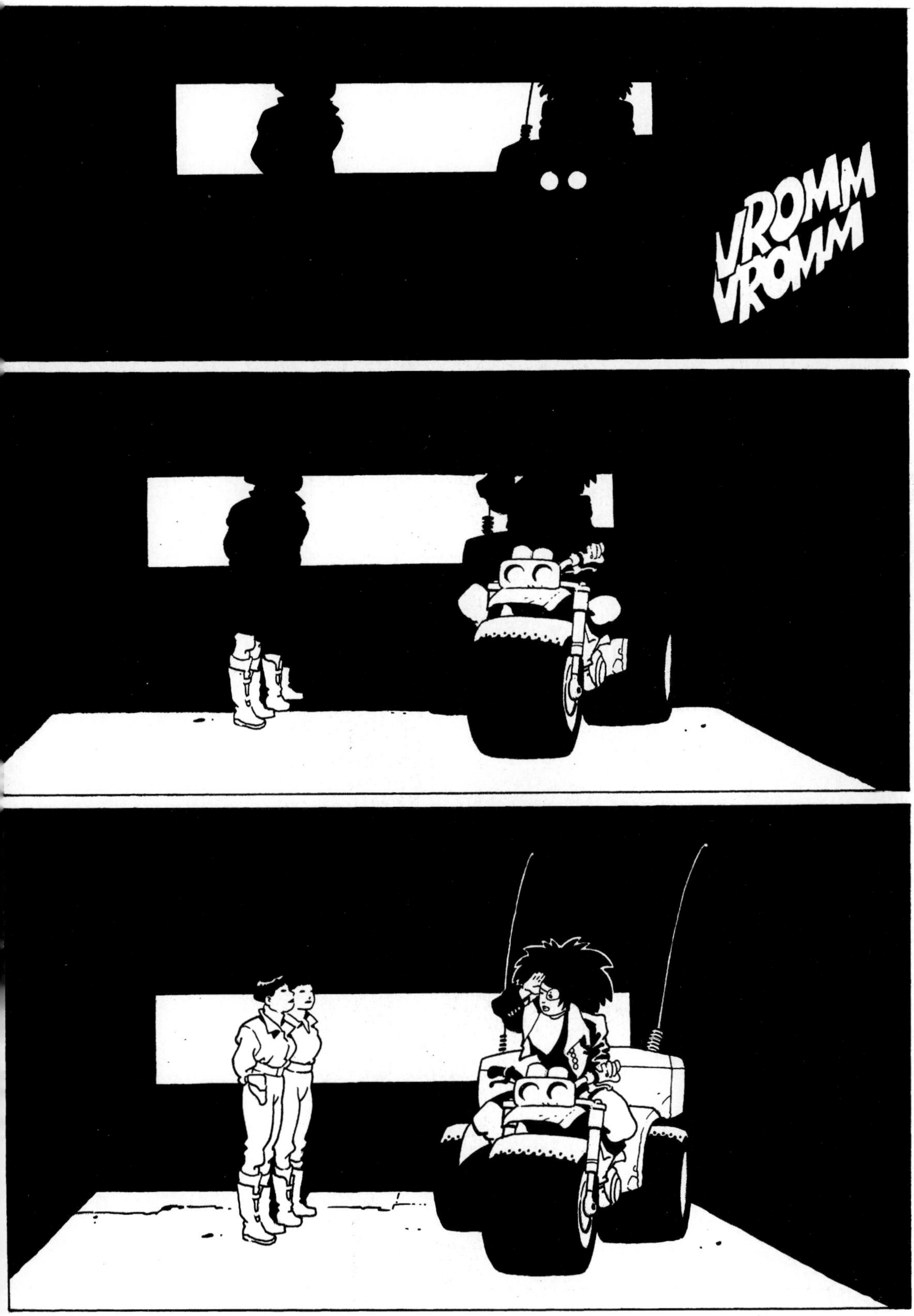
VROMM
VROMM

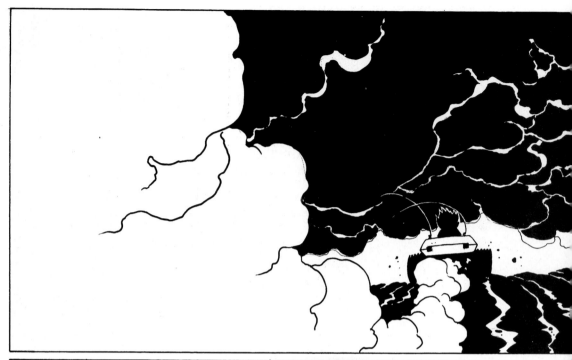

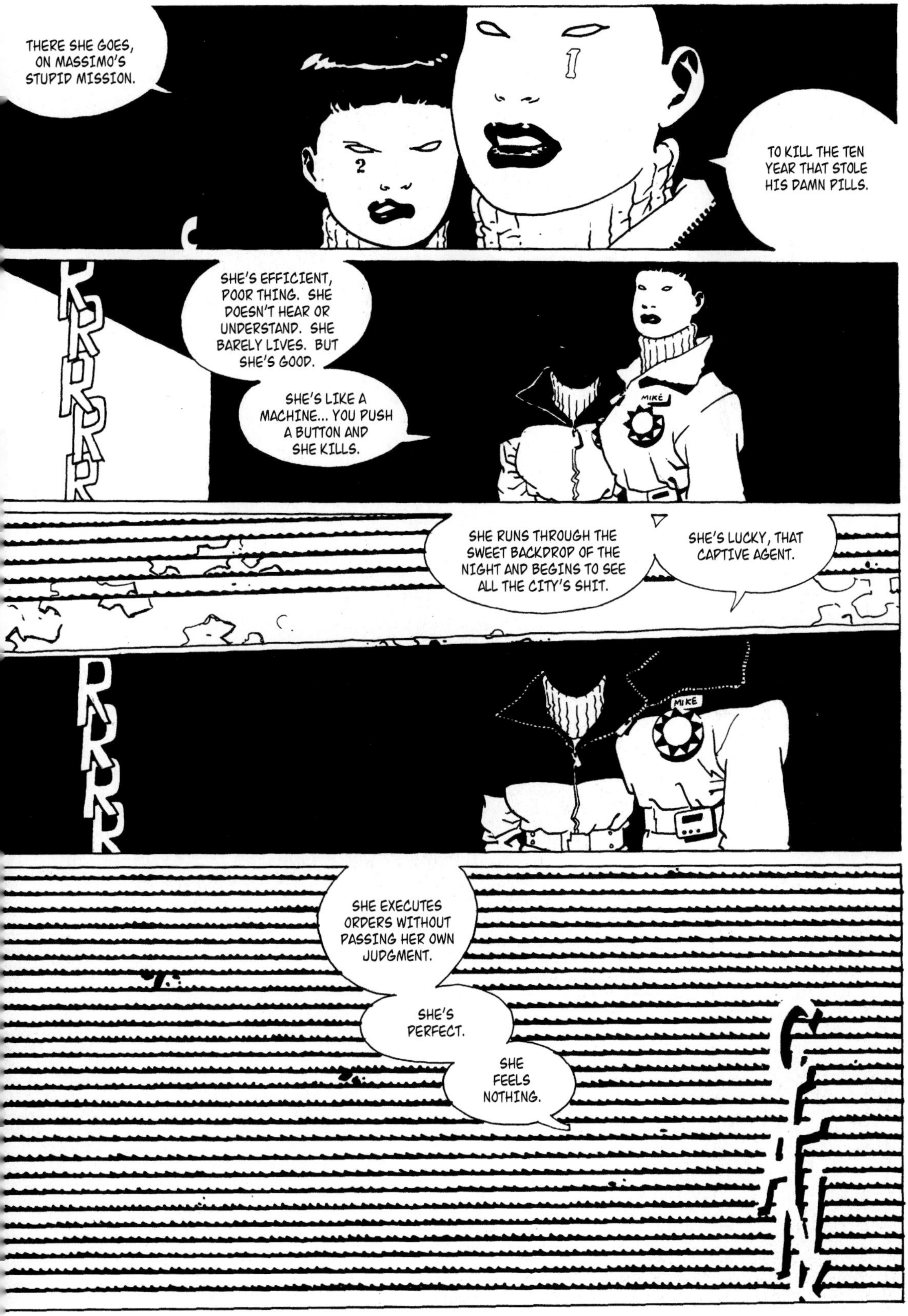

THERE SHE GOES, ON MASSIMO'S STUPID MISSION.
TO KILL THE TEN YEAR THAT STOLE HIS DAMN PILLS.
RRRRRR
SHE'S EFFICIENT, POOR THING. SHE DOESN'T HEAR OR UNDERSTAND. SHE BARELY LIVES. BUT SHE'S GOOD.
SHE'S LIKE A MACHINE... YOU PUSH A BUTTON AND SHE KILLS.
MIKE
SHE RUNS THROUGH THE SWEET BACKDROP OF THE NIGHT AND BEGINS TO SEE ALL THE CITY'S SHIT.
SHE'S LUCKY, THAT CAPTIVE AGENT.
RRRRR
MIKE
SHE EXECUTES ORDERS WITHOUT PASSING HER OWN JUDGMENT.
SHE'S PERFECT.
SHE FEELS NOTHING.

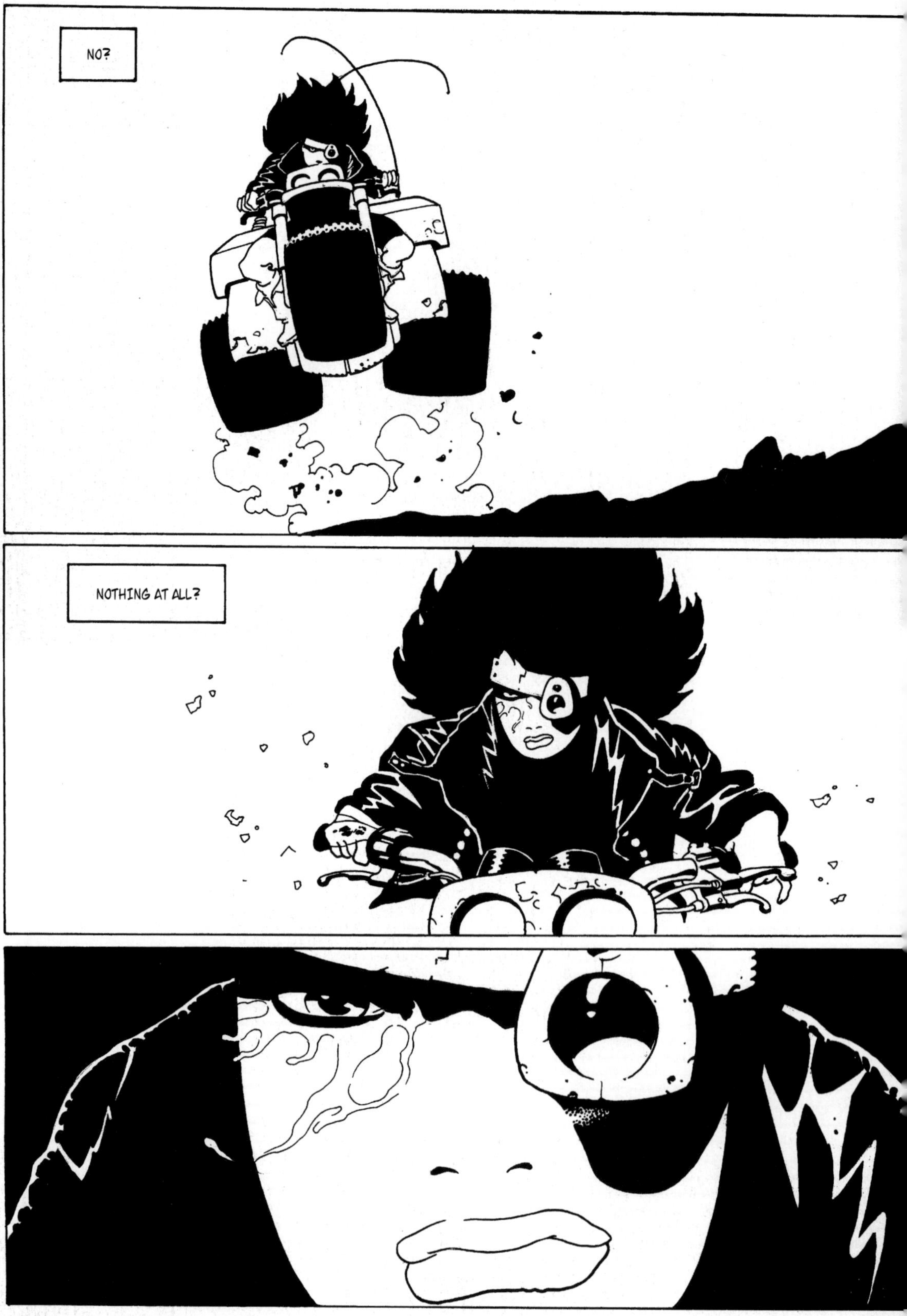
NO?
NOTHING AT ALL?

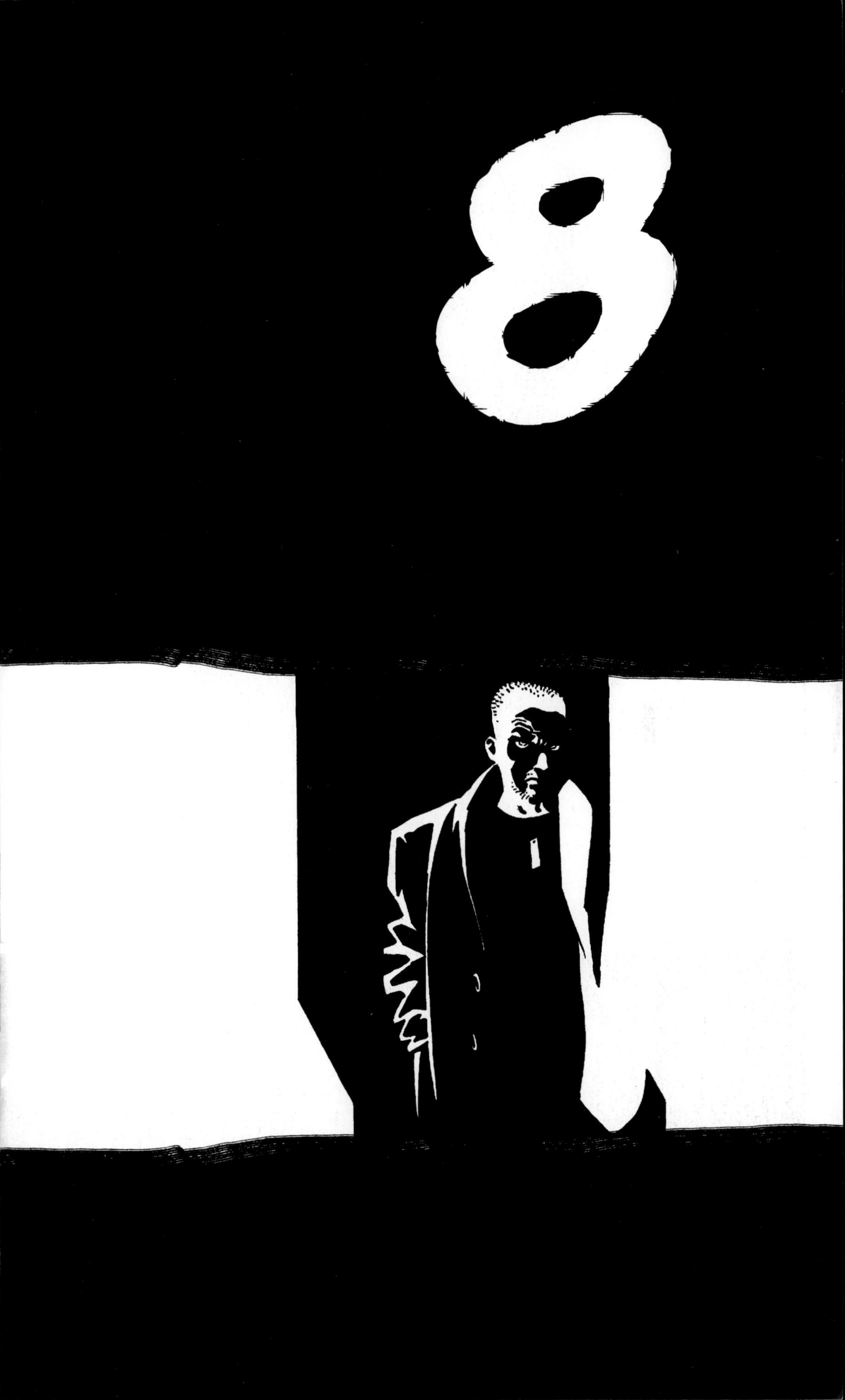
8

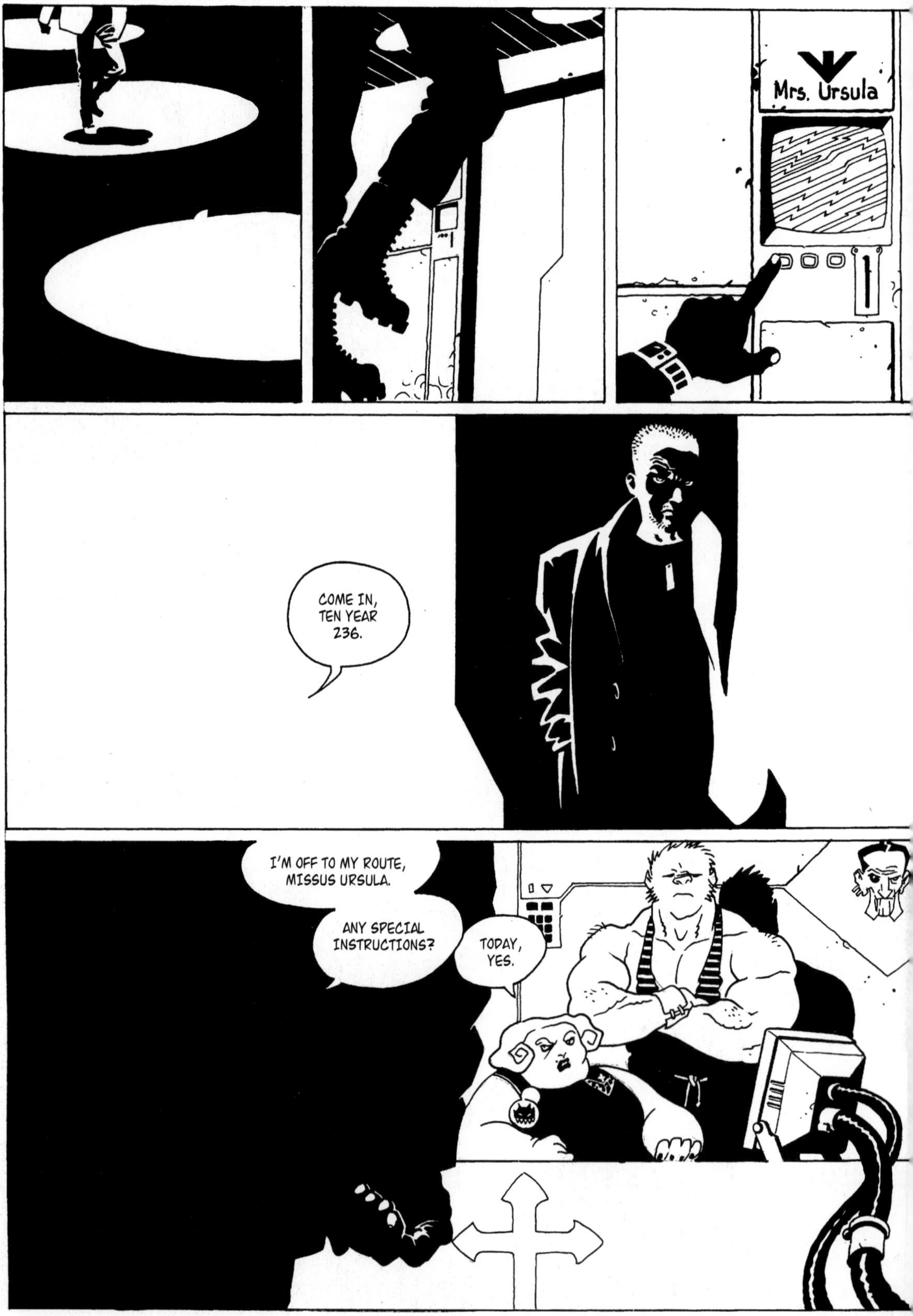
Mrs. Ursula
COME IN, TEN YEAR 236.
I'M OFF TO MY ROUTE, MISSUS URSULA.
ANY SPECIAL INSTRUCTIONS?
TODAY, YES.

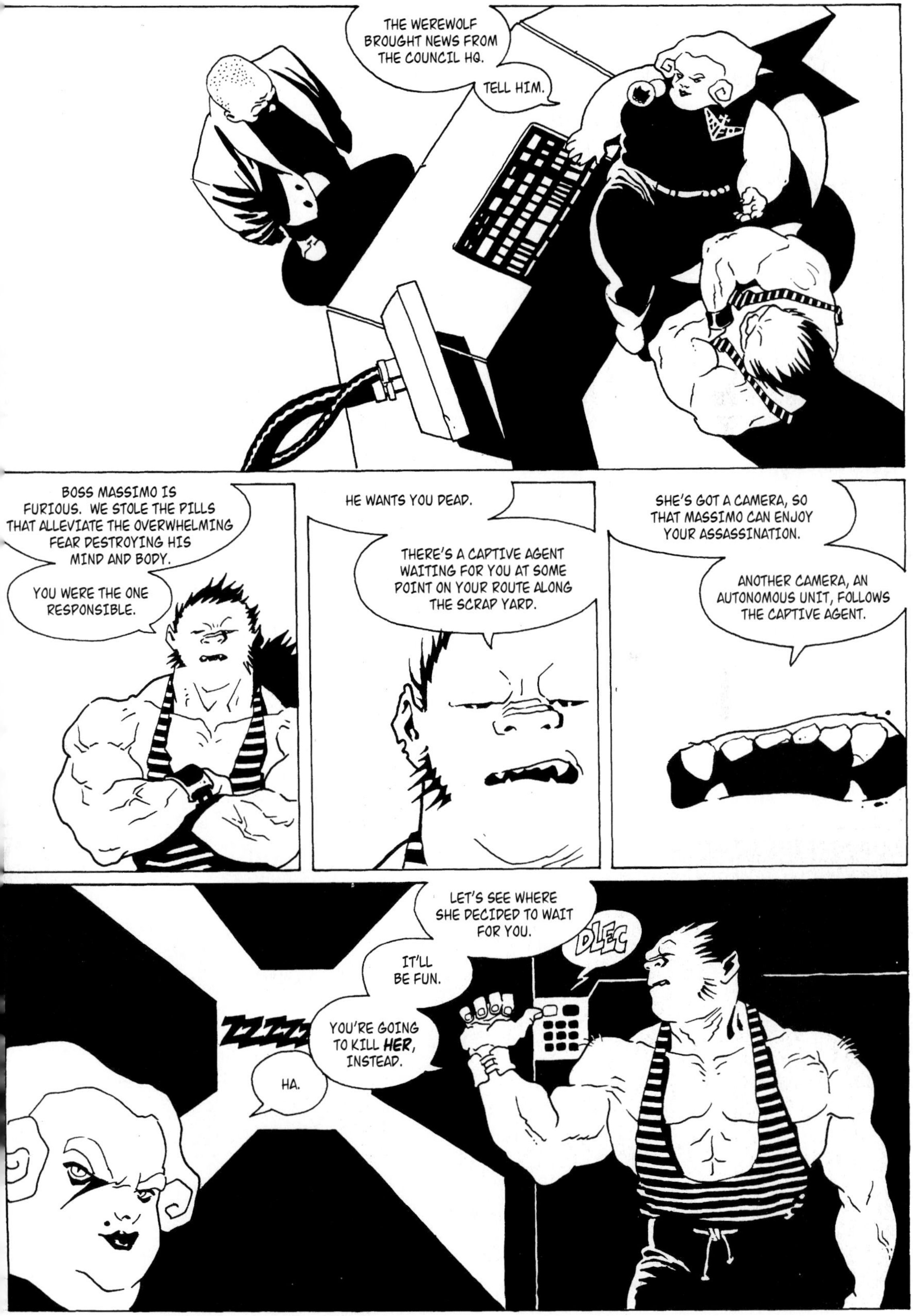
THE WEREWOLF BROUGHT NEWS FROM THE COUNCIL HQ.
TELL HIM.
BOSS MASSIMO IS FURIOUS. WE STOLE THE PILLS THAT ALLEVIATE THE OVERWHELMING FEAR DESTROYING HIS MIND AND BODY.
YOU WERE THE ONE RESPONSIBLE.
HE WANTS YOU DEAD.
THERE'S A CAPTIVE AGENT WAITING FOR YOU AT SOME POINT ON YOUR ROUTE ALONG THE SCRAP YARD.
SHE'S GOT A CAMERA, SO THAT MASSIMO CAN ENJOY YOUR ASSASSINATION.
ANOTHER CAMERA, AN AUTONOMOUS UNIT, FOLLOWS THE CAPTIVE AGENT.
LET'S SEE WHERE SHE DECIDED TO WAIT FOR YOU.
DLEC
IT'LL BE FUN.
ZZZZ
YOU'RE GOING TO KILL **HER**, INSTEAD.
HA.

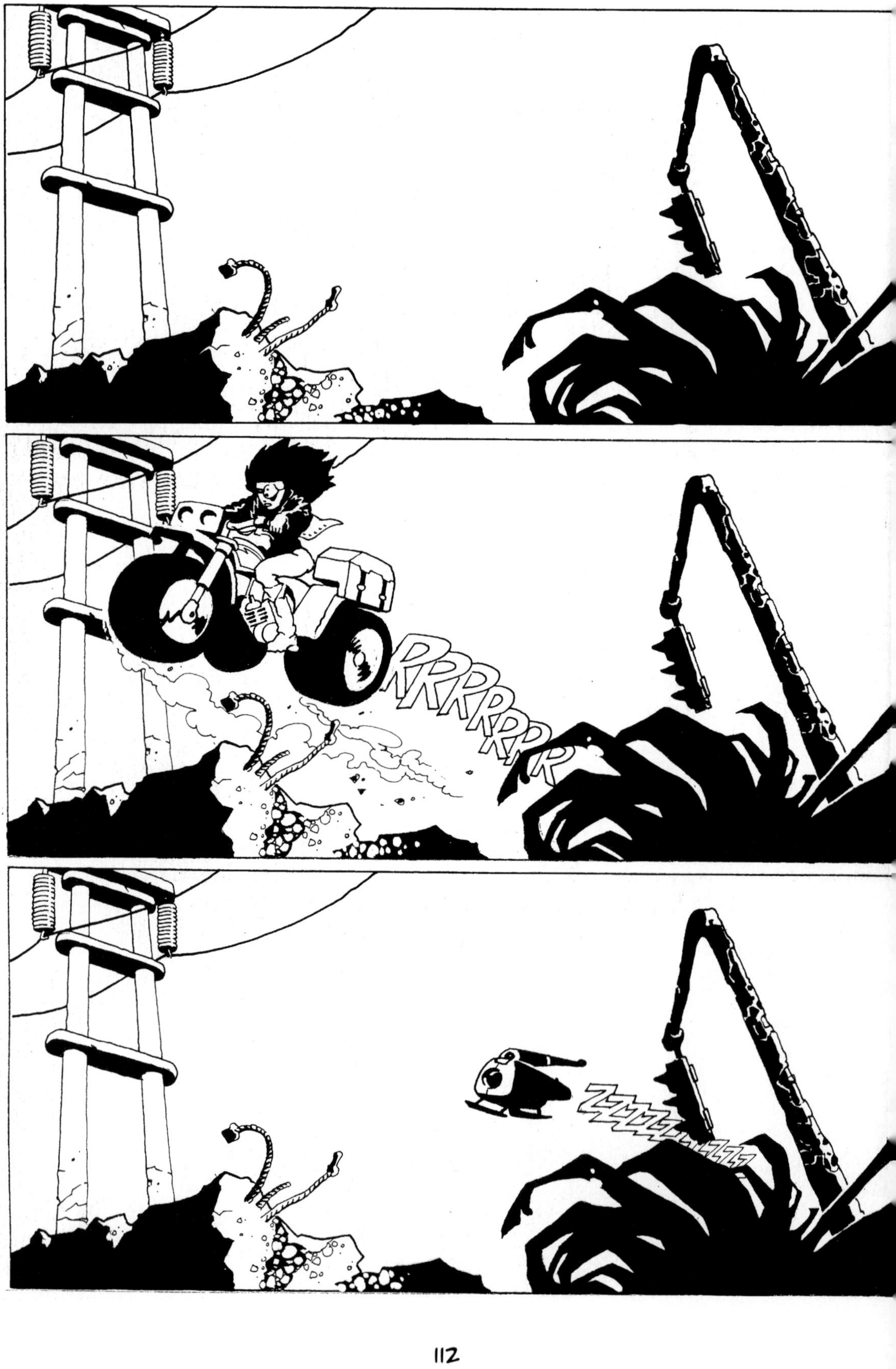
RRRRRRRRR
ZZZZZZZZZZ

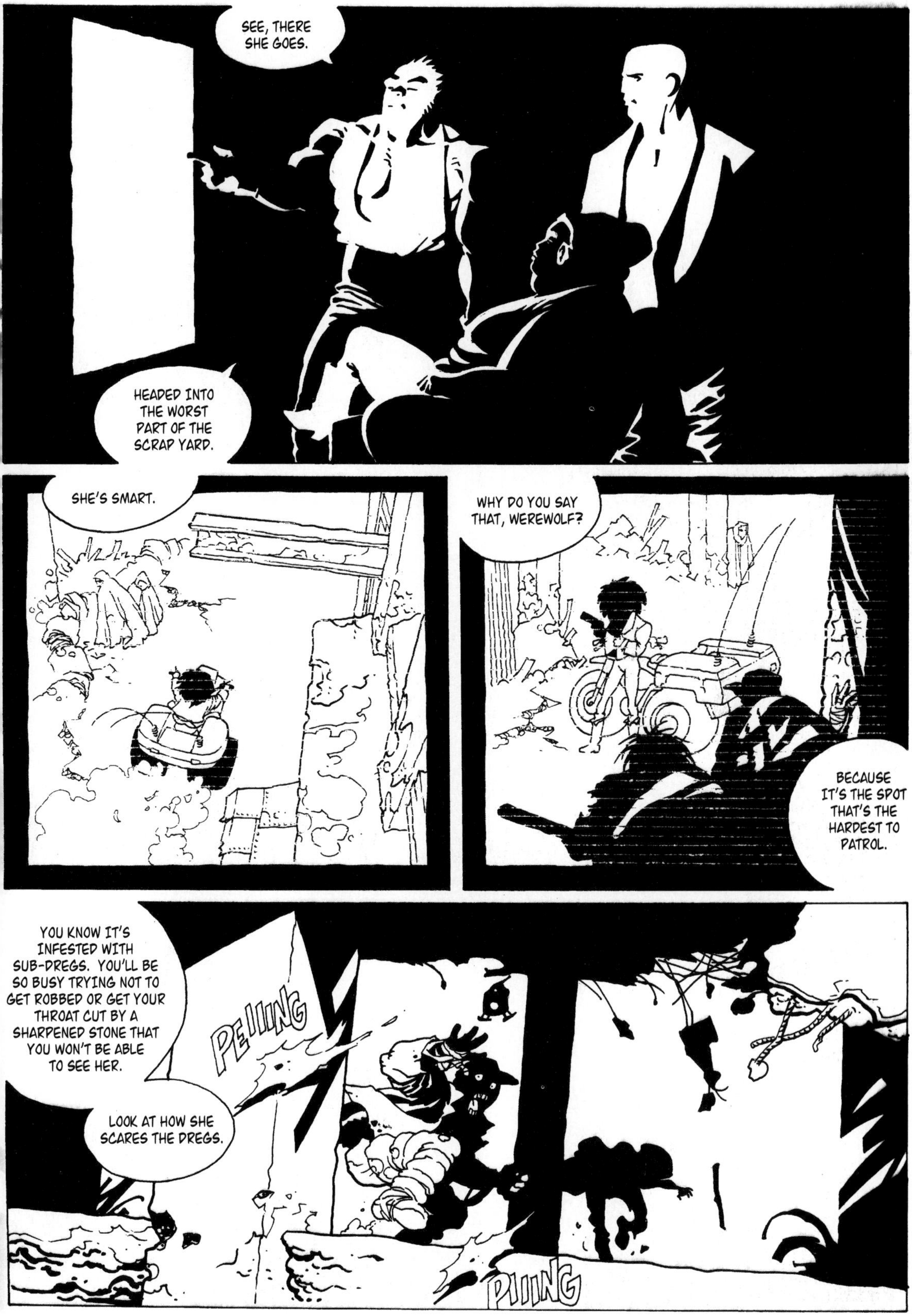
SEE, THERE SHE GOES.
HEADED INTO THE WORST PART OF THE SCRAP YARD.
SHE'S SMART.
WHY DO YOU SAY THAT, WEREWOLF?
BECAUSE IT'S THE SPOT THAT'S THE HARDEST TO PATROL.
YOU KNOW IT'S INFESTED WITH SUB-DREGS. YOU'LL BE SO BUSY TRYING NOT TO GET ROBBED OR GET YOUR THROAT CUT BY A SHARPENED STONE THAT YOU WON'T BE ABLE TO SEE HER.
PEIIING
LOOK AT HOW SHE SCARES THE DREGS.
PIIING

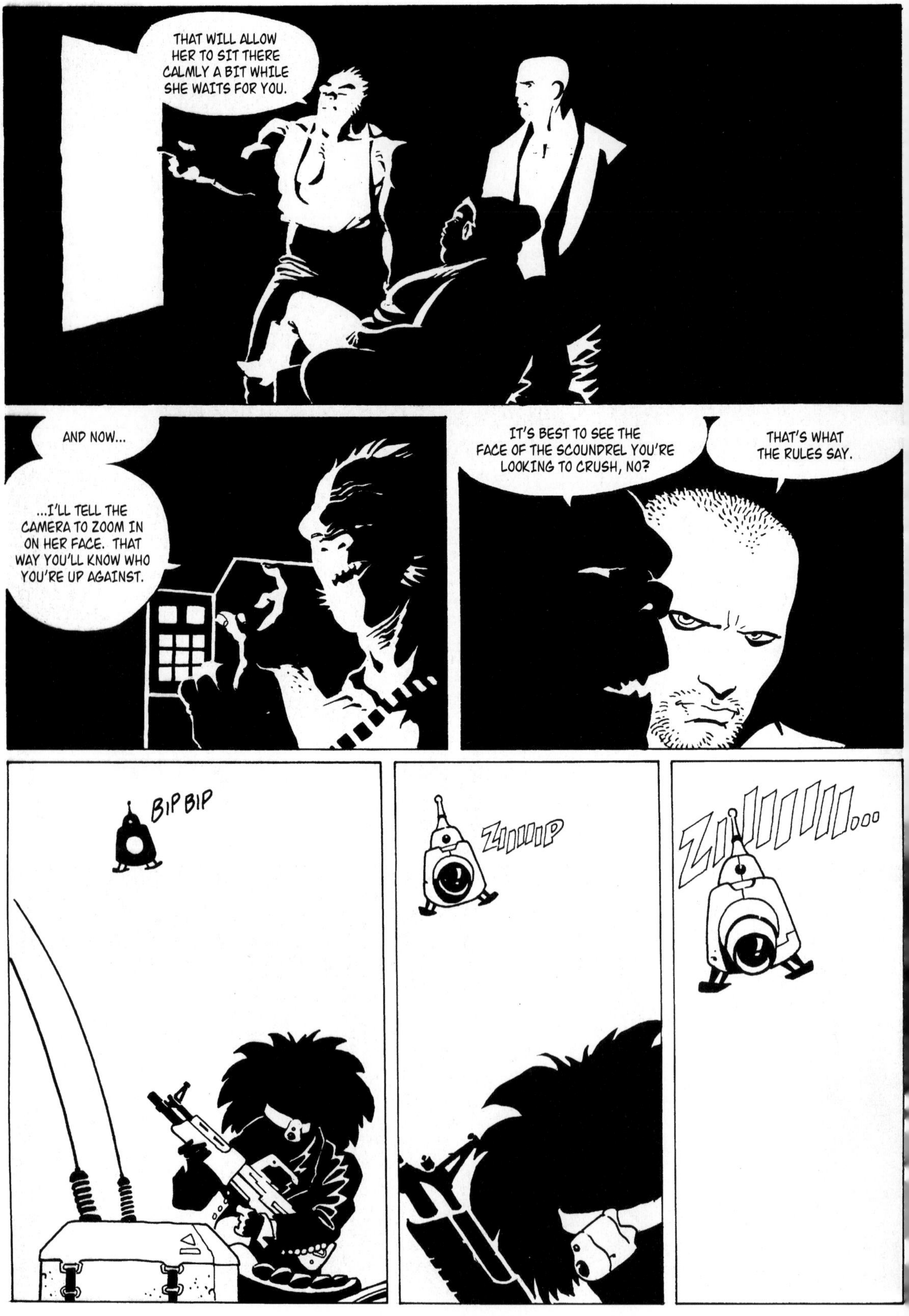
THAT WILL ALLOW HER TO SIT THERE CALMLY A BIT WHILE SHE WAITS FOR YOU.
AND NOW...
...I'LL TELL THE CAMERA TO ZOOM IN ON HER FACE. THAT WAY YOU'LL KNOW WHO YOU'RE UP AGAINST.
IT'S BEST TO SEE THE FACE OF THE SCOUNDREL YOU'RE LOOKING TO CRUSH, NO?
THAT'S WHAT THE RULES SAY.
BIP BIP
ZIIIIIP
ZIIIIIIII...

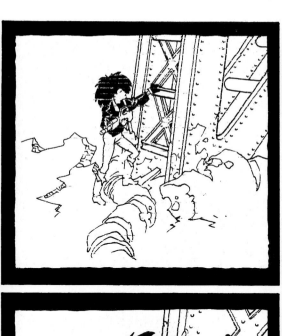

I...

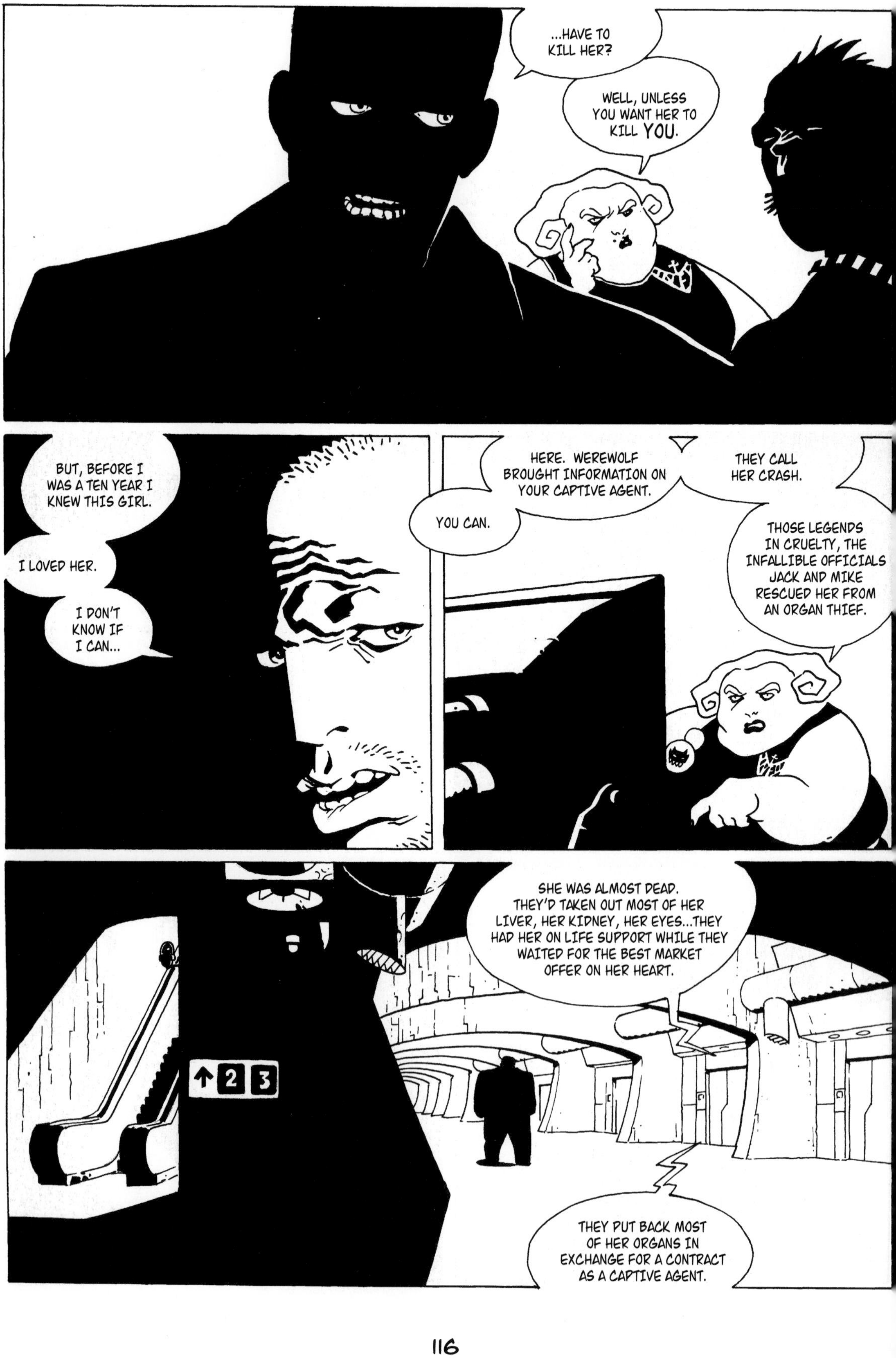

...HAVE TO KILL HER?
WELL, UNLESS YOU WANT HER TO KILL YOU.
BUT, BEFORE I WAS A TEN YEAR I KNEW THIS GIRL.
I LOVED HER.
I DON'T KNOW IF I CAN...
YOU CAN.
HERE. WEREWOLF BROUGHT INFORMATION ON YOUR CAPTIVE AGENT.
THEY CALL HER CRASH.
THOSE LEGENDS IN CRUELTY, THE INFALLIBLE OFFICIALS JACK AND MIKE RESCUED HER FROM AN ORGAN THIEF.
SHE WAS ALMOST DEAD. THEY'D TAKEN OUT MOST OF HER LIVER, HER KIDNEY, HER EYES...THEY HAD HER ON LIFE SUPPORT WHILE THEY WAITED FOR THE BEST MARKET OFFER ON HER HEART.
↑ 2 3
THEY PUT BACK MOST OF HER ORGANS IN EXCHANGE FOR A CONTRACT AS A CAPTIVE AGENT.

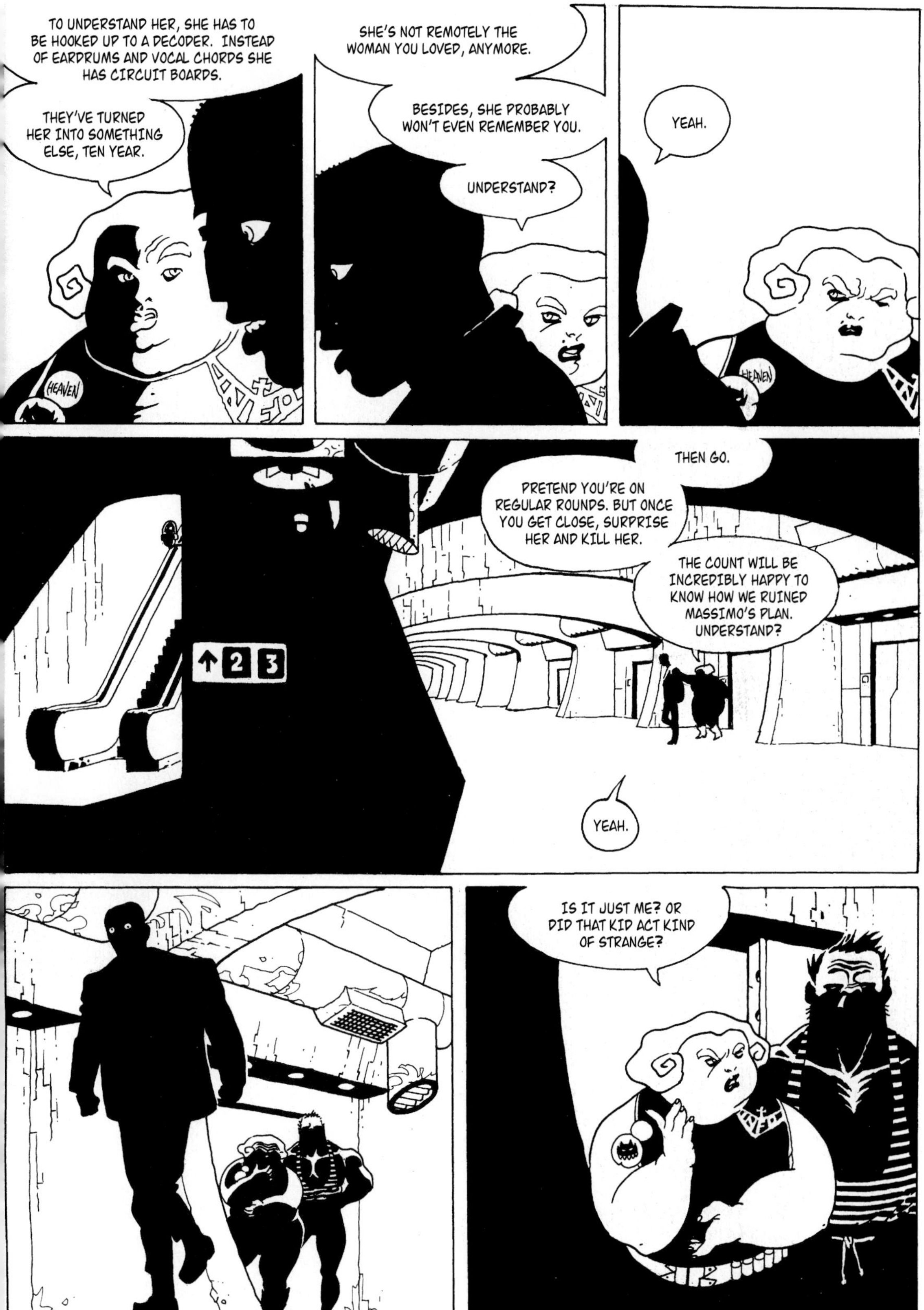
TO UNDERSTAND HER, SHE HAS TO BE HOOKED UP TO A DECODER. INSTEAD OF EARDRUMS AND VOCAL CHORDS SHE HAS CIRCUIT BOARDS.
THEY'VE TURNED HER INTO SOMETHING ELSE, TEN YEAR.
HEAVEN
SHE'S NOT REMOTELY THE WOMAN YOU LOVED, ANYMORE.
BESIDES, SHE PROBABLY WON'T EVEN REMEMBER YOU.
UNDERSTAND?
YEAH.
HEAVEN
THEN GO.
PRETEND YOU'RE ON REGULAR ROUNDS. BUT ONCE YOU GET CLOSE, SURPRISE HER AND KILL HER.
THE COUNT WILL BE INCREDIBLY HAPPY TO KNOW HOW WE RUINED MASSIMO'S PLAN. UNDERSTAND?
↑ 2 3
YEAH.
IS IT JUST ME? OR DID THAT KID ACT KIND OF STRANGE?

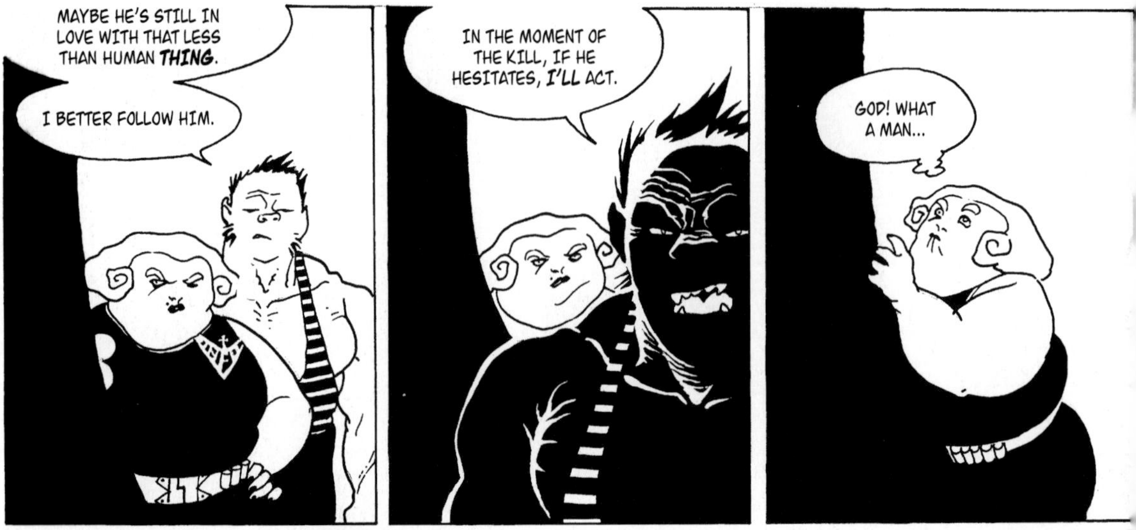
MAYBE HE'S STILL IN LOVE WITH THAT LESS THAN HUMAN **THING**.
I BETTER FOLLOW HIM.
IN THE MOMENT OF THE KILL, IF HE HESITATES, ***I'LL*** ACT.
GOD! WHAT A MAN...

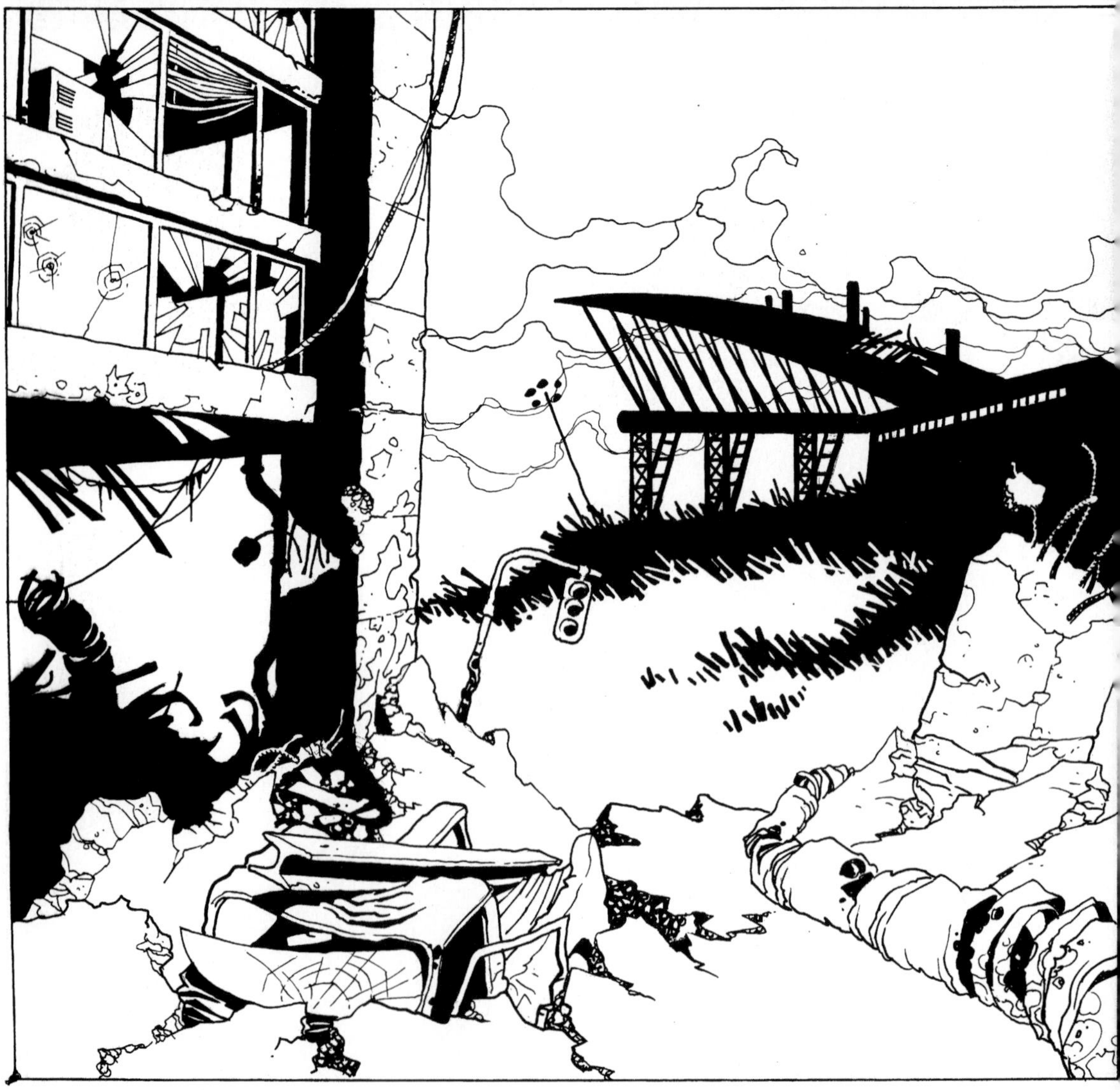

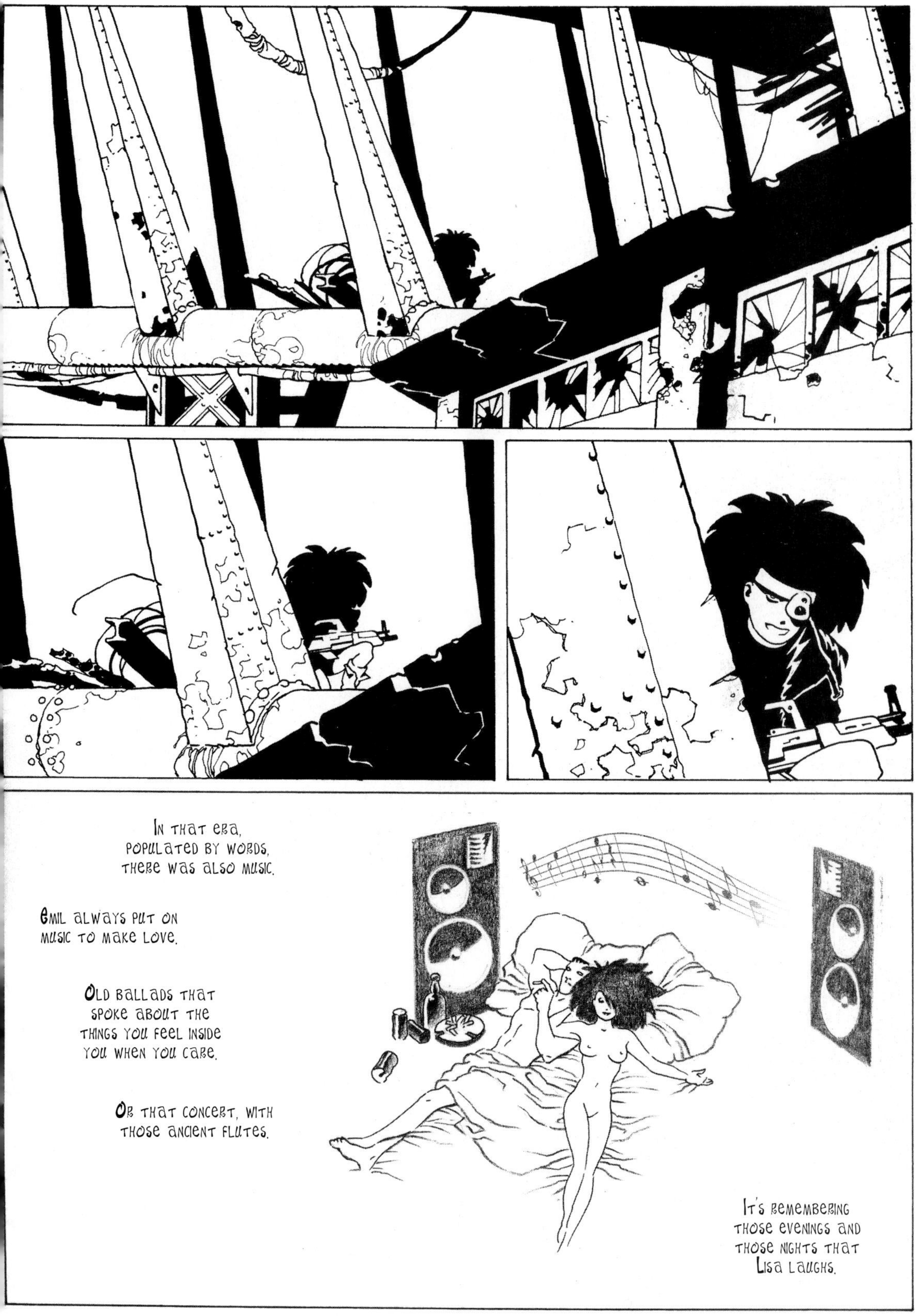
In that era, populated by words, there was also music.
Emil always put on music to make love.
Old ballads that spoke about the things you feel inside you when you care.
Or that concert, with those ancient flutes.
It's remembering those evenings and those nights that Lisa laughs.

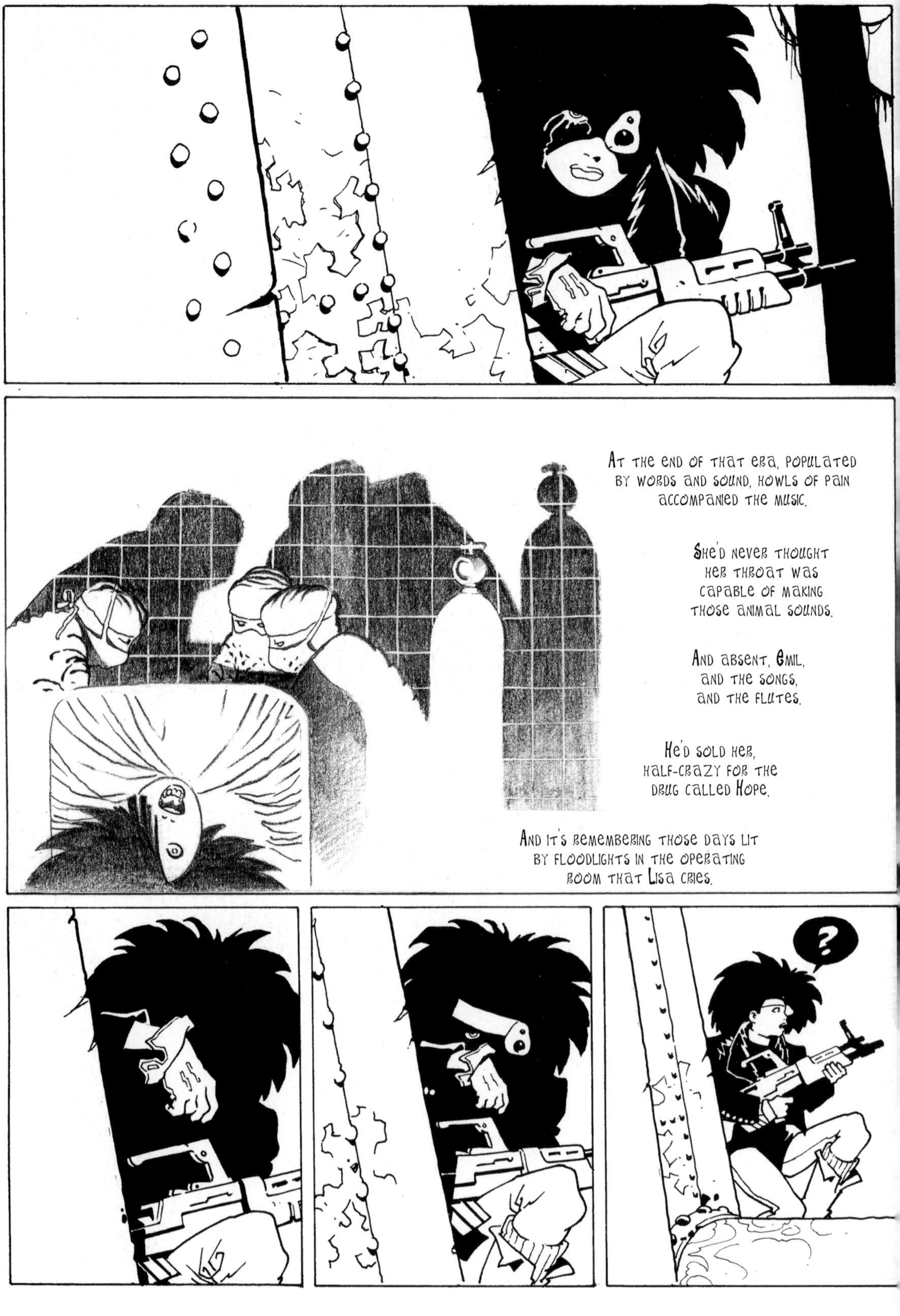
At the end of that era, populated by words and sound, howls of pain accompanied the music.
She'd never thought her throat was capable of making those animal sounds.
And absent, Emil, and the songs, and the flutes.
He'd sold her, half-crazy for the drug called Hope.
And it's remembering those days lit by floodlights in the operating room that Lisa cries.
?

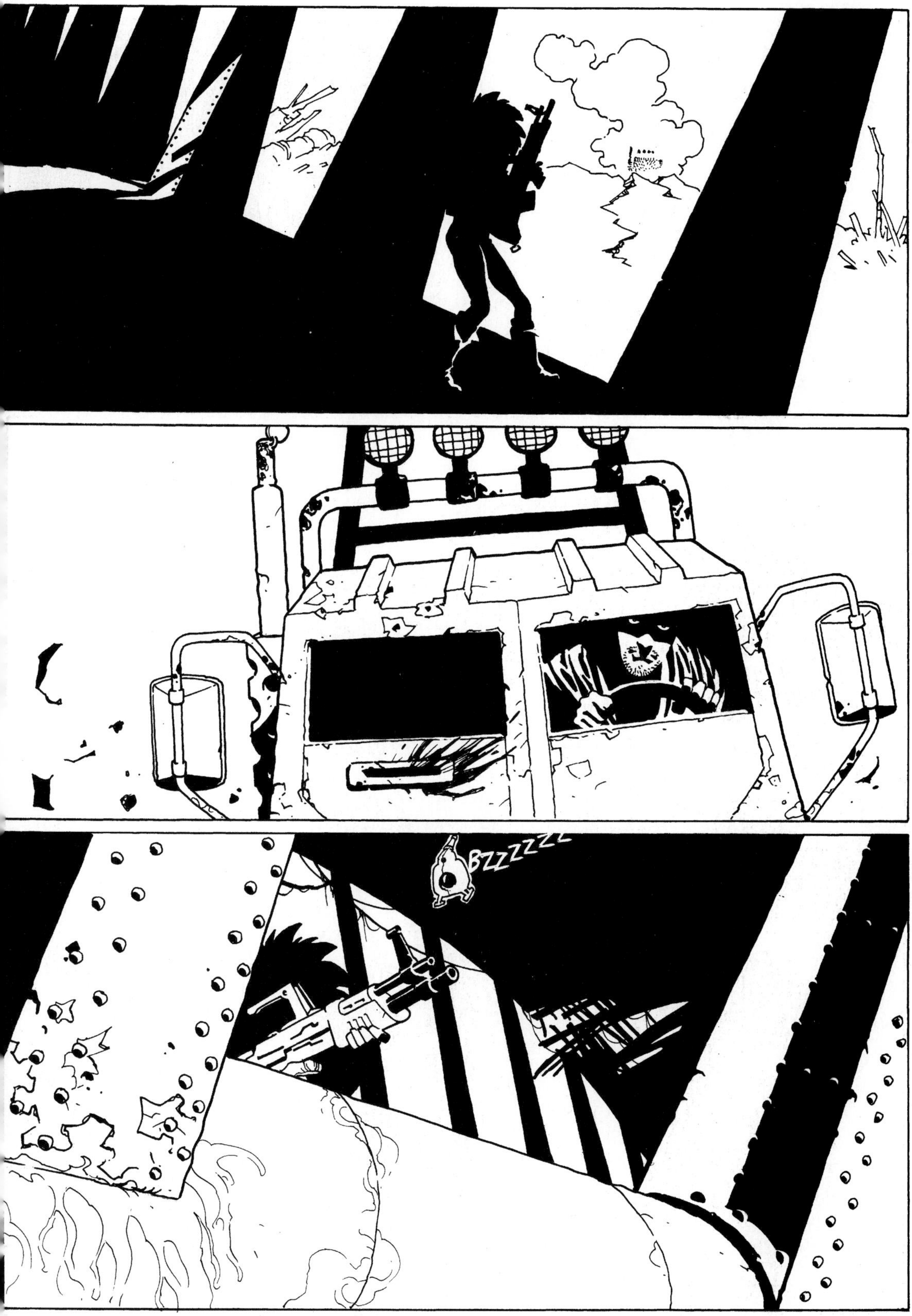
BZZZZZZ

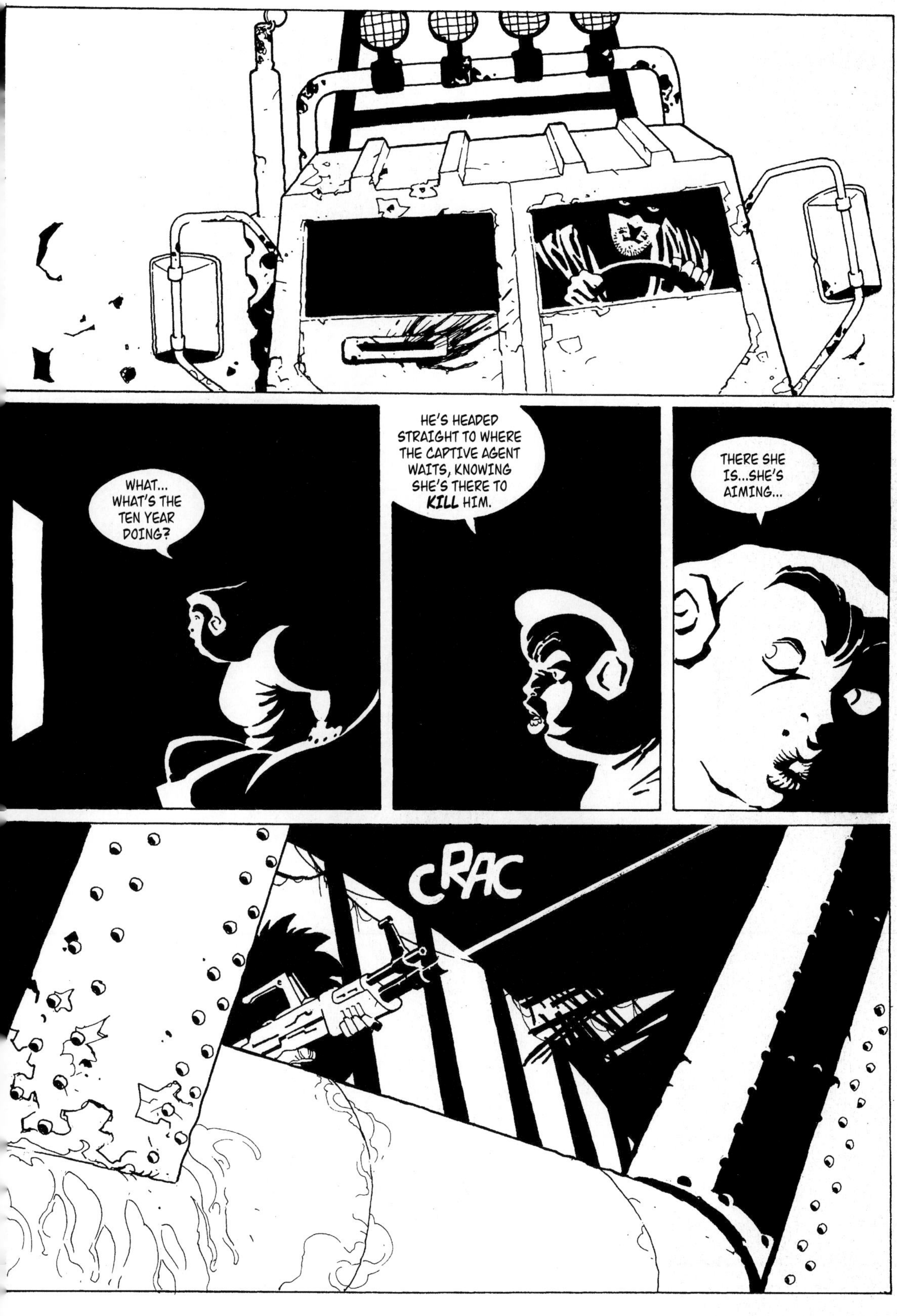

WHAT... WHAT'S THE TEN YEAR DOING?
HE'S HEADED STRAIGHT TO WHERE THE CAPTIVE AGENT WAITS, KNOWING SHE'S THERE TO **KILL** HIM.
THERE SHE IS...SHE'S AIMING...
CRAC

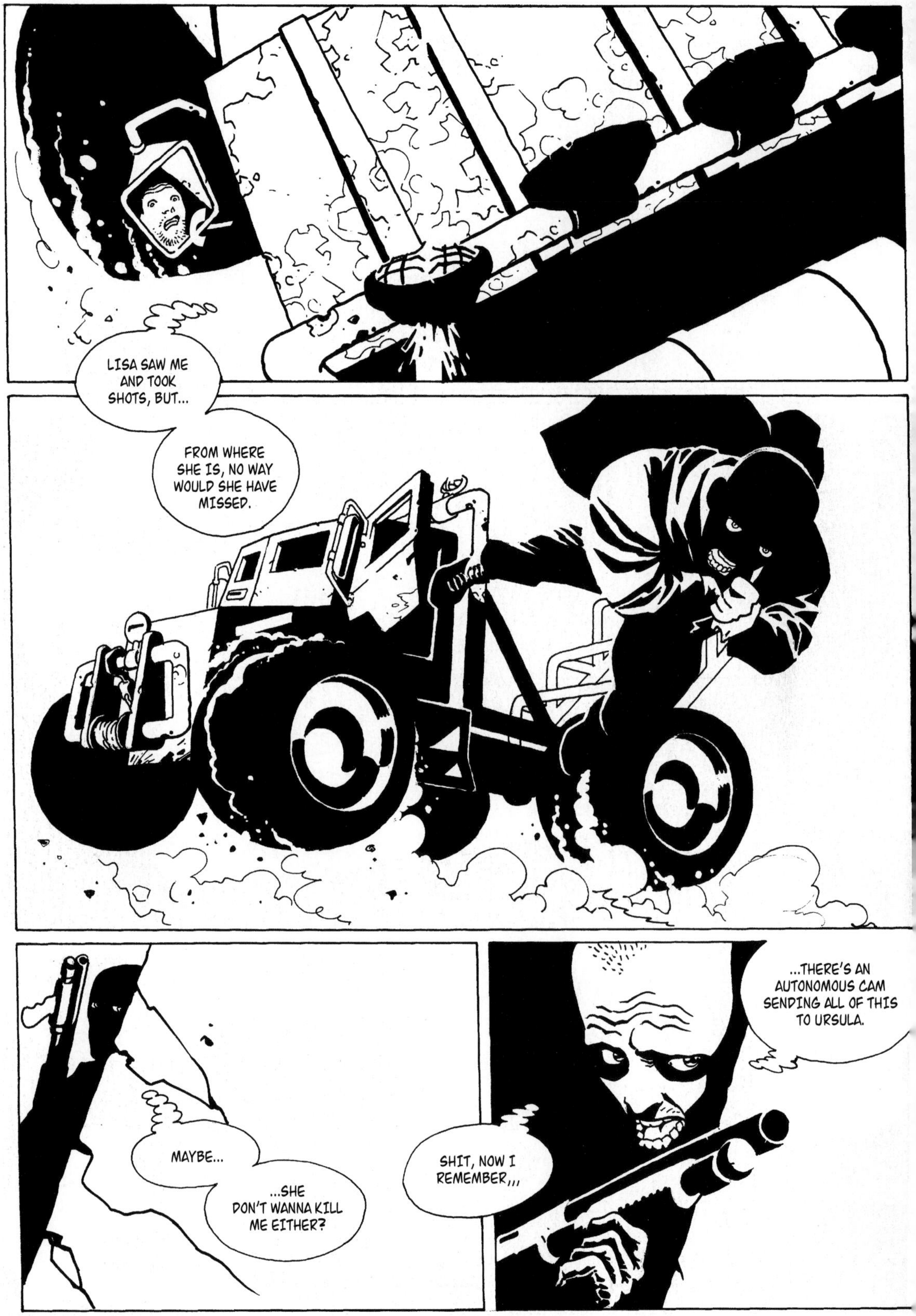
LISA SAW ME AND TOOK SHOTS, BUT...
FROM WHERE SHE IS, NO WAY WOULD SHE HAVE MISSED.
MAYBE...
...SHE DON'T WANNA KILL ME EITHER?
SHIT, NOW I REMEMBER,,,
...THERE'S AN AUTONOMOUS CAM SENDING ALL OF THIS TO URSULA.

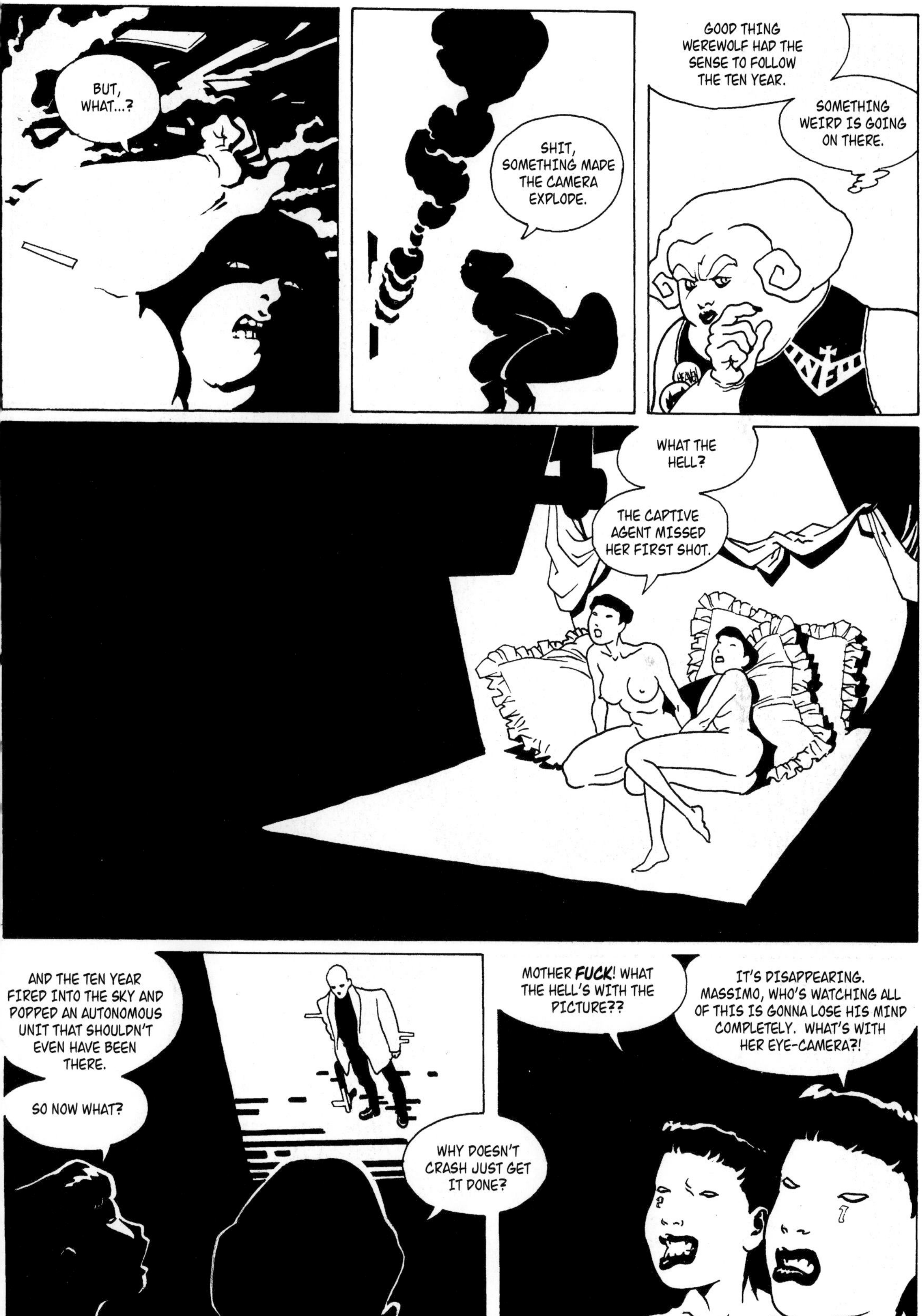
BUT, WHAT...?
SHIT, SOMETHING MADE THE CAMERA EXPLODE.
GOOD THING WEREWOLF HAD THE SENSE TO FOLLOW THE TEN YEAR.
SOMETHING WEIRD IS GOING ON THERE.
WHAT THE HELL?
THE CAPTIVE AGENT MISSED HER FIRST SHOT.
AND THE TEN YEAR FIRED INTO THE SKY AND POPPED AN AUTONOMOUS UNIT THAT SHOULDN'T EVEN HAVE BEEN THERE.
SO NOW WHAT?
WHY DOESN'T CRASH JUST GET IT DONE?
MOTHER **FUCK**! WHAT THE HELL'S WITH THE PICTURE??
IT'S DISAPPEARING. MASSIMO, WHO'S WATCHING ALL OF THIS IS GONNA LOSE HIS MIND COMPLETELY. WHAT'S WITH HER EYE-CAMERA?!

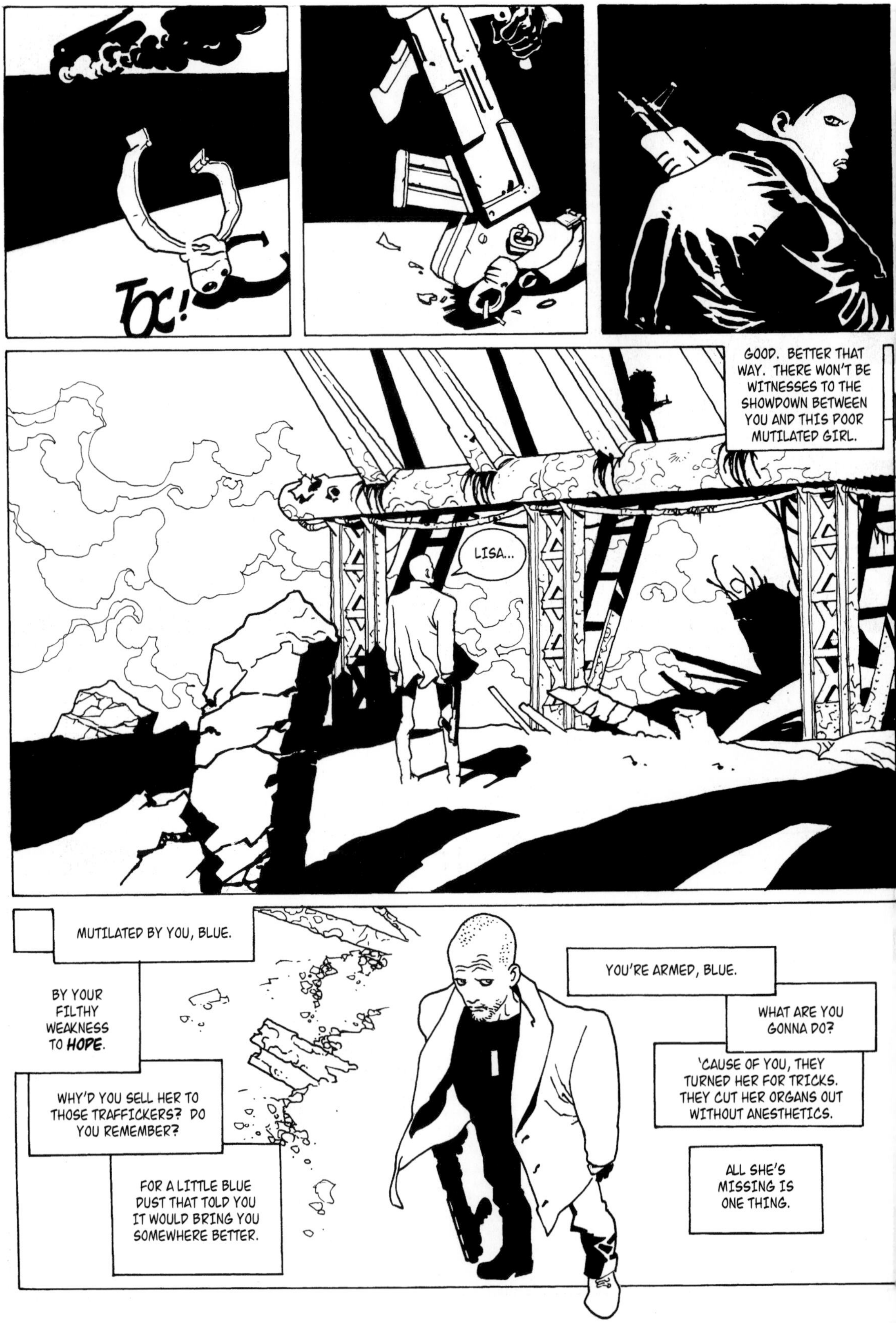
TOC!
GOOD. BETTER THAT WAY. THERE WON'T BE WITNESSES TO THE SHOWDOWN BETWEEN YOU AND THIS POOR MUTILATED GIRL.
LISA...
MUTILATED BY YOU, BLUE.
BY YOUR FILTHY WEAKNESS TO HOPE.
WHY'D YOU SELL HER TO THOSE TRAFFICKERS? DO YOU REMEMBER?
FOR A LITTLE BLUE DUST THAT TOLD YOU IT WOULD BRING YOU SOMEWHERE BETTER.
YOU'RE ARMED, BLUE.
WHAT ARE YOU GONNA DO?
'CAUSE OF YOU, THEY TURNED HER FOR TRICKS. THEY CUT HER ORGANS OUT WITHOUT ANESTHETICS.
ALL SHE'S MISSING IS ONE THING.

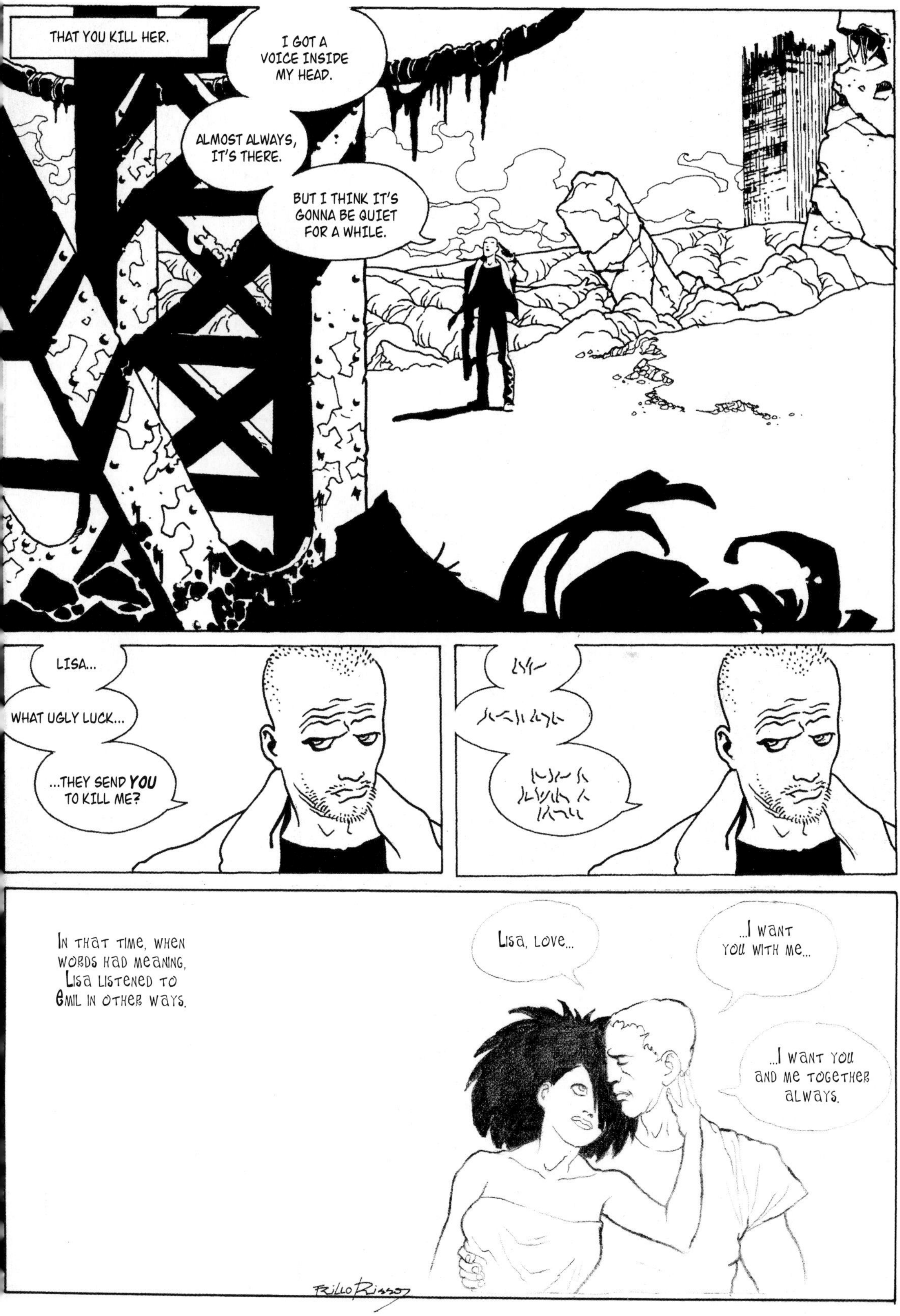

THAT YOU KILL HER.
I GOT A VOICE INSIDE MY HEAD.
ALMOST ALWAYS, IT'S THERE.
BUT I THINK IT'S GONNA BE QUIET FOR A WHILE.
LISA...
WHAT UGLY LUCK...
...THEY SEND **YOU** TO KILL ME?
IN THAT TIME, WHEN WORDS HAD MEANING, LISA LISTENED TO EMIL IN OTHER WAYS.
LISA, LOVE...
...I WANT YOU WITH ME...
...I WANT YOU AND ME TOGETHER ALWAYS.

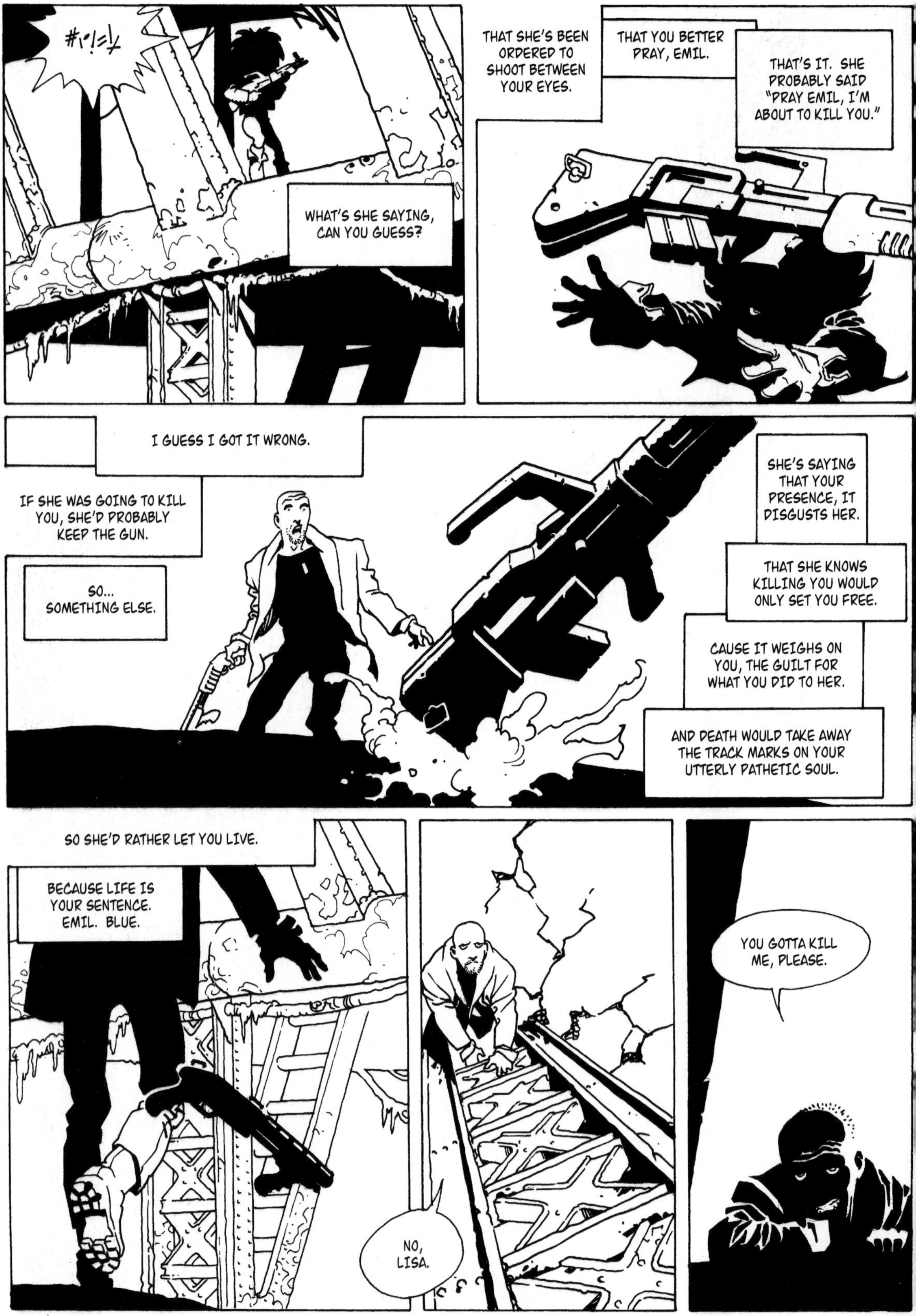
#!@=!%
WHAT'S SHE SAYING, CAN YOU GUESS?
THAT SHE'S BEEN ORDERED TO SHOOT BETWEEN YOUR EYES.
THAT YOU BETTER PRAY, EMIL.
THAT'S IT. SHE PROBABLY SAID "PRAY EMIL, I'M ABOUT TO KILL YOU."
I GUESS I GOT IT WRONG.
IF SHE WAS GOING TO KILL YOU, SHE'D PROBABLY KEEP THE GUN.
SO... SOMETHING ELSE.
SHE'S SAYING THAT YOUR PRESENCE, IT DISGUSTS HER.
THAT SHE KNOWS KILLING YOU WOULD ONLY SET YOU FREE.
CAUSE IT WEIGHS ON YOU, THE GUILT FOR WHAT YOU DID TO HER.
AND DEATH WOULD TAKE AWAY THE TRACK MARKS ON YOUR UTTERLY PATHETIC SOUL.
SO SHE'D RATHER LET YOU LIVE.
BECAUSE LIFE IS YOUR SENTENCE. EMIL. BLUE.
NO, LISA.
YOU GOTTA KILL ME, PLEASE.

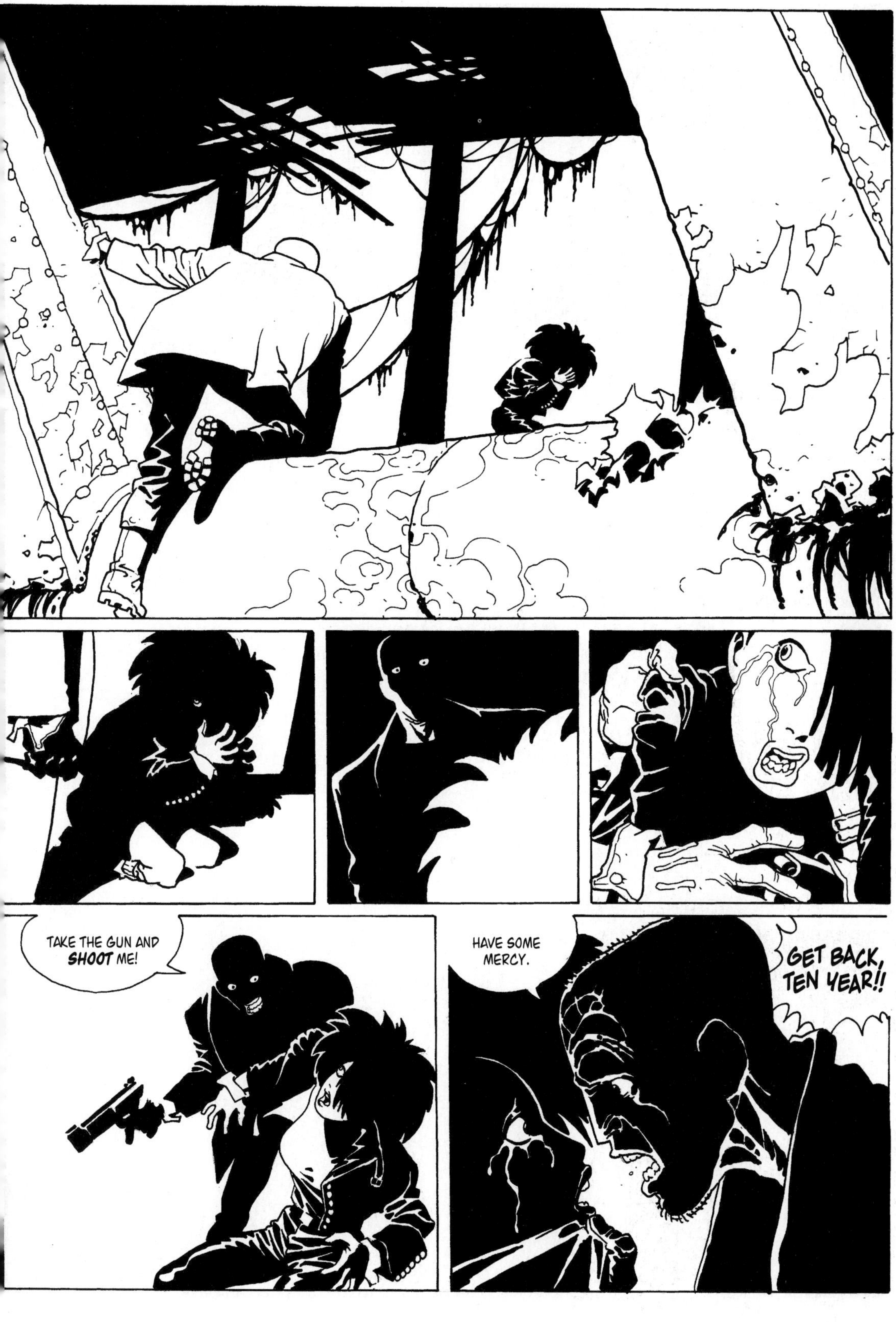
TAKE THE GUN AND SHOOT ME!
HAVE SOME MERCY.
GET BACK, TEN YEAR!!

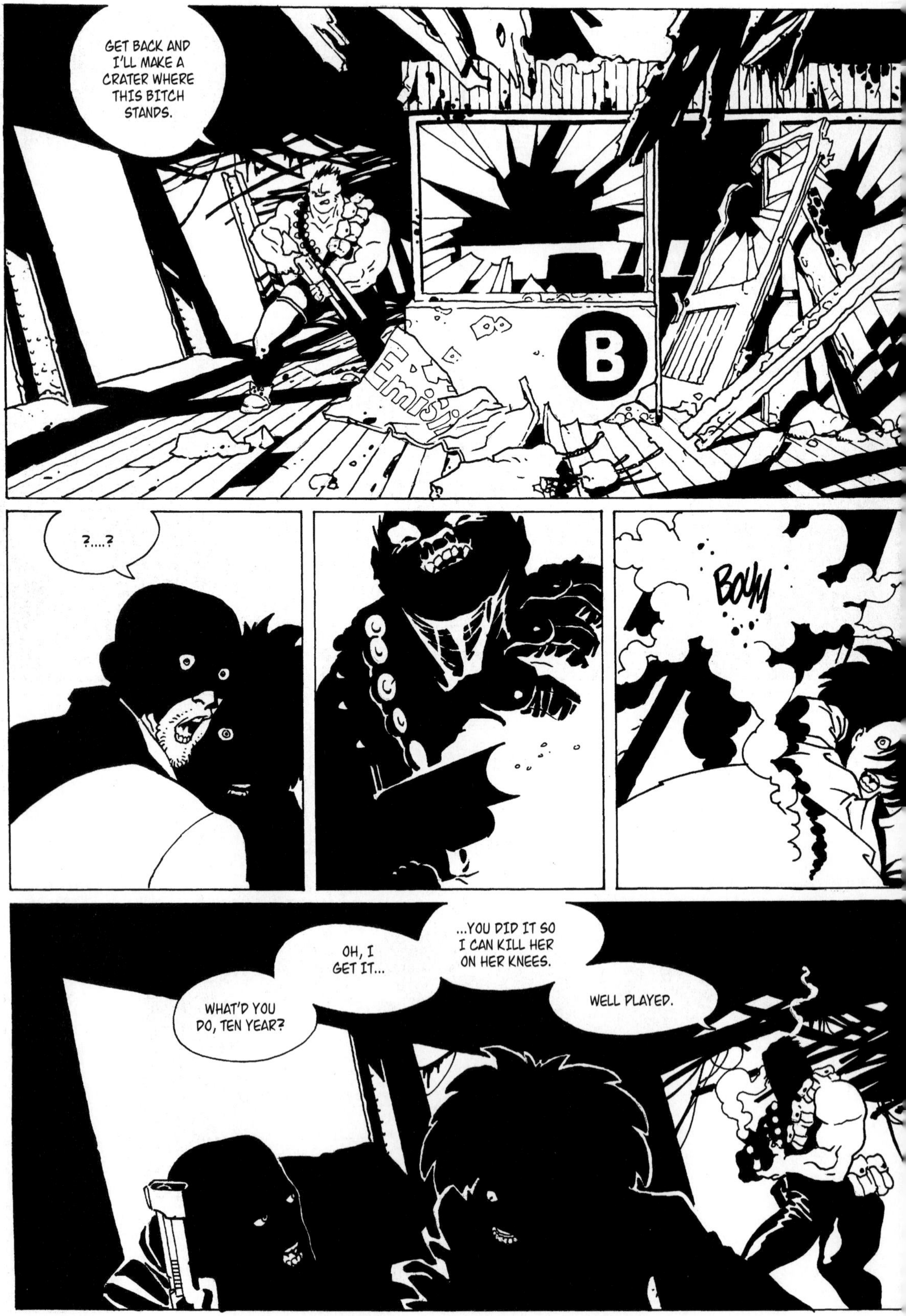
GET BACK AND I'LL MAKE A CRATER WHERE THIS BITCH STANDS.
B
?....?
BOUM
WHAT'D YOU DO, TEN YEAR?
OH, I GET IT...
...YOU DID IT SO I CAN KILL HER ON HER KNEES.
WELL PLAYED.

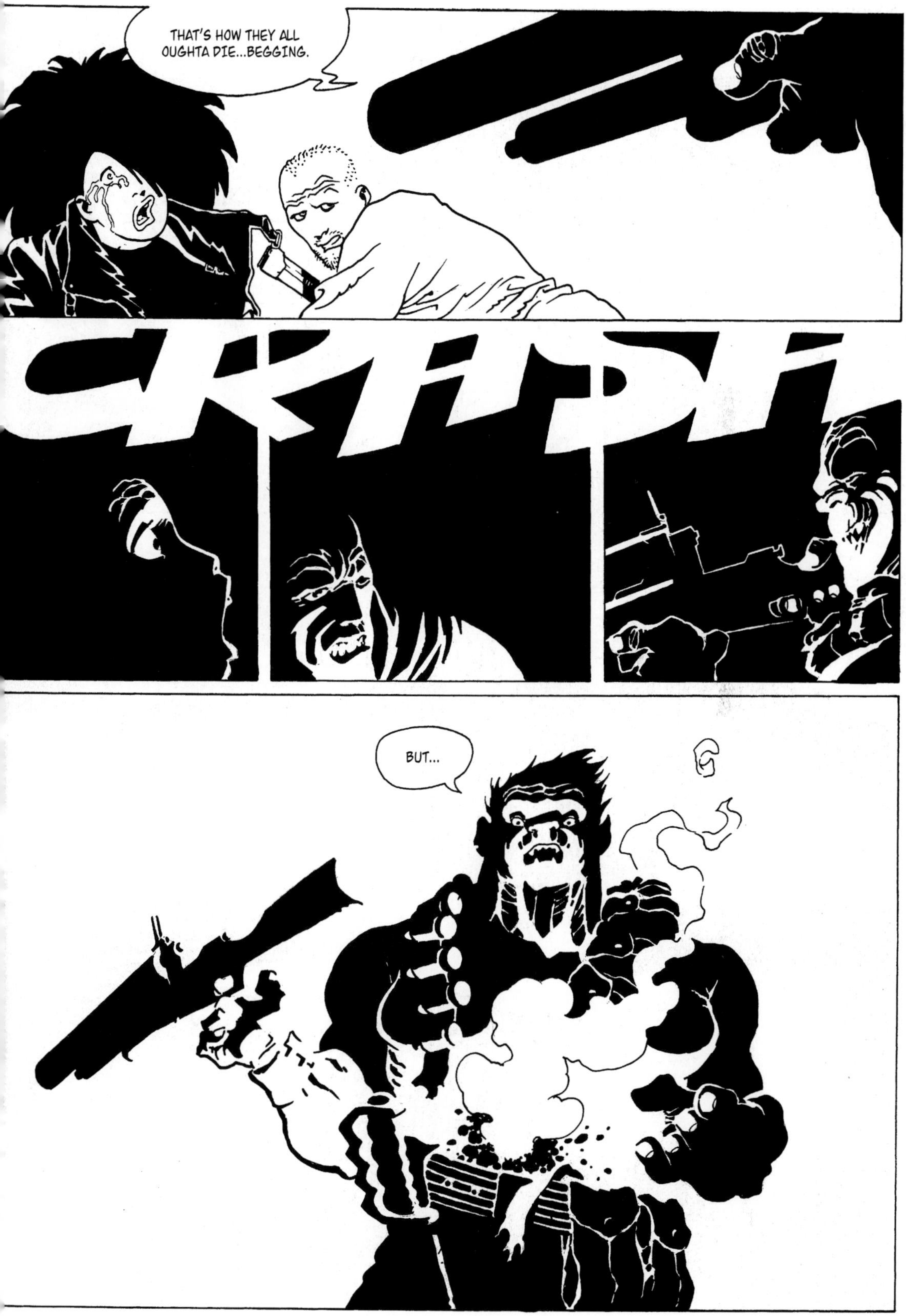
THAT'S HOW THEY ALL OUGHTA DIE...BEGGING.
BUT...

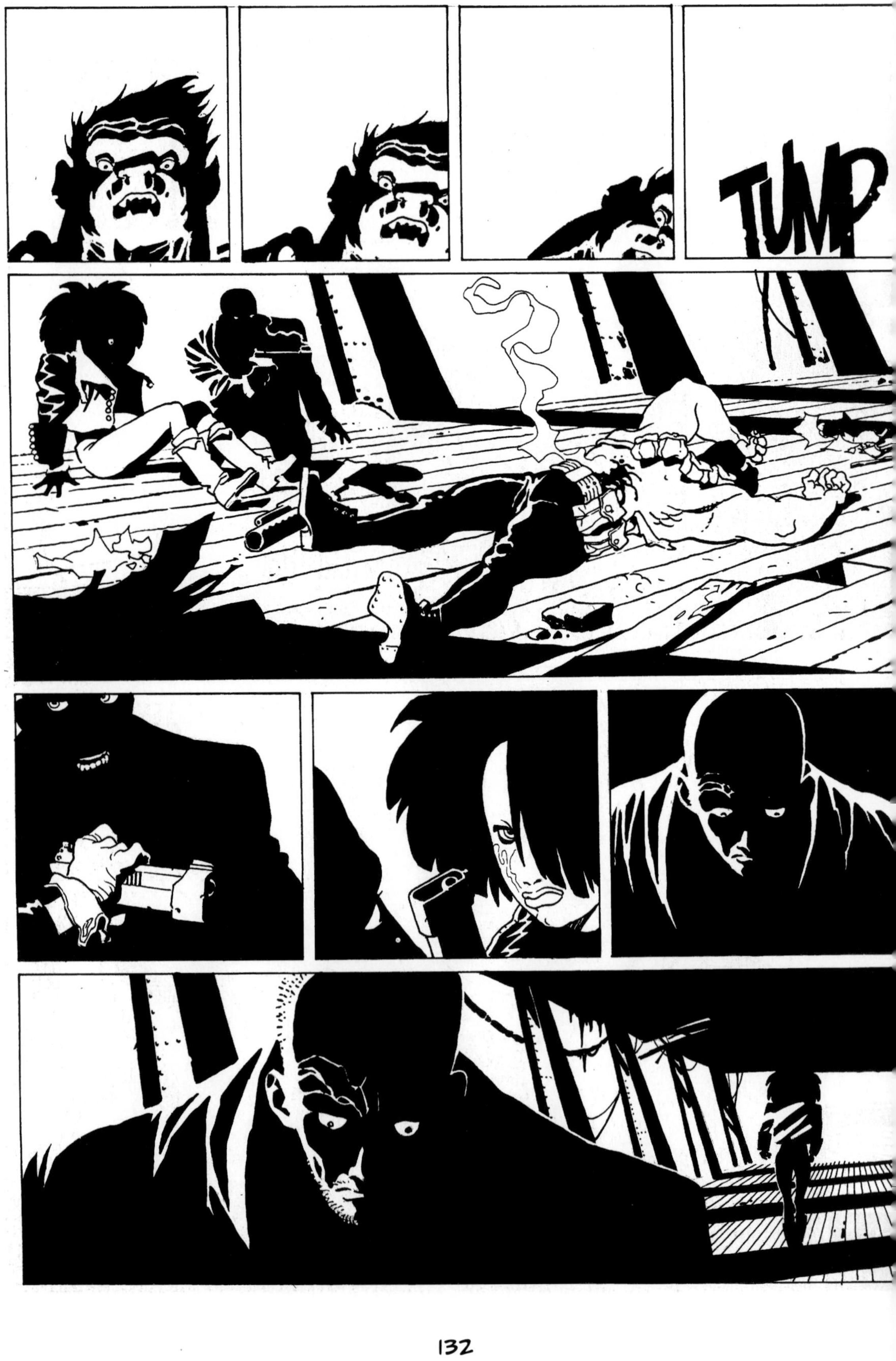
TUMP

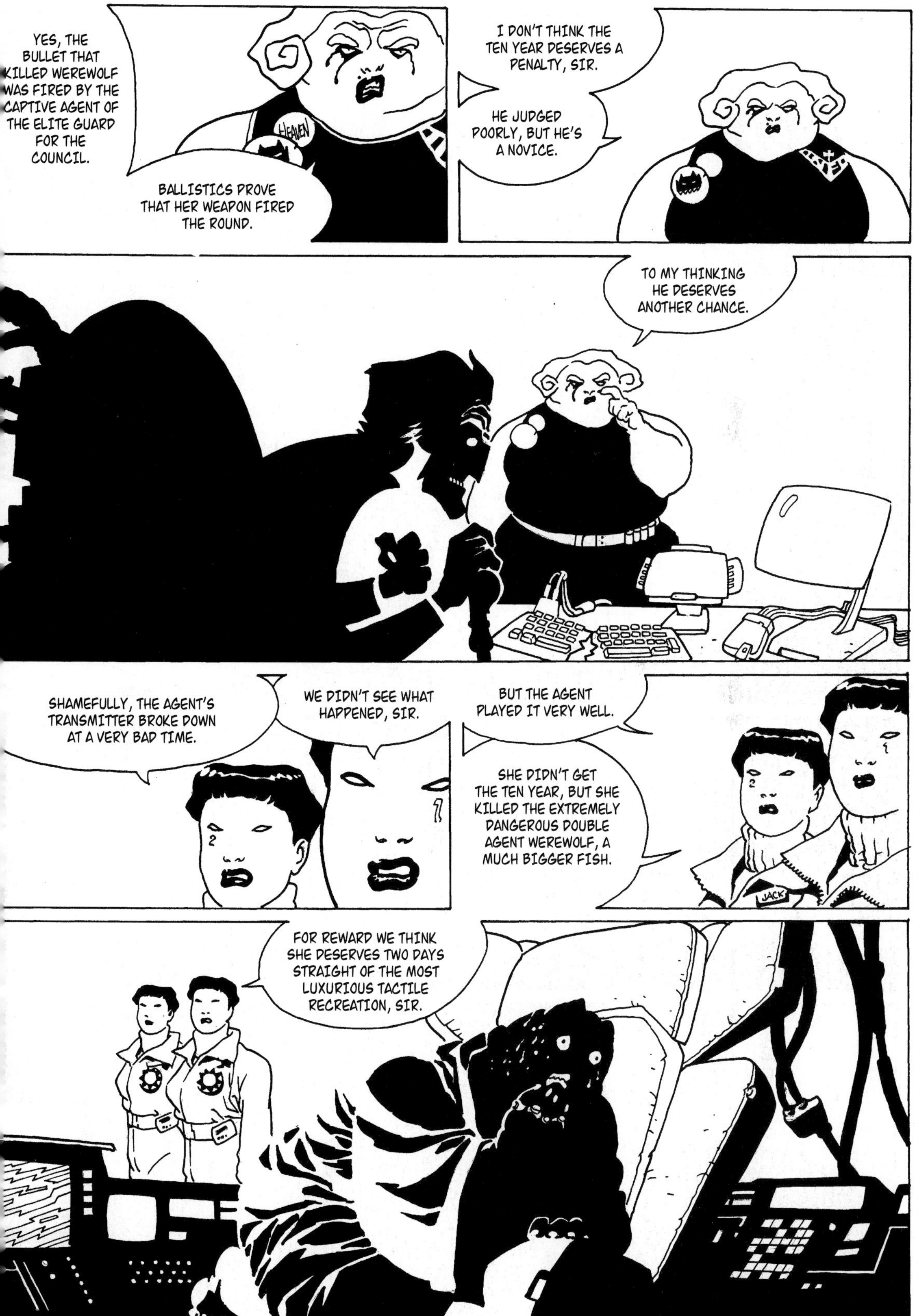

YES, THE BULLET THAT KILLED WEREWOLF WAS FIRED BY THE CAPTIVE AGENT OF THE ELITE GUARD FOR THE COUNCIL.
BALLISTICS PROVE THAT HER WEAPON FIRED THE ROUND.
HEAVEN
I DON'T THINK THE TEN YEAR DESERVES A PENALTY, SIR.
HE JUDGED POORLY, BUT HE'S A NOVICE.
TO MY THINKING HE DESERVES ANOTHER CHANCE.
SHAMEFULLY, THE AGENT'S TRANSMITTER BROKE DOWN AT A VERY BAD TIME.
WE DIDN'T SEE WHAT HAPPENED, SIR.
BUT THE AGENT PLAYED IT VERY WELL.
SHE DIDN'T GET THE TEN YEAR, BUT SHE KILLED THE EXTREMELY DANGEROUS DOUBLE AGENT WEREWOLF, A MUCH BIGGER FISH.
JACK
FOR REWARD WE THINK SHE DESERVES TWO DAYS STRAIGHT OF THE MOST LUXURIOUS TACTILE RECREATION, SIR.

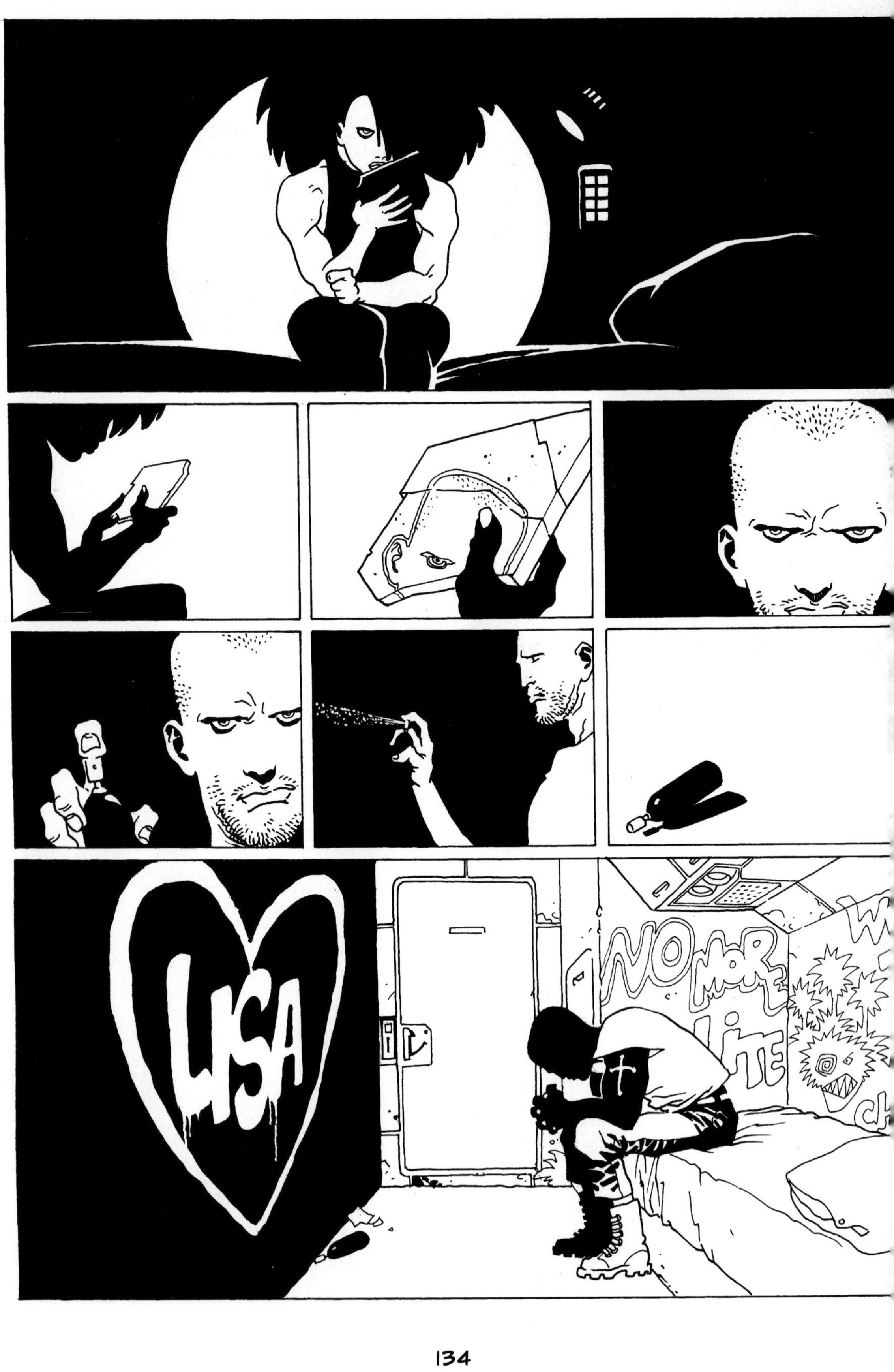
LISA
NO MORE

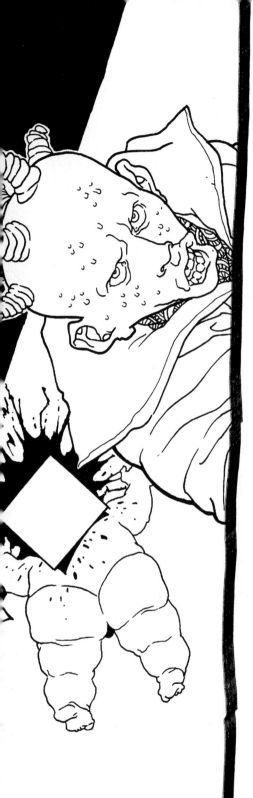

10

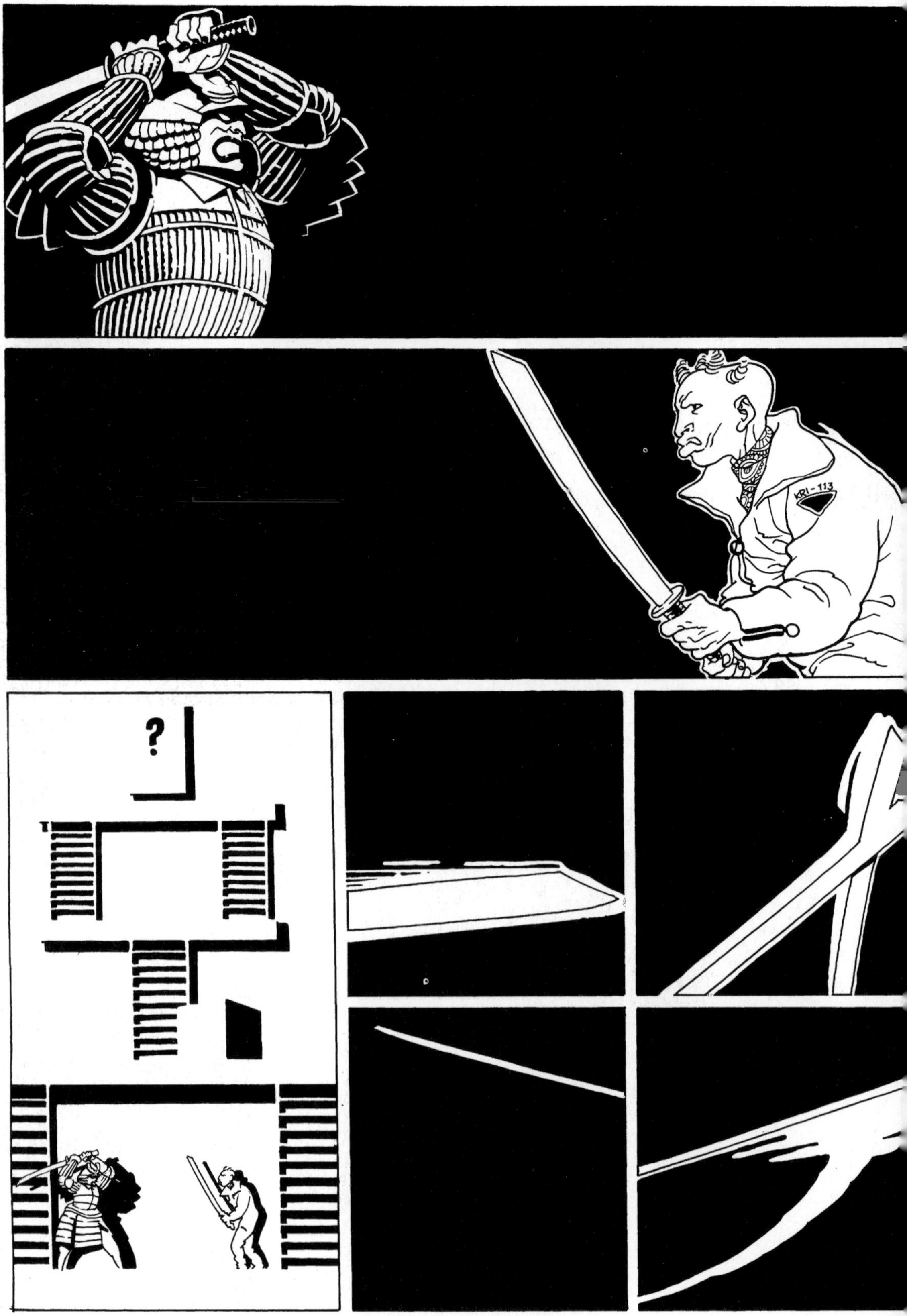
KRI-113
?

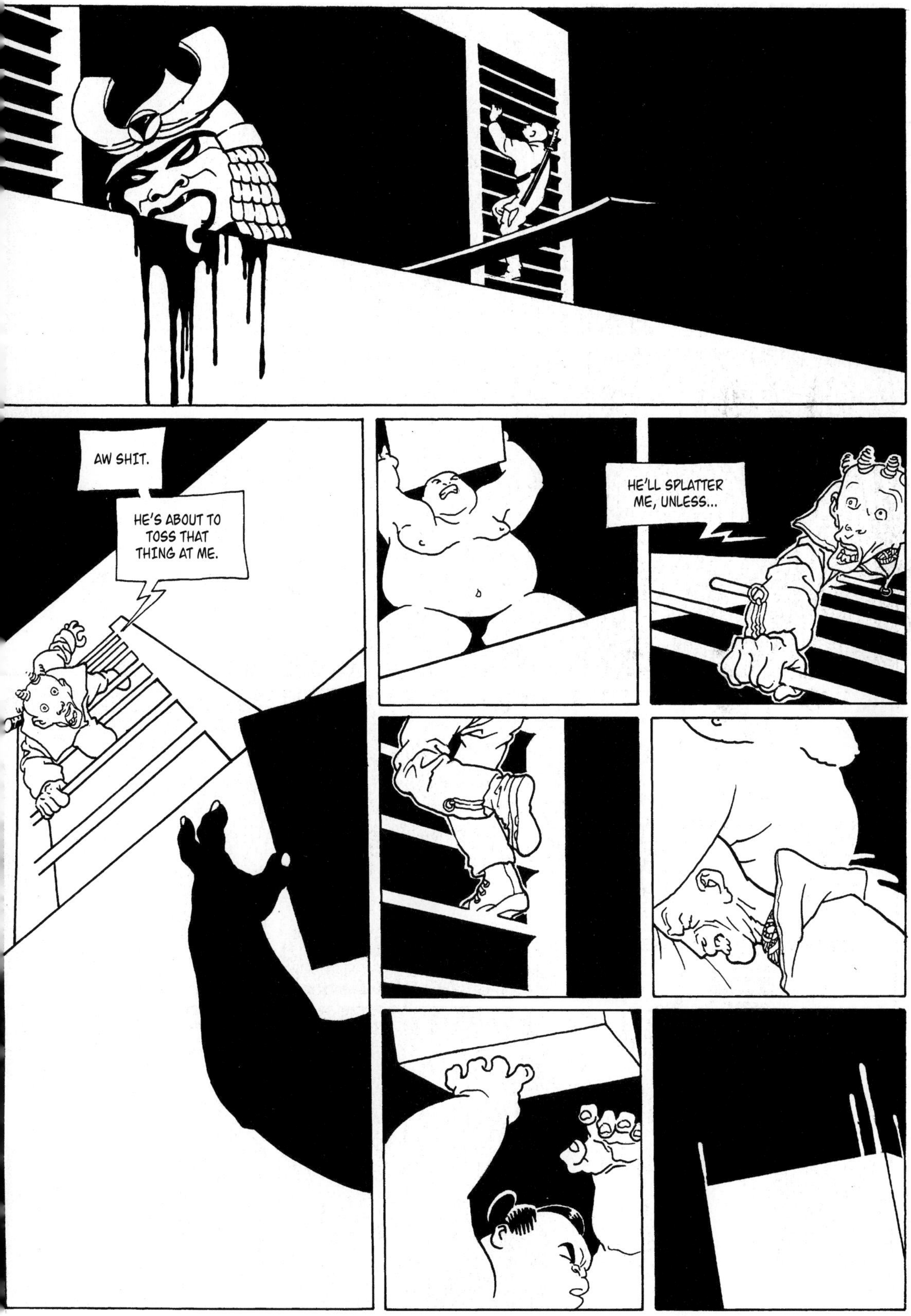
AW SHIT.
HE'S ABOUT TO TOSS THAT THING AT ME.
HE'LL SPLATTER ME, UNLESS...

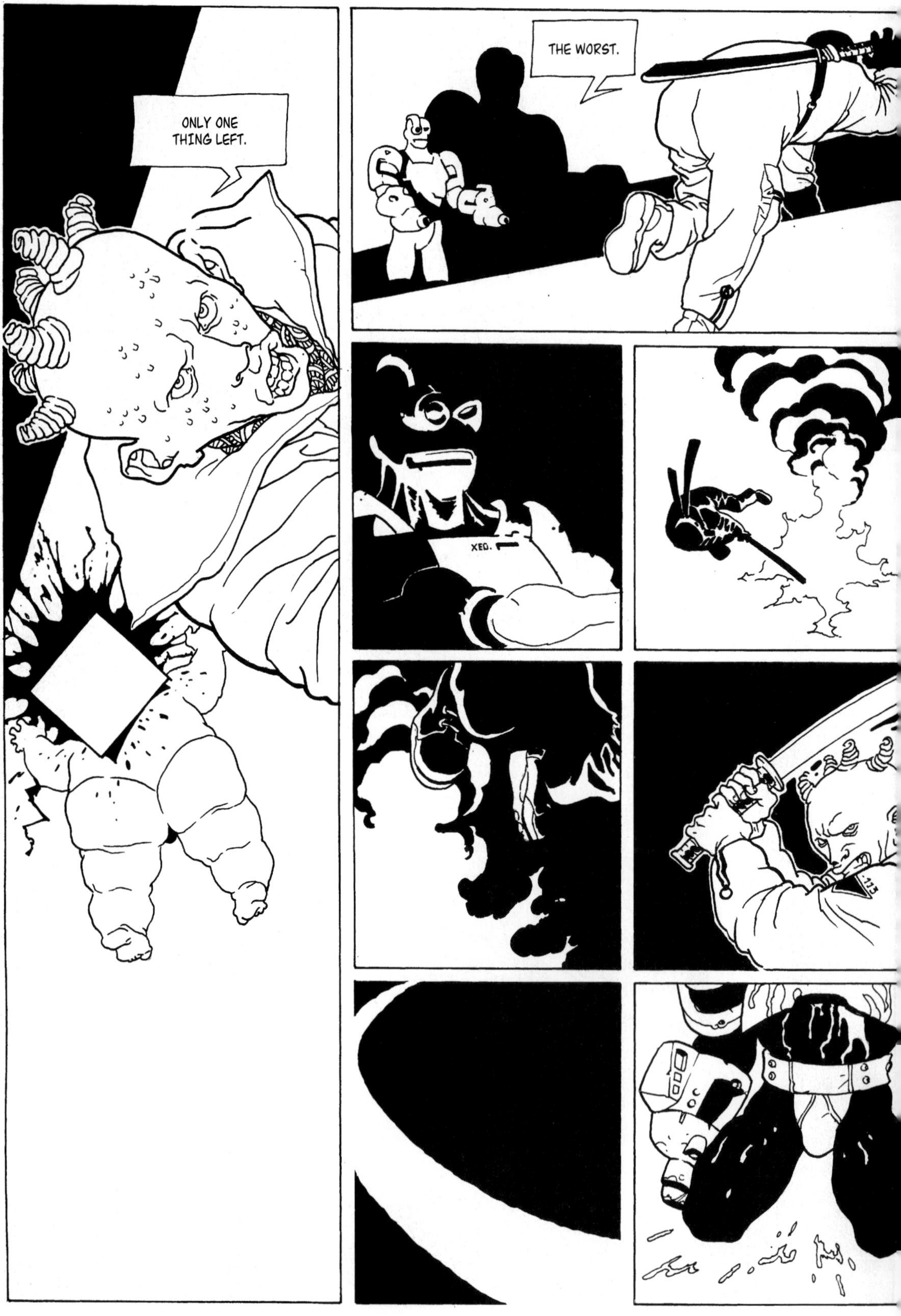
ONLY ONE THING LEFT.
THE WORST.
XEO.

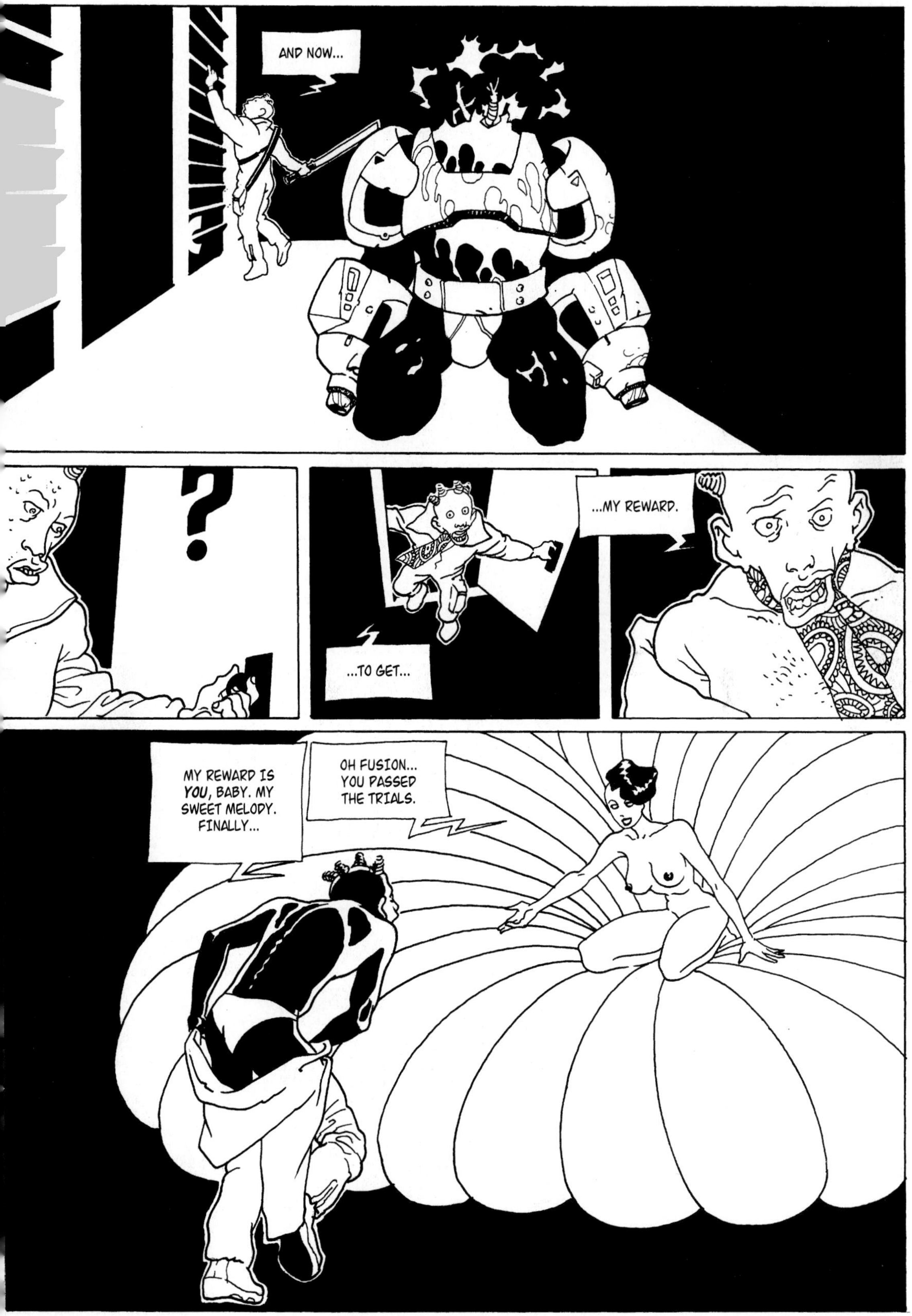
AND NOW...
?
...TO GET...
...MY REWARD.
MY REWARD IS YOU, BABY. MY SWEET MELODY. FINALLY...
OH FUSION... YOU PASSED THE TRIALS.

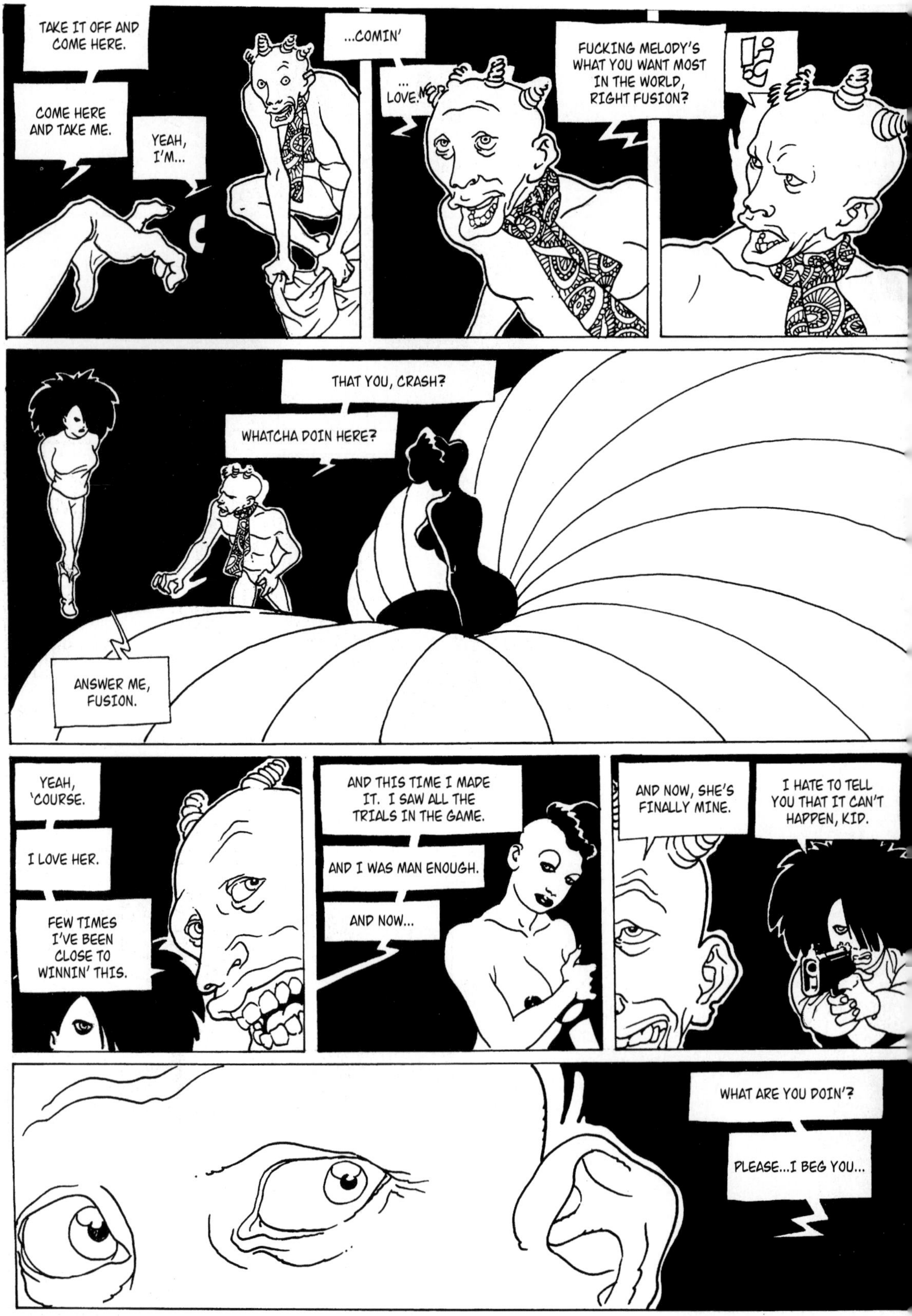
TAKE IT OFF AND COME HERE.
COME HERE AND TAKE ME.
YEAH, I'M...
...COMIN'
... LOVE.
FUCKING MELODY'S WHAT YOU WANT MOST IN THE WORLD, RIGHT FUSION?
THAT YOU, CRASH?
WHATCHA DOIN HERE?
ANSWER ME, FUSION.
YEAH, 'COURSE.
I LOVE HER.
FEW TIMES I'VE BEEN CLOSE TO WINNIN' THIS.
AND THIS TIME I MADE IT. I SAW ALL THE TRIALS IN THE GAME.
AND I WAS MAN ENOUGH.
AND NOW...
AND NOW, SHE'S FINALLY MINE.
I HATE TO TELL YOU THAT IT CAN'T HAPPEN, KID.
WHAT ARE YOU DOIN'?
PLEASE...I BEG YOU...

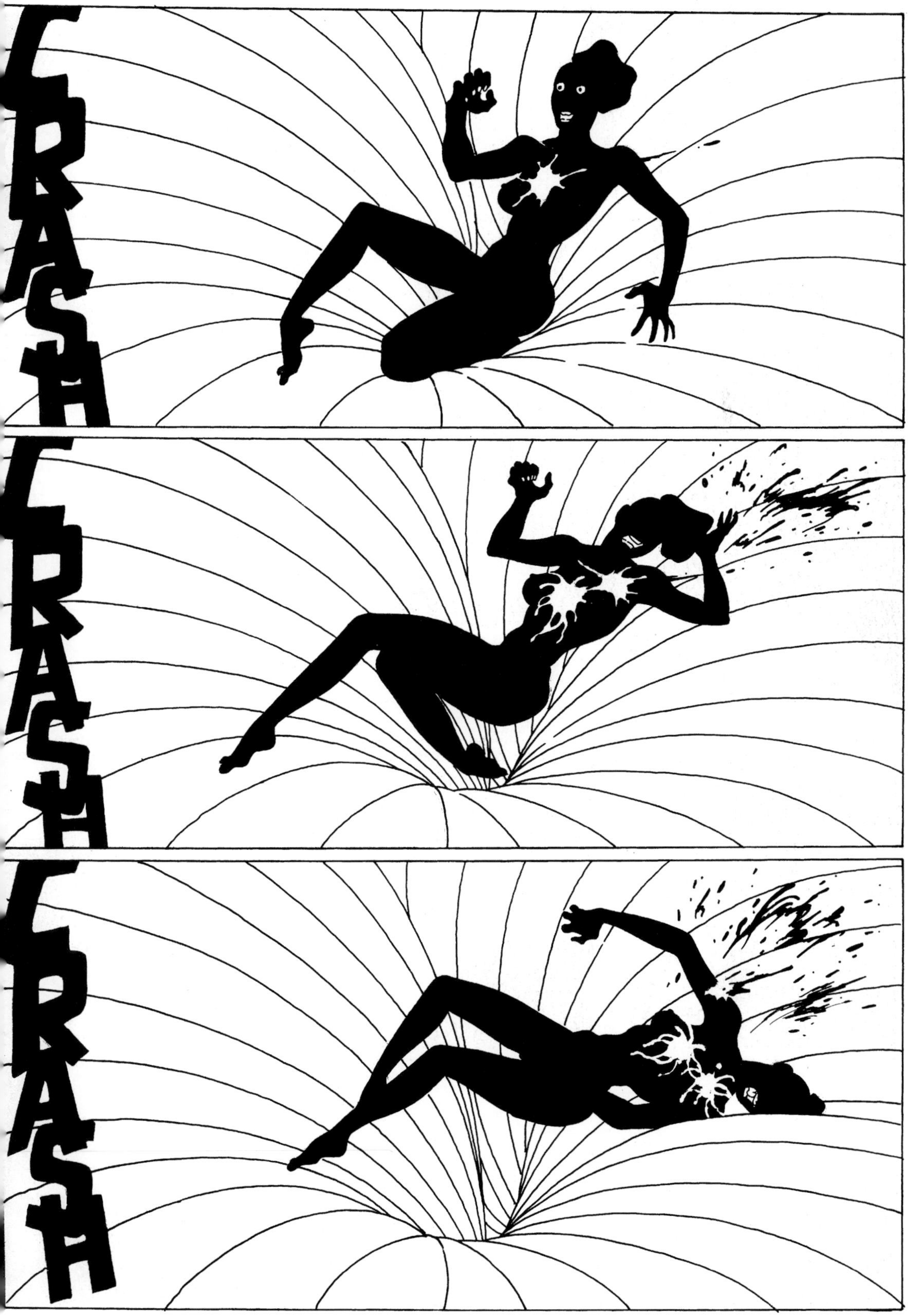
CRASH
CRASH
CRASH

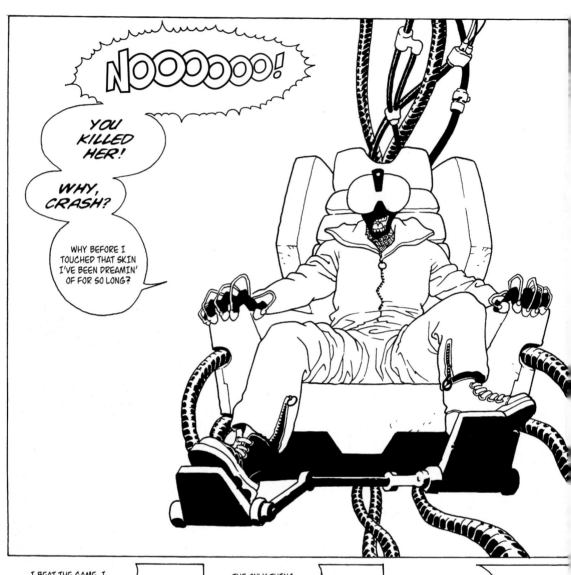

NOOOOOO!

YOU KILLED HER!

WHY, CRASH?

WHY BEFORE I TOUCHED THAT SKIN I'VE BEEN DREAMIN' OF FOR SO LONG?

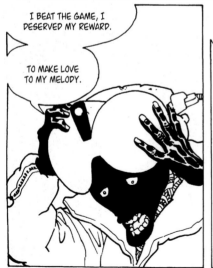

I BEAT THE GAME, I DESERVED MY REWARD.

TO MAKE LOVE TO MY MELODY.

THE ONLY THING I CARED ABOUT IN THE WORLD.

AND NOW...

...NOW I GOT NO REASON TO KEEP LIVING. SON OF A BITCH, SON OF A BITCH, SON OF A **BITCH**.

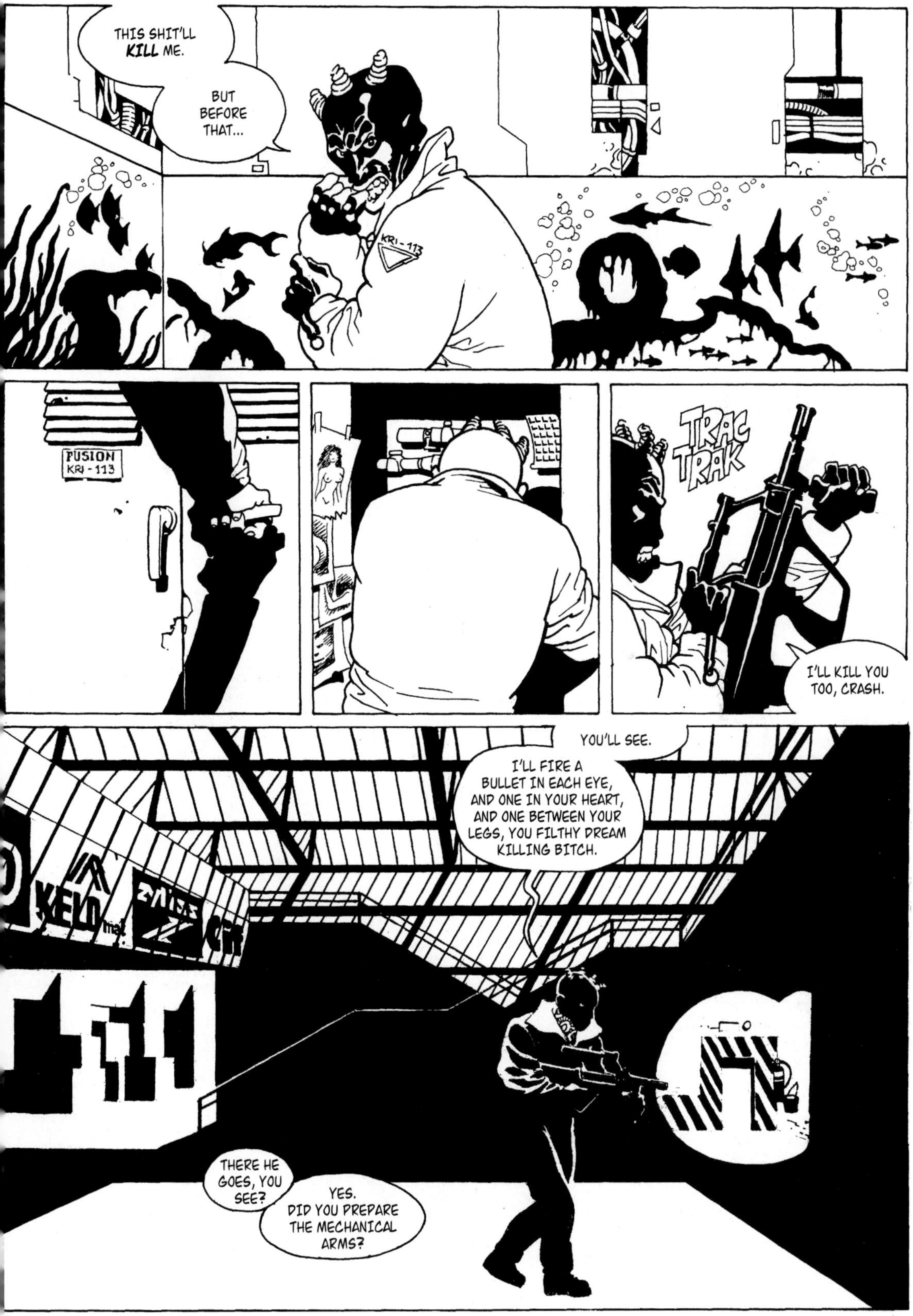
THIS SHIT'LL KILL ME.
BUT BEFORE THAT...
KRI - 113
FUSION KRI - 113
TRAC TRAK
I'LL KILL YOU TOO, CRASH.
YOU'LL SEE.
I'LL FIRE A BULLET IN EACH EYE, AND ONE IN YOUR HEART, AND ONE BETWEEN YOUR LEGS, YOU FILTHY DREAM KILLING BITCH.
THERE HE GOES, YOU SEE?
YES. DID YOU PREPARE THE MECHANICAL ARMS?

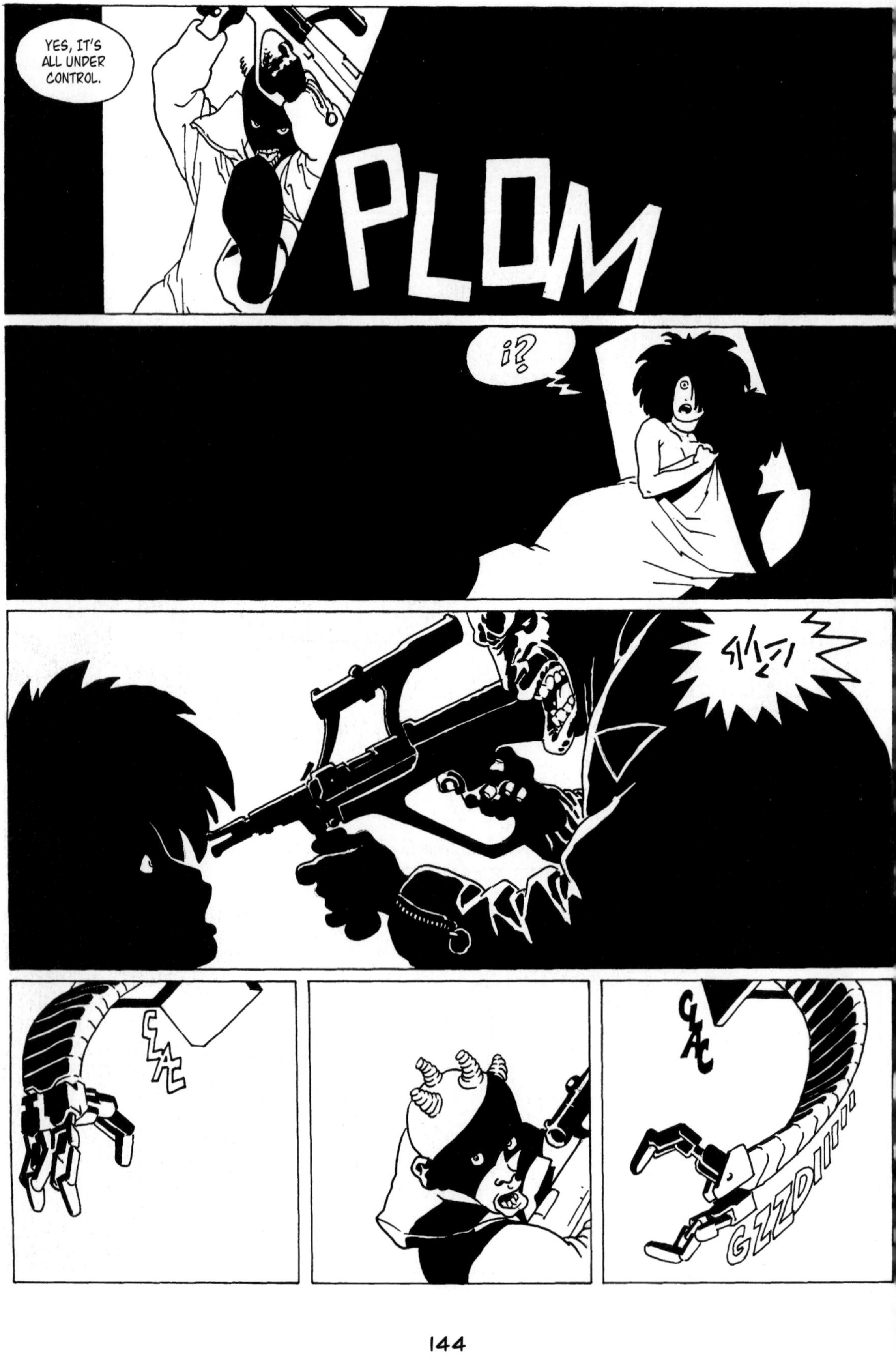
YES, IT'S ALL UNDER CONTROL.
PLOM
¿?
GZZDIII

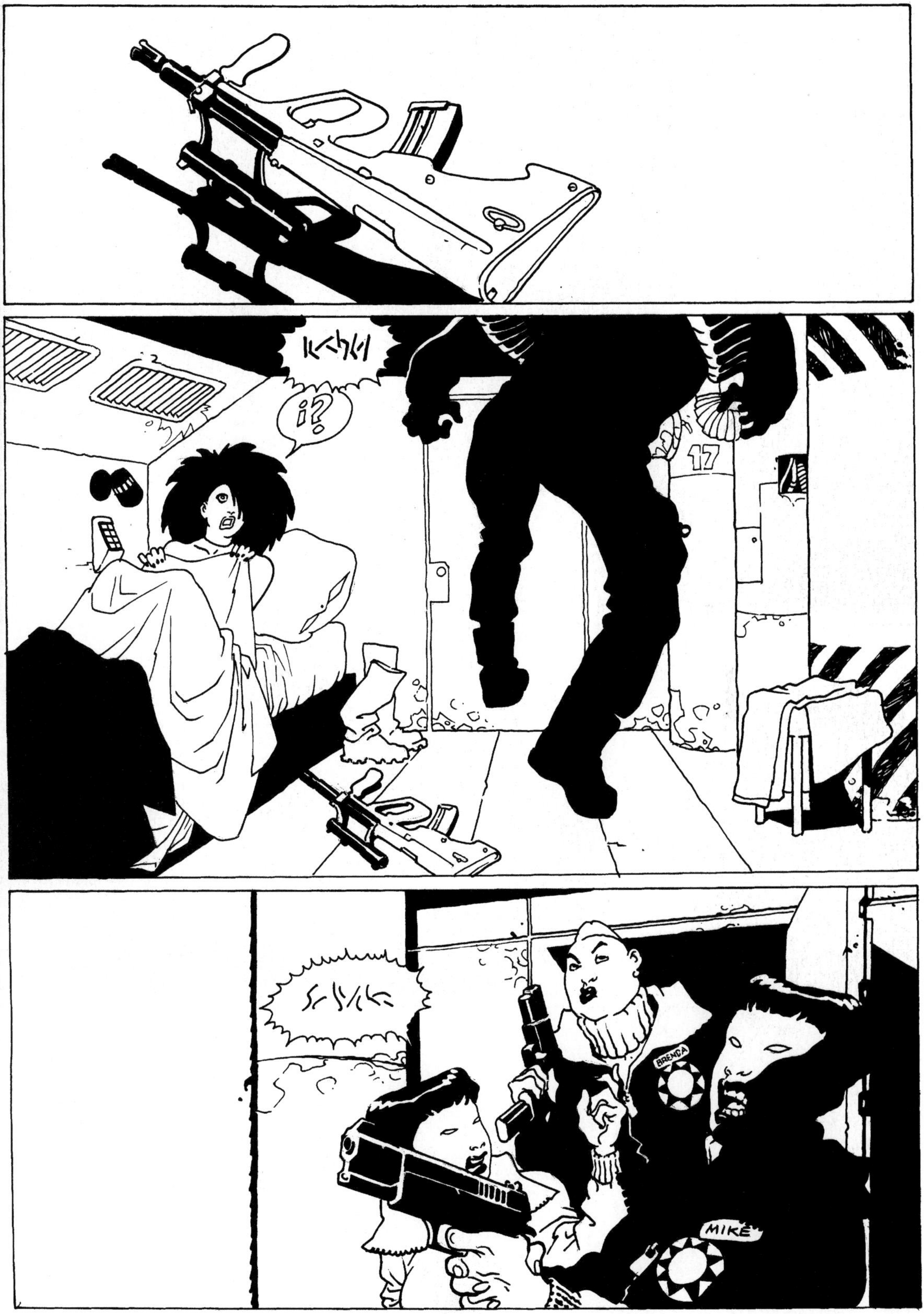
¿?
BRENDA
MIKE

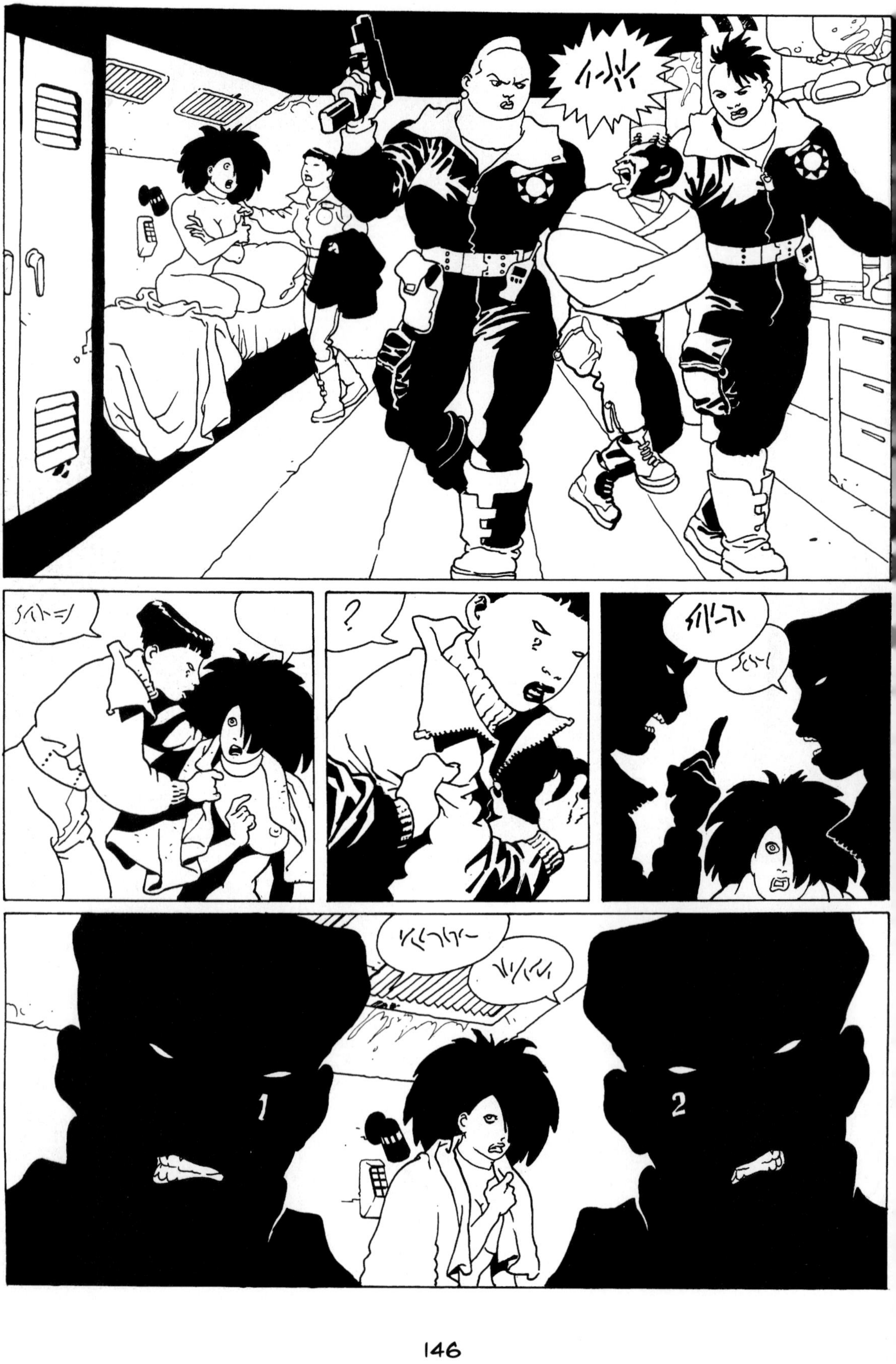
?
1
2

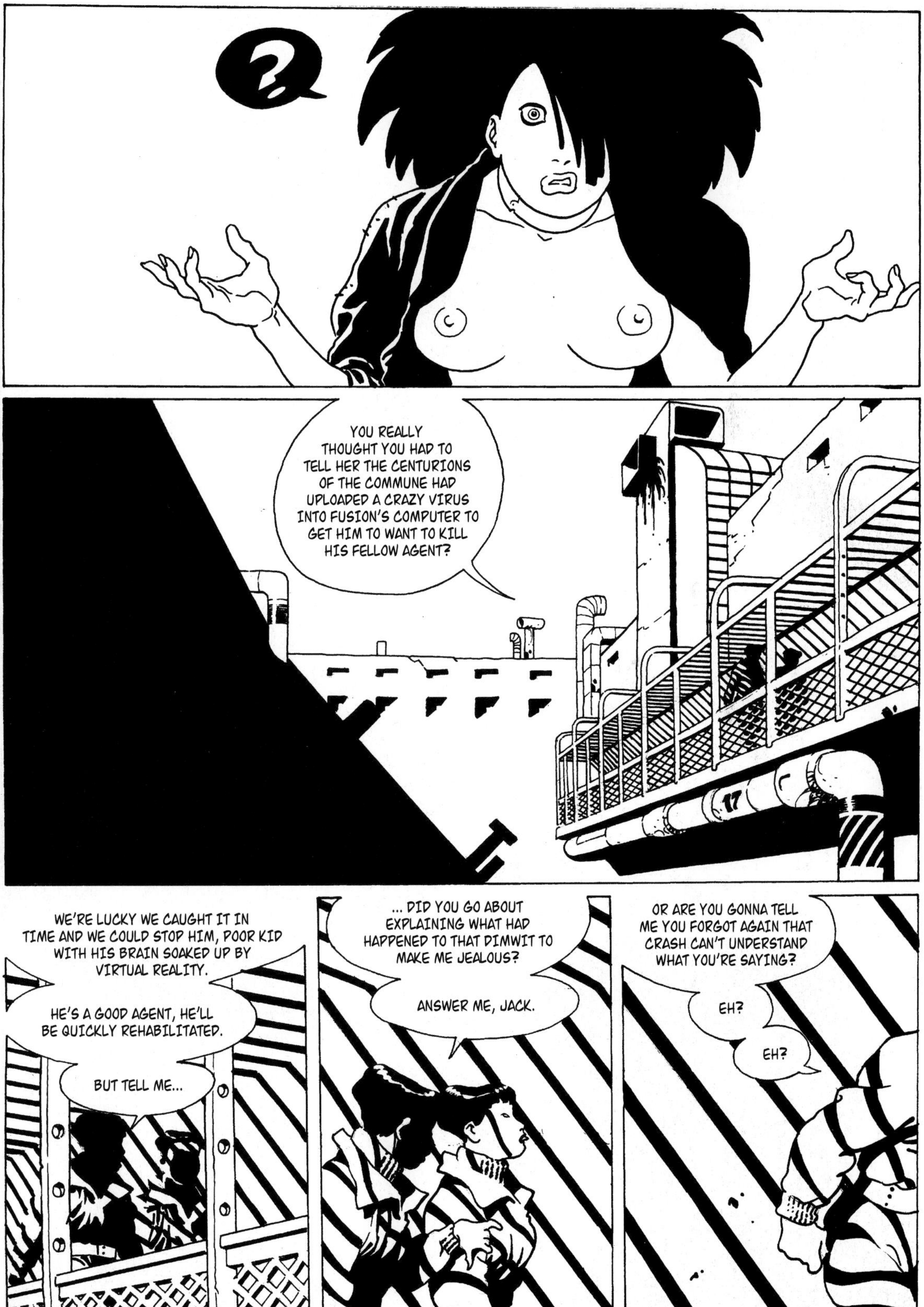
?
YOU REALLY THOUGHT YOU HAD TO TELL HER THE CENTURIONS OF THE COMMUNE HAD UPLOADED A CRAZY VIRUS INTO FUSION'S COMPUTER TO GET HIM TO WANT TO KILL HIS FELLOW AGENT?
WE'RE LUCKY WE CAUGHT IT IN TIME AND WE COULD STOP HIM, POOR KID WITH HIS BRAIN SOAKED UP BY VIRTUAL REALITY.
HE'S A GOOD AGENT, HE'LL BE QUICKLY REHABILITATED.
BUT TELL ME...
... DID YOU GO ABOUT EXPLAINING WHAT HAD HAPPENED TO THAT DIMWIT TO MAKE ME JEALOUS?
ANSWER ME, JACK.
OR ARE YOU GONNA TELL ME YOU FORGOT AGAIN THAT CRASH CAN'T UNDERSTAND WHAT YOU'RE SAYING?
EH?
EH?

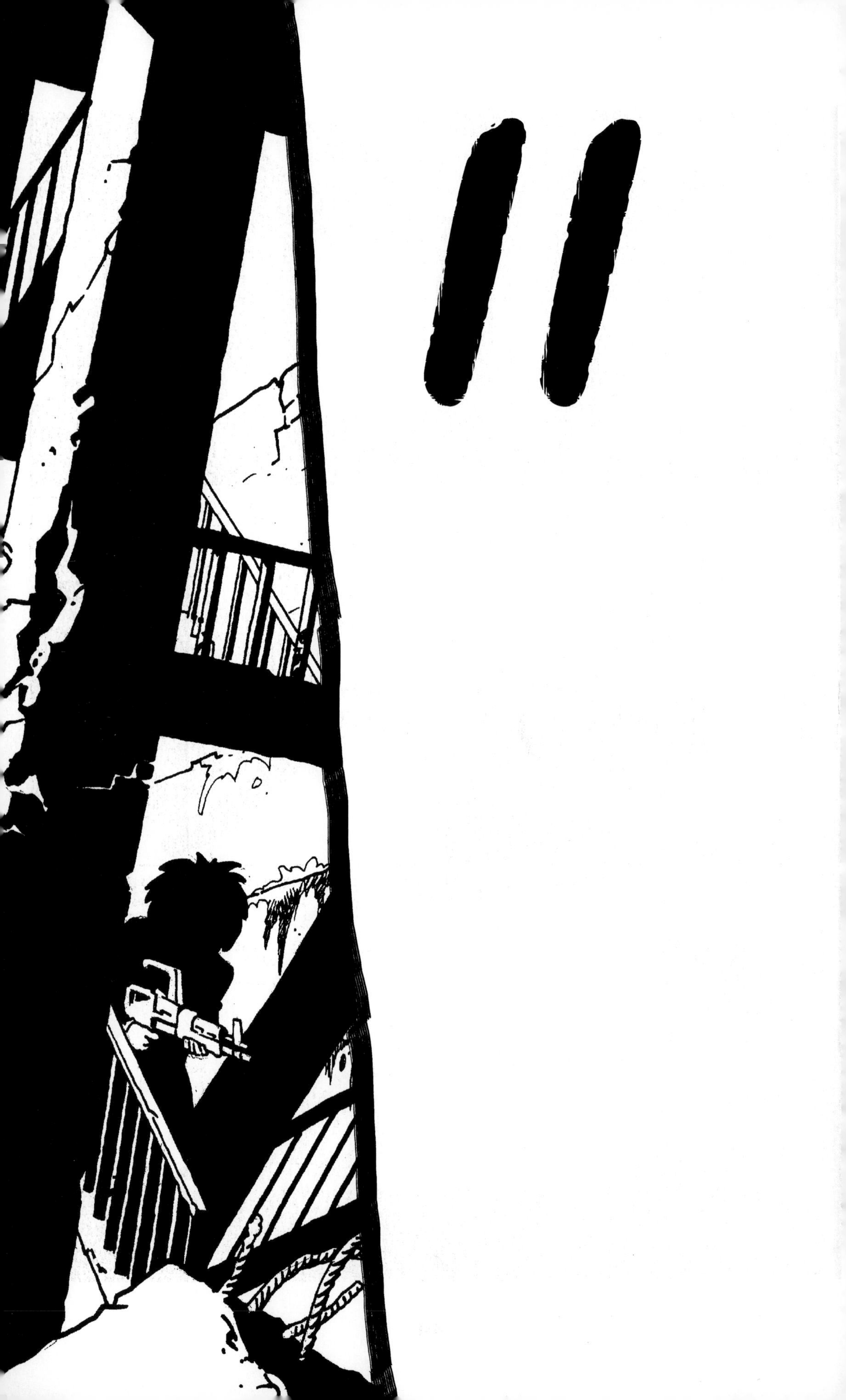

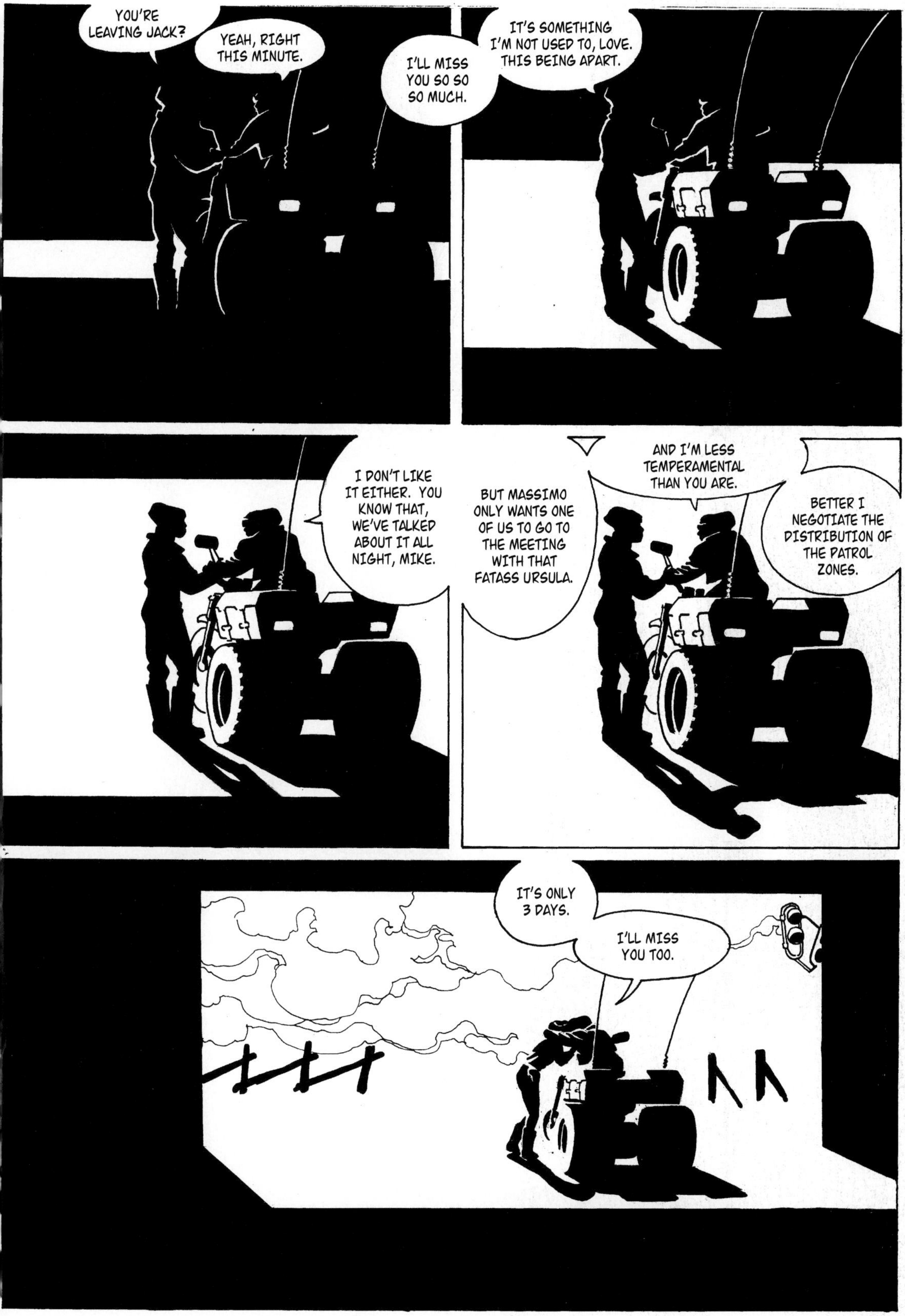
YOU'RE LEAVING JACK?
YEAH, RIGHT THIS MINUTE.
I'LL MISS YOU SO SO SO MUCH.
IT'S SOMETHING I'M NOT USED TO, LOVE. THIS BEING APART.
I DON'T LIKE IT EITHER. YOU KNOW THAT, WE'VE TALKED ABOUT IT ALL NIGHT, MIKE.
BUT MASSIMO ONLY WANTS ONE OF US TO GO TO THE MEETING WITH THAT FATASS URSULA.
AND I'M LESS TEMPERAMENTAL THAN YOU ARE.
BETTER I NEGOTIATE THE DISTRIBUTION OF THE PATROL ZONES.
IT'S ONLY 3 DAYS.
I'LL MISS YOU TOO.

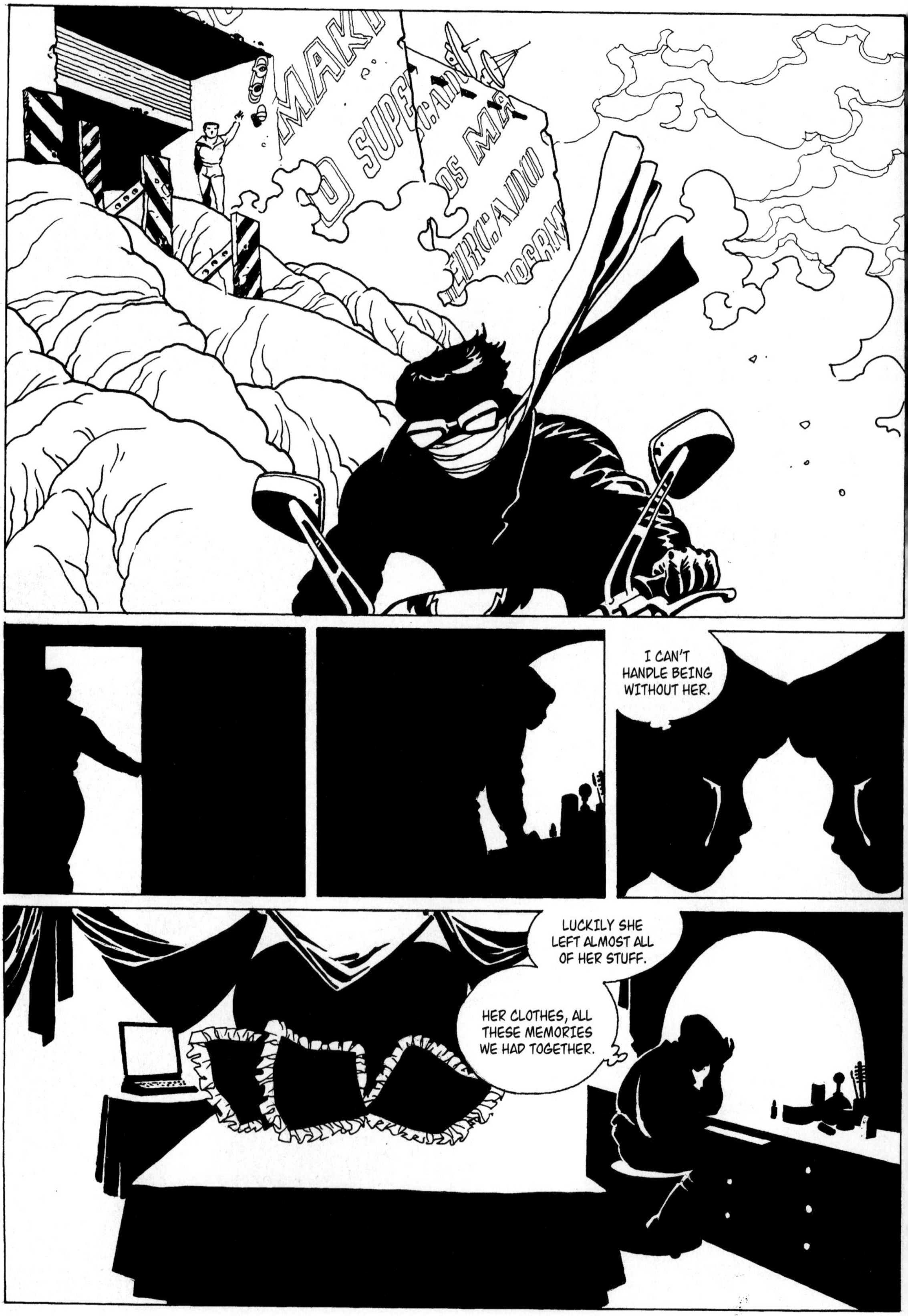
I CAN'T HANDLE BEING WITHOUT HER.
LUCKILY SHE LEFT ALMOST ALL OF HER STUFF.
HER CLOTHES, ALL THESE MEMORIES WE HAD TOGETHER.

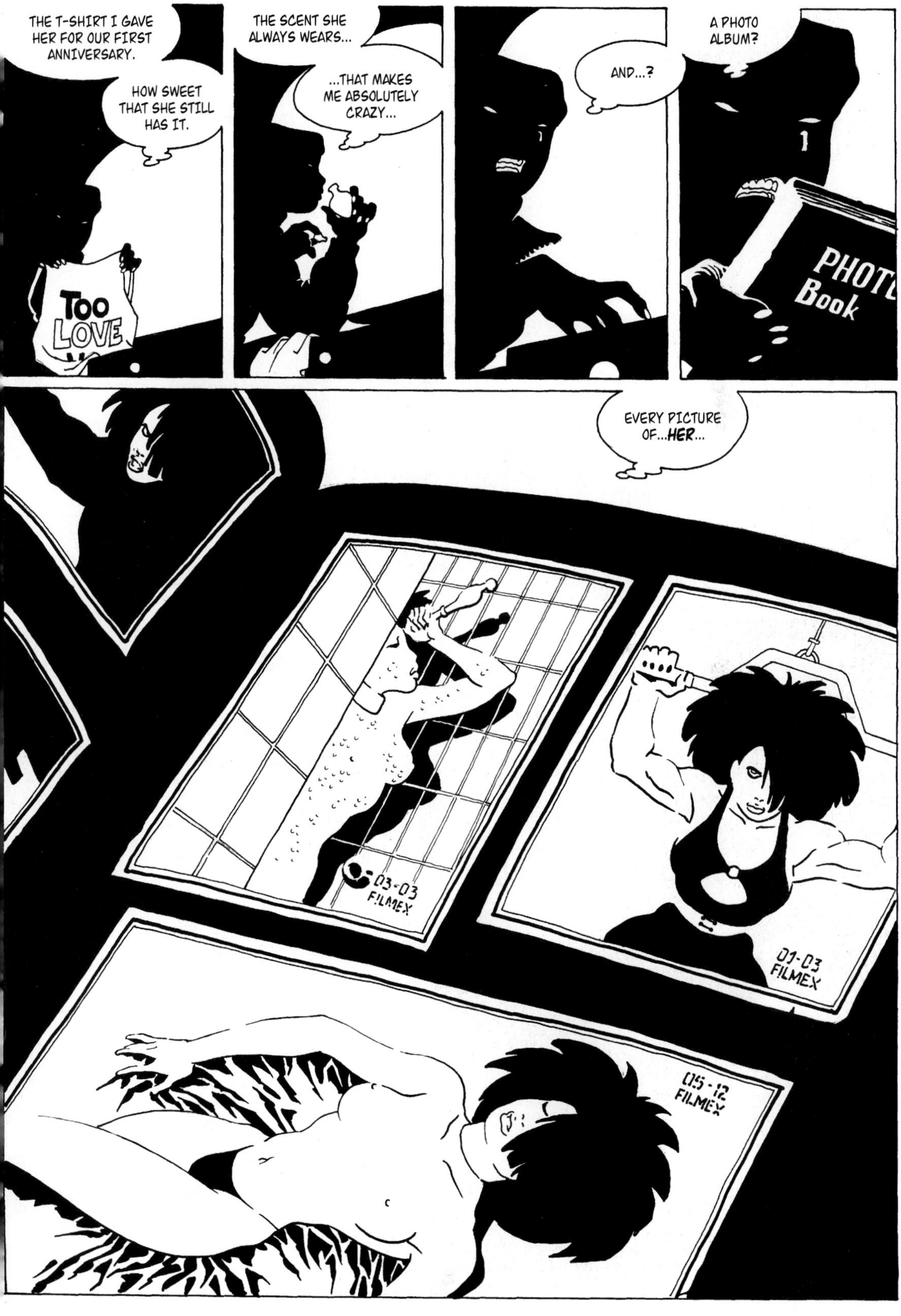
THE T-SHIRT I GAVE HER FOR OUR FIRST ANNIVERSARY.
HOW SWEET THAT SHE STILL HAS IT.
TOO LOVE
THE SCENT SHE ALWAYS WEARS...
...THAT MAKES ME ABSOLUTELY CRAZY...
AND...?
A PHOTO ALBUM?
PHOTO Book
EVERY PICTURE OF...**HER**...
03-03 FILMEX
01-03 FILMEX
05-12 FILMEX

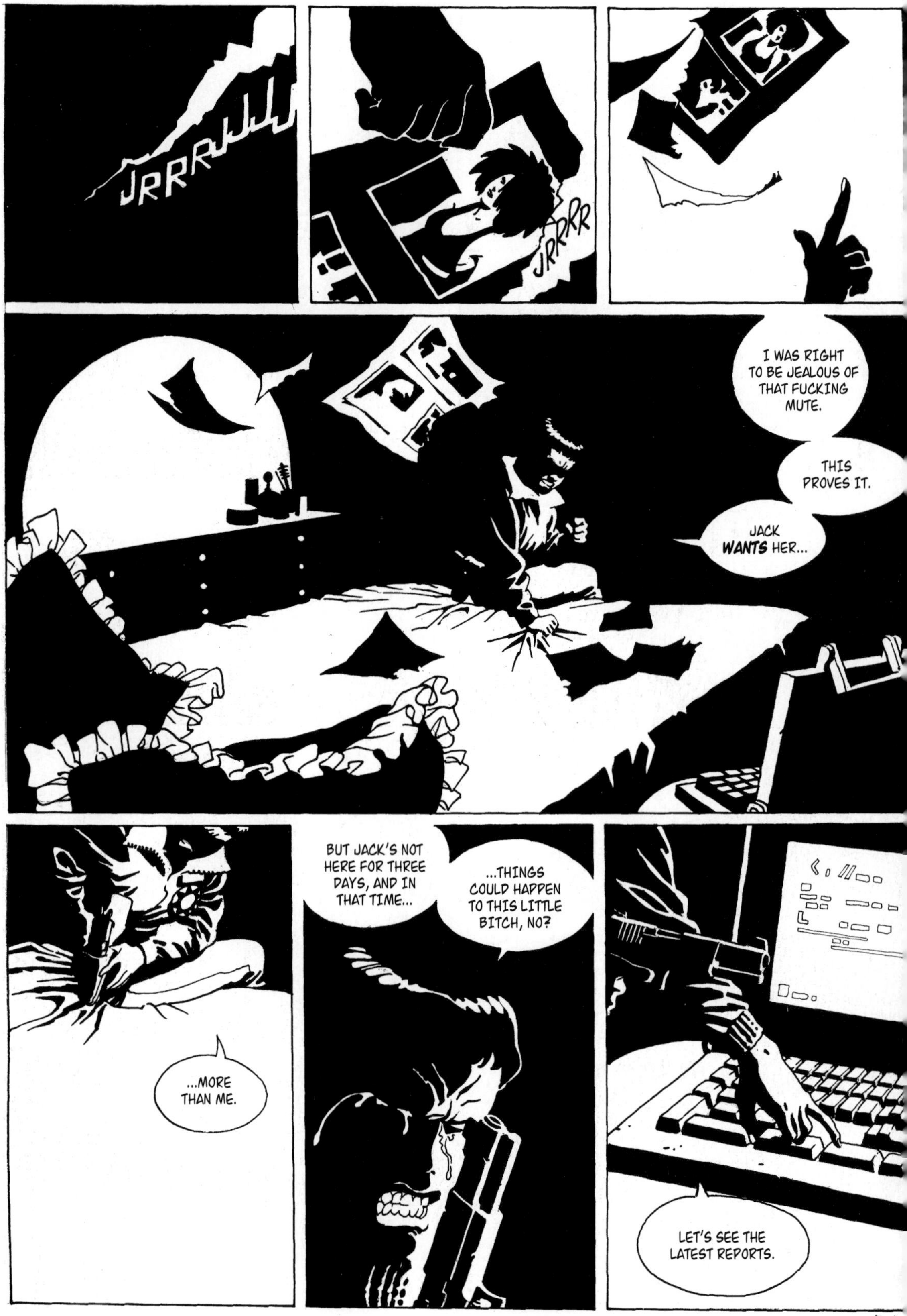
JRRRJJJJ
JRRRR
I WAS RIGHT TO BE JEALOUS OF THAT FUCKING MUTE.
THIS PROVES IT.
JACK **WANTS** HER...
...MORE THAN ME.
BUT JACK'S NOT HERE FOR THREE DAYS, AND IN THAT TIME...
...THINGS COULD HAPPEN TO THIS LITTLE BITCH, NO?
LET'S SEE THE LATEST REPORTS.

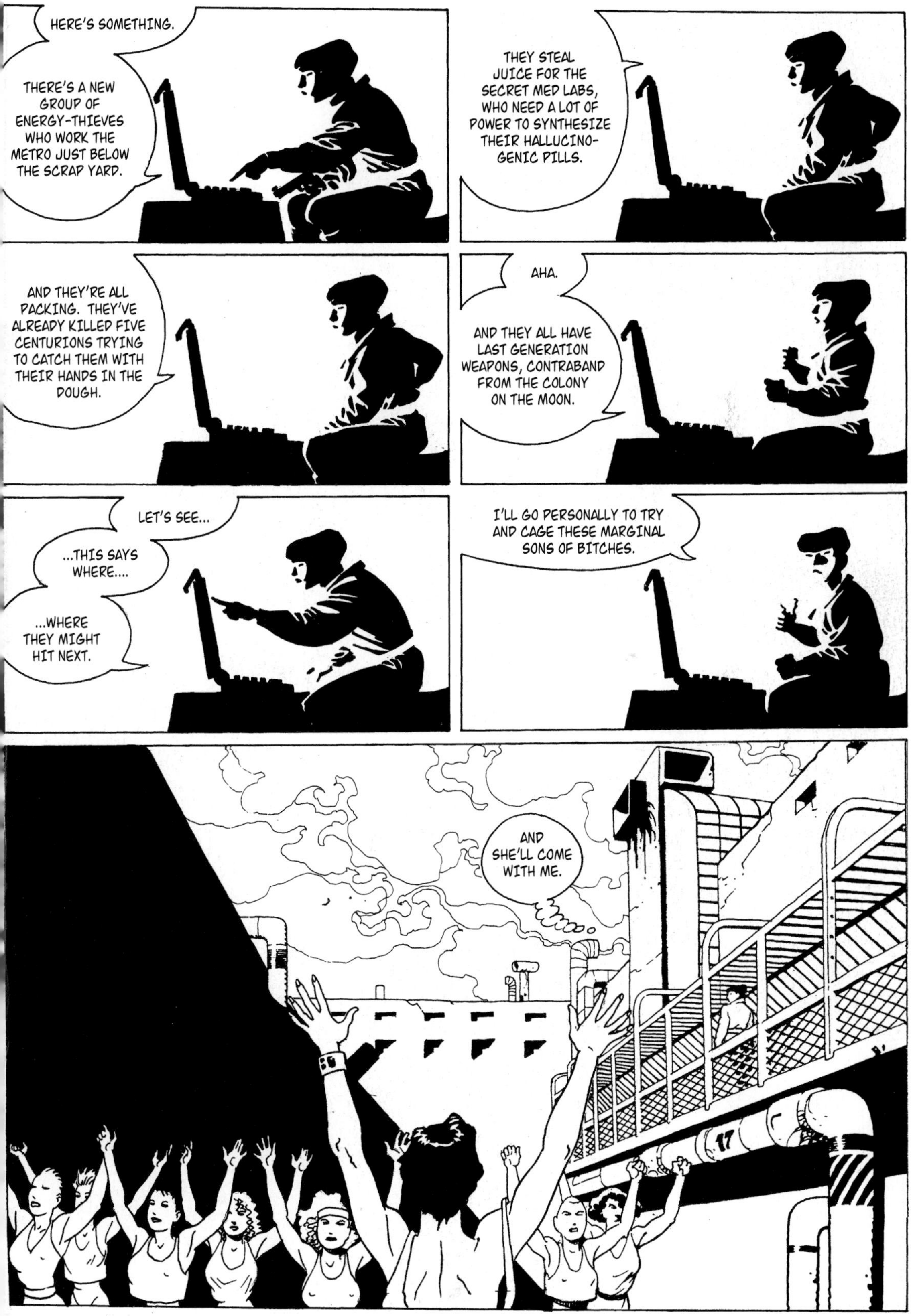
HERE'S SOMETHING.
THERE'S A NEW GROUP OF ENERGY-THIEVES WHO WORK THE METRO JUST BELOW THE SCRAP YARD.
THEY STEAL JUICE FOR THE SECRET MED LABS, WHO NEED A LOT OF POWER TO SYNTHESIZE THEIR HALLUCINO-GENIC PILLS.
AND THEY'RE ALL PACKING. THEY'VE ALREADY KILLED FIVE CENTURIONS TRYING TO CATCH THEM WITH THEIR HANDS IN THE DOUGH.
AHA.
AND THEY ALL HAVE LAST GENERATION WEAPONS, CONTRABAND FROM THE COLONY ON THE MOON.
LET'S SEE...
...THIS SAYS WHERE....
...WHERE THEY MIGHT HIT NEXT.
I'LL GO PERSONALLY TO TRY AND CAGE THESE MARGINAL SONS OF BITCHES.
AND SHE'LL COME WITH ME.
17

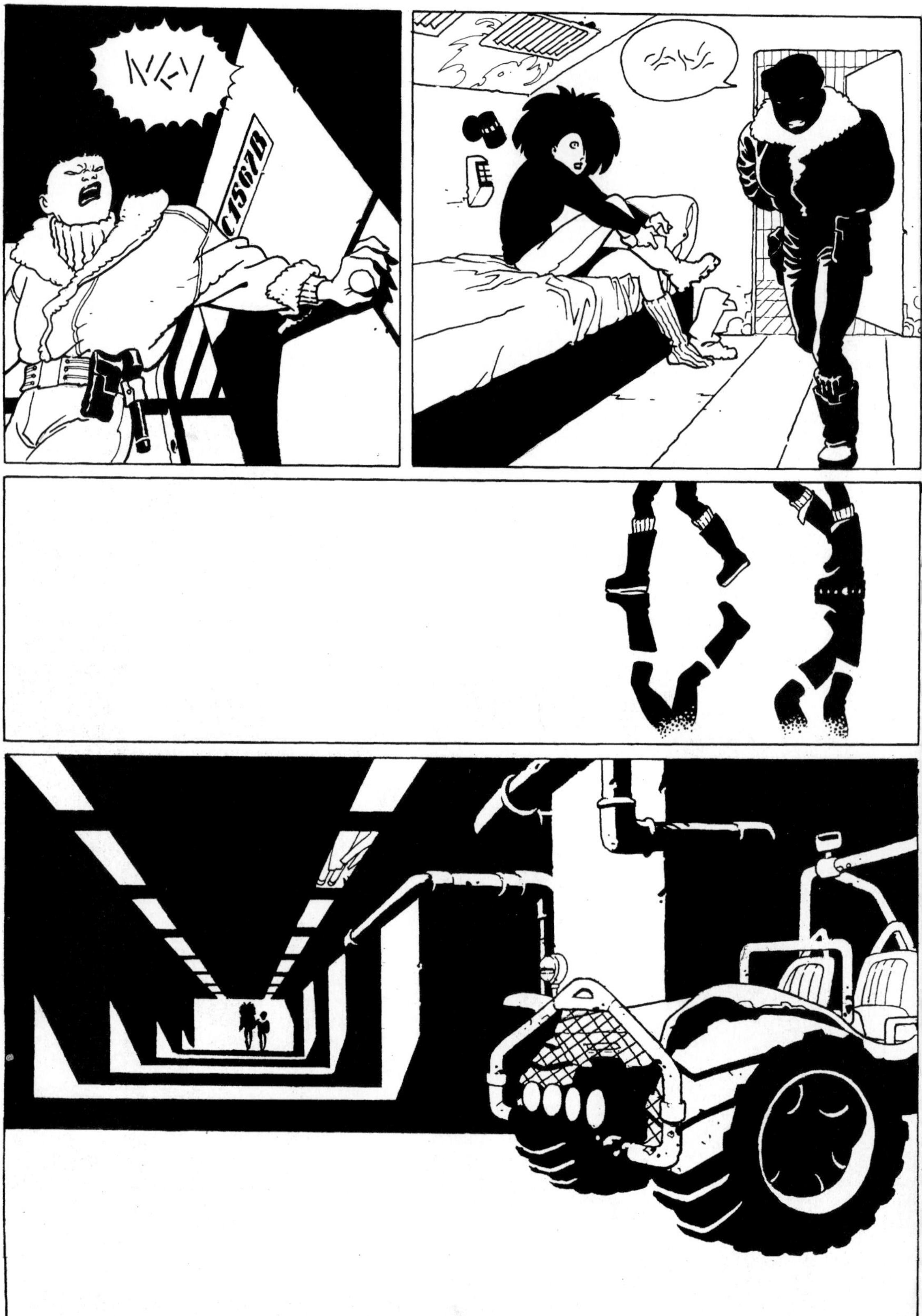
C1567B

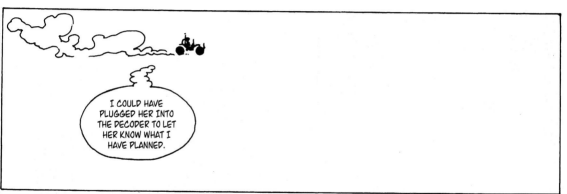

I COULD HAVE PLUGGED HER INTO THE DECODER TO LET HER KNOW WHAT I HAVE PLANNED.

BUT I'D RATHER SHE DIE WITHOUT A CLUE, FOR BEING A WHORE.

SHIT.

SENSOR SHOWS THAT...

DEP... DEP...

...A HEAVILY ARMED GROUP IS MANIPULATING THE FLUID TRANSFER CABLES JUST BELOW WHERE WE STAND.

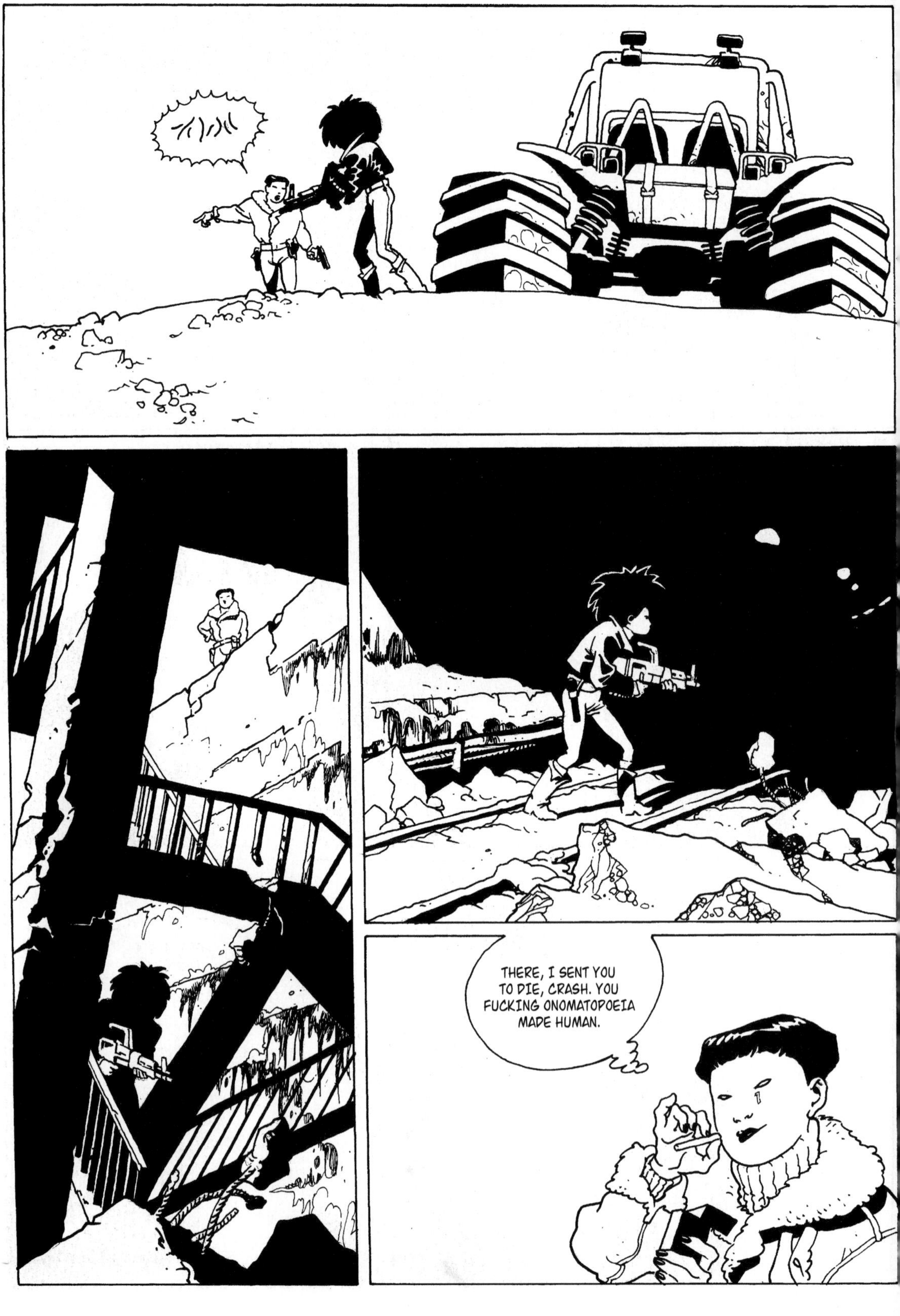
THERE, I SENT YOU TO DIE, CRASH. YOU FUCKING ONOMATOPOEIA MADE HUMAN.

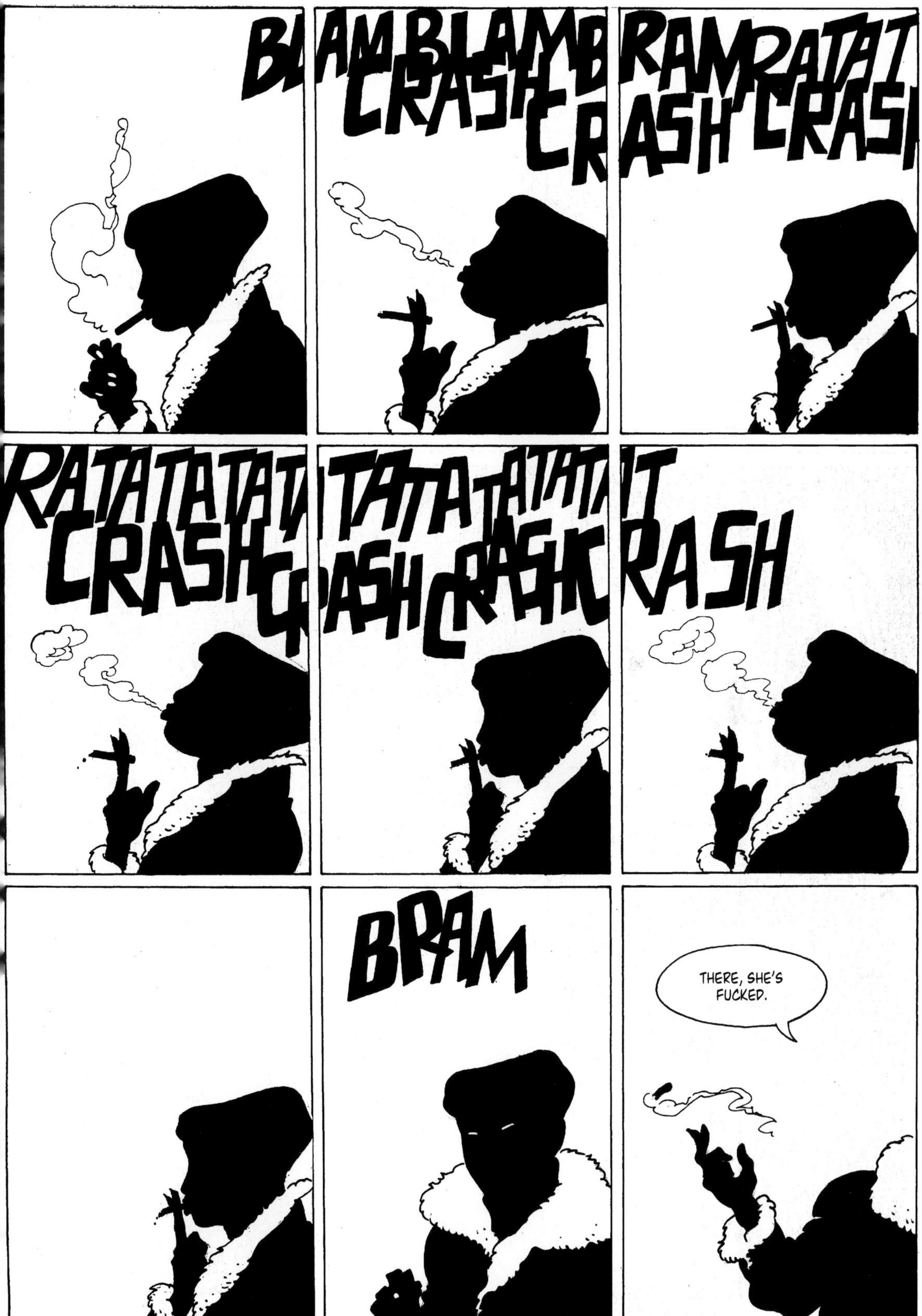
BLAM BLAM B
CRASH CR
RAM RATATAT
ASH CRASH
RATATATATATATATATATAT
CRASH CRASH CRASH CRASH
BRAM
THERE, SHE'S FUCKED.

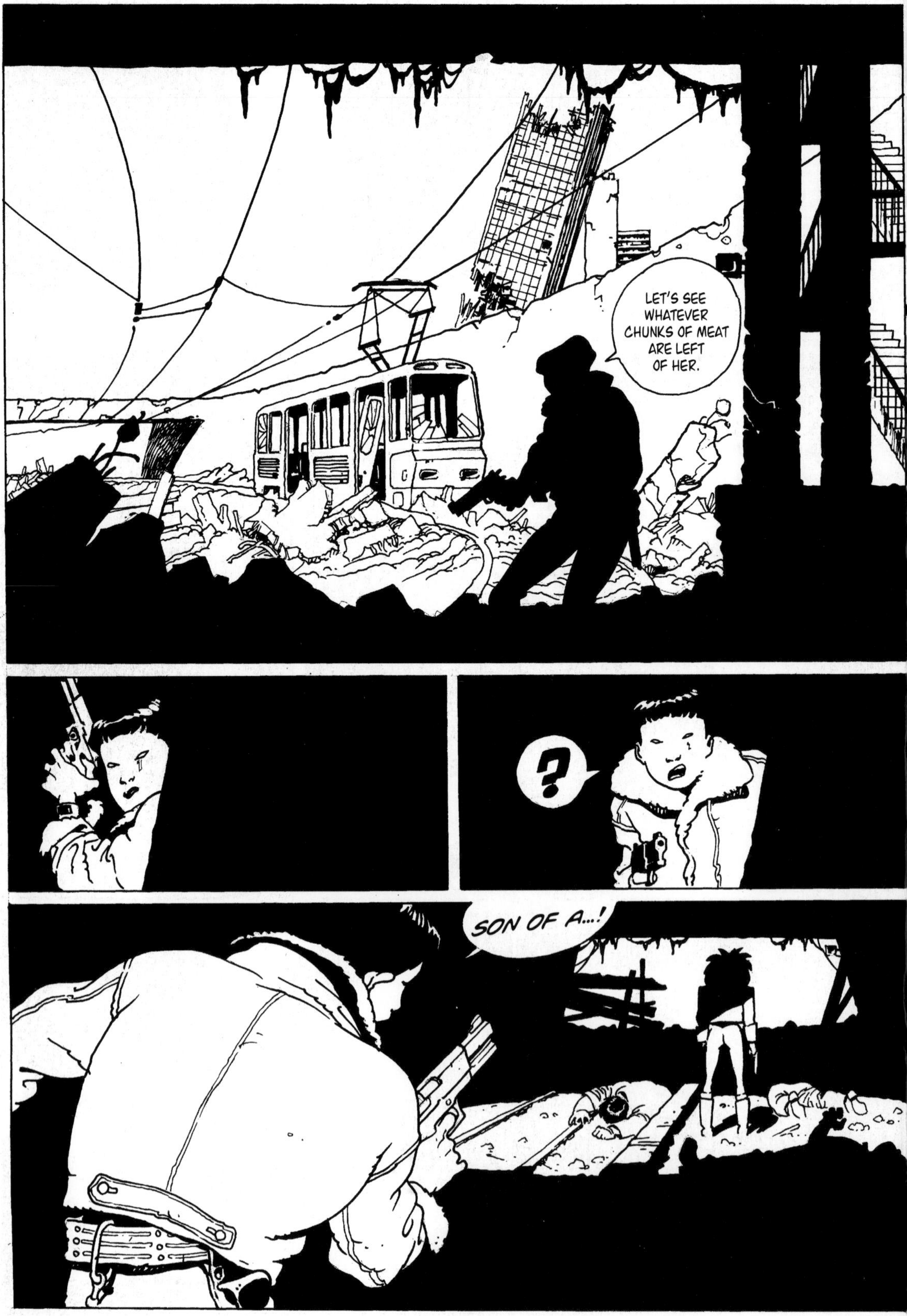
LET'S SEE WHATEVER CHUNKS OF MEAT ARE LEFT OF HER.
?
SON OF A...!

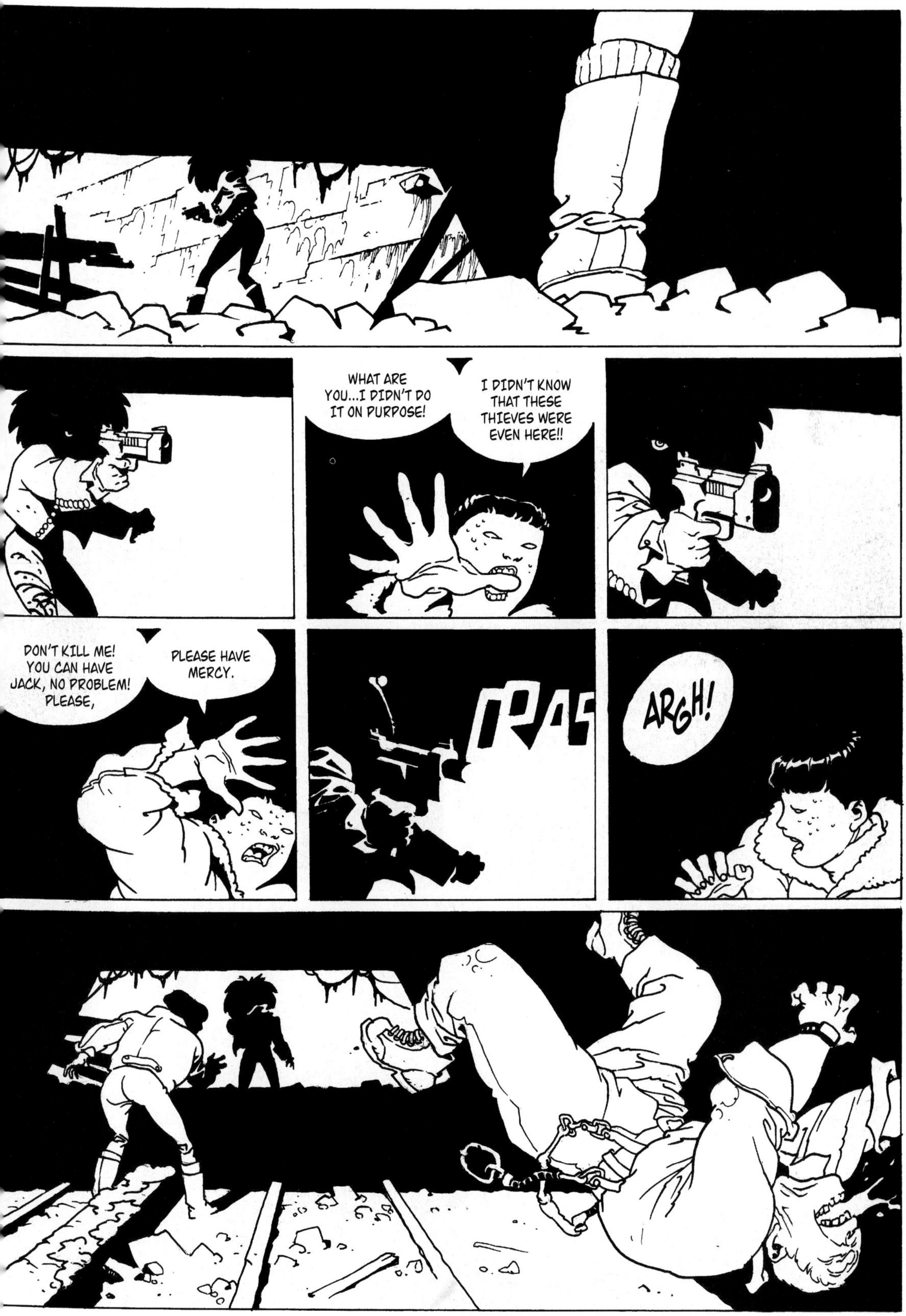
WHAT ARE YOU...I DIDN'T DO IT ON PURPOSE!
I DIDN'T KNOW THAT THESE THIEVES WERE EVEN HERE!!
DON'T KILL ME! YOU CAN HAVE JACK, NO PROBLEM! PLEASE,
PLEASE HAVE MERCY.
ARGH!

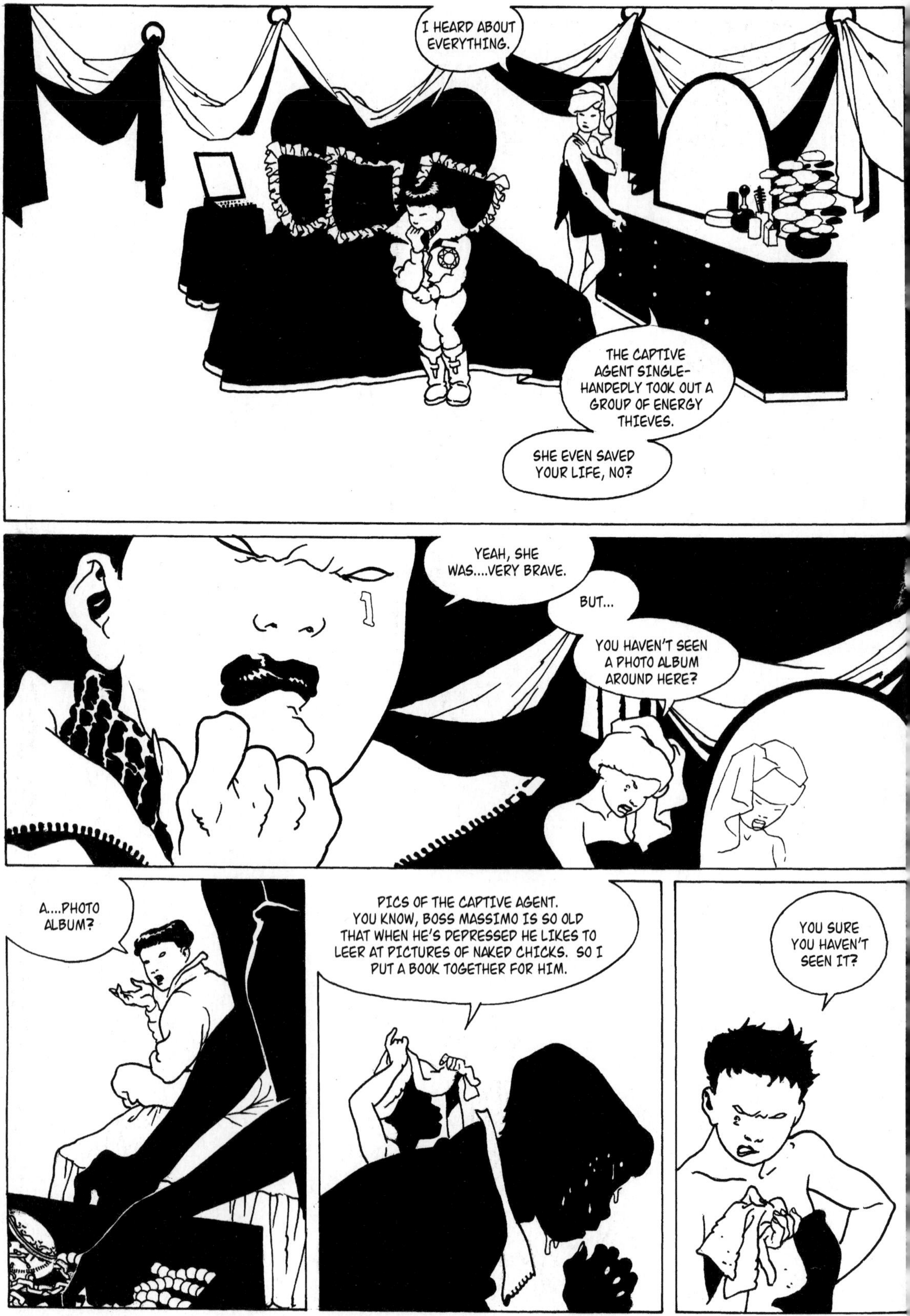
I HEARD ABOUT EVERYTHING.
THE CAPTIVE AGENT SINGLE-HANDEDLY TOOK OUT A GROUP OF ENERGY THIEVES.
SHE EVEN SAVED YOUR LIFE, NO?
YEAH, SHE WAS....VERY BRAVE.
BUT...
YOU HAVEN'T SEEN A PHOTO ALBUM AROUND HERE?
A....PHOTO ALBUM?
PICS OF THE CAPTIVE AGENT. YOU KNOW, BOSS MASSIMO IS SO OLD THAT WHEN HE'S DEPRESSED HE LIKES TO LEER AT PICTURES OF NAKED CHICKS. SO I PUT A BOOK TOGETHER FOR HIM.
YOU SURE YOU HAVEN'T SEEN IT?

TO BE CONTINUED IN VOLUME 2 OF BORDERLINE